UNSOLVED

UNSOLVED

BARRY CUMMINS

Gill & Macmillan

*For every murder victim
still awaiting justice*

Gill & Macmillan Ltd
Hume Avenue, Park West, Dublin 12
with associated companies throughout the world
www.gillmacmillan.ie

978 07171 4250 7

Typography design by Make Communication
Print origination by Carole Lynch
Printed by Nørhaven Paperback A/S, Denmark

This book is typeset in Linotype Minion and Neue Helvetica.

The paper used in this book comes from the wood pulp of
managed forests. For every tree felled, at least one tree is
planted, thereby renewing natural resources.

A CIP catalogue record for this book is available
from the British Library.

5 4 3 2

CONTENTS

ACKNOWLEDGEMENTS

First and foremost I would like to thank each and every family who spoke to me during my research for this book. The grief that these families experience every day is compounded by the fact that their loved one's murder remains unsolved. These families gave generously not only of their time but also of their memories of, and feelings for, their murdered loved ones.

Many close friends of the murder victims also spoke to me, and I would like to acknowledge their kind assistance and helpfulness towards me.

Thank you to the staff of the Garda Press Office for assistance with historical research in respect of two chapters in this book. Thank you in particular to Superintendent Kevin Donohoe and Sergeant Ken Hill, and thank you also to Jim Kirwan at Garda Headquarters. Thank you to the Garda Commissioner for facilitating this aspect of my research.

Thank you to Gail McGreevy, head of news, and to Acting Inspector June McHugh in the Press Office of the Police Service of Northern Ireland. Thank you also to the staff of the Kent Police Press Office.

Many other people also provided invaluable assistance during my research. Thank you to Lorraine Murphy and all the staff of the Dublin City Coroner's Court, and thanks also to the Dublin City Coroner, Dr Brian Farrell. Thank you to Catherine Brennan in the Laois Coroner's Court, and the Wicklow Coroner, Cathal Louth. Thank you to Gerry Curran, media relations adviser with the Courts Service, and thank you to Kevin Fidgeon at the Dublin County Registrar's Office, to Verona Lambe, Offaly County Registrar, to Eithne Coughlan, Kildare County Registrar, and to Catherine and Nuala and the staff of the Kildare Circuit Court Office.

I would also like to thank everyone in the Department of Justice Press Office, Crimestoppers, the Prison Officers' Association, the

Office of Births, Deaths and Marriages, the National Archives, Coco Television, and Photolabs.

Because of the sensitivity of the information provided to me by a number of sources, there are dozens of people whom I cannot acknowledge publicly. Without their assistance the level of detail in this book would not have been possible, and I sincerely thank each and every one of them for their time and trust.

Thank you again to all at Gill & Macmillan, especially Fergal Tobin, publishing director, for his support. Also thank you to Nicki Howard, Deirdre Rennison Kunz, Antoinette Doddy, Liz Raleigh, Lisa Buckley, Patricia Hannon and Helen Thompson.

As always, thank you to my former boss at Midlands Radio 3, Barry Flynn, and to Noel Shannon, Cathy Farrell, and all at Today FM News. Thank you also to my colleagues in RTE, especially the news editors Ray Burke, Fiona Mitchell and Mary Campbell. Thank you to all my friends in journalism, both in crime reporting and beyond.

Thank you, as always, to all the staff at my former schools, St Mark's primary and secondary schools in Tallaght.

Thank you to my parents, Patricia O'Neill and Barry Cummins, and to my brother Mark for their constant support and interest.

Finally, thank you especially to my wife, Grace, for her constant support, advice, ideas, motivation and guidance and without whom I could not have written this book.

For further information visit www.barrycummins.com. E-mail the author at unsolved@barrycummins.com.

01 | THE MURDER OF BERNADETTE CONNOLLY

Ten-year-old Bernadette Connolly had gone on a quick errand for her mother when she was abducted and murdered in Co. Sligo on Friday 17 April 1970. Bernadette had cycled a mile and a half along quiet roads towards a neighbour's house, but she never made it to her destination. Somewhere along the route her killer struck, taking her off her red-and-gold bike and putting her into a car or a van. The killer placed Bernadette's bike up on an embankment five feet above the narrow road; he then drove away with Bernadette, leaving her mother's purse lying on the grass verge.

Minutes earlier, Bernadette had been at home with her mother, Maureen. It was shortly before 4:30 p.m. when her mother asked her to cycle to Ellen Molloy's house to collect messages for dinner. Ellen was a friend of Maureen's and they had spoken earlier that day. Ellen said she was heading into the nearby town of Collooney to do some shopping, and Maureen had asked her to buy some fish for her. The Connollys were going to have smoked haddock and potatoes for their tea. Bernadette's father, Gerry, would be home from work soon and her older sister Ann would be arriving back from school too. It was time to cycle to the Molloy house and collect the messages, and Bernadette took her mother's purse to pay Mrs Molloy for the fish and potatoes.

A steady stream of rain was falling outside as Bernadette prepared to leave the house. She was glad to get out for a cycle, as she had been off school sick for the previous few days. But she was feeling better now and looking forward to a journey on the Raleigh Astronaut bike she had got from Santa the previous Christmas. She put her mother's purse in the front basket of the bike and put on her brown anorak and light-brown woollen gloves. She pulled up the hood of the corduroy anorak to shield herself from the rain and called out goodbye to her mother.

Underneath her anorak Bernadette was wearing a blue blouse and light-brown pinafore dress with box pleats. She was also wearing a white vest with three religious medals pinned to it. These medals would later help in the provisional identification of Bernadette's body.

As Bernadette began her journey to the Molloys' she may have been thinking about the excitement of the Apollo space mission that was being shown all day on television. The *Apollo 13* spacecraft was coming back to earth after a failed attempt to reach the moon. There was much concern for the safety of the three astronauts on board, and RTE television was showing news reports. It had been a topic of discussion in Bernadette's school, where teachers asked the pupils what they knew about the astronauts. Bernadette had missed the discussion through being at home sick, but she had previously written in her English copybook about another space flight, that of *Apollo 12*. 'They stayed on the moon for thirty hours, then they went back to the mother ship,' she wrote. 'They were going at a speed of 3,000 m.p.h. Some people say it is all a waste of money. Other people say it is really useful.'

Bernadette had cycled two hundred yards from her house when she overtook twelve-year-old Oliver Flynn, who was carrying a load of coal by donkey and cart. Oliver's mother, Kathleen, was cycling behind him. Bernadette called out 'Hello' to her neighbours as she pedalled past them; it was raining quite heavily, and Kathleen saw that Bernadette was wearing her hood up. Kathleen had been talking to Maureen Connolly earlier in the day and

Maureen had mentioned that she would be sending Bernadette out to get some groceries.

Bernadette was cycling at a good pace and was soon out of sight of Kathleen and Oliver. Within minutes she would be abducted.

Bernadette Connolly was born in Birmingham in 1959, the second-eldest of six children born to Gerry and Maureen Connolly. Gerry was originally from Co. Sligo while Maureen was born in Co. Kerry but had lived in England from her mid-teens. The couple had met in London in the 1950s and had moved to Aston in north Birmingham. Gerry knew people from Co. Sligo who had settled in Birmingham, and the couple became part of a vibrant Irish community in the city. Their first child, Ann, was born in 1956, Bernadette was born in 1959, and their first son, Tommy, arrived three years later. Their three other children—Patricia, Gerard and Kerrie—were born in Ireland when the family eventually returned to Co. Sligo in the mid-60s.

On meeting Bernadette's three sisters in Collooney it is evident that they have a shared sense of heartbreak and loss, while each has different memories of growing up without their sister. Ann was thirteen when Bernadette vanished, Patricia was four, and Kerrie was not yet born. Patricia and Kerrie listen intently when Ann speaks about the time that Bernadette was taken from them, but even now Ann finds it difficult to talk about memories that are with her every day. It was Ann who found her sister's bike abandoned on the roadside and who found her mother's wet purse on the road; it was Ann who had to tell her mother and father that Bernadette had never arrived at the Molloys' house and that she was missing. It was Ann who later stood beside her mother and father at the cemetery in Collooney and watched as Bernadette's white coffin was lowered into the ground. Amid tears, Ann recounts her memories of the day that Bernadette went missing.

> Bernie was off school that week because she was sick, and I had to get up to catch the bus at the gate. The last time I actually saw her she was turning over asleep in bed that morning, and I was thinking how lucky she was to still be in bed. That was

the last I saw of her. Then when I came home I was sent out to find her. Bernie had been gone from the house for over an hour and should have been home by then. I was sent to Molloys' house to see what was keeping Bernie, why was she not home yet. I remember I was giving out as I cycled along; I was giving out that I had to go out and look for her. I was just a kid, and I know kids say those kinds of things, but those thoughts haunt me now.

Ann and Bernie were close, and they played together a lot at home. By April 1970 Ann was in secondary school in Ballymote, while Bernie was still in the national school in Collooney, but they spent a lot of time together outside school. They would cuddle up in bed together and play make-believe.

We pretended we had our own houses. My house was one side of the bedroom and hers was the other side. And we decided we were going to marry twin brothers. And I remember Bernie was so tickly, and I used to tickle her to make her laugh.

It was after 5:30 p.m. when Ann left the family home to go and look for Bernadette. She cycled a short distance along the road towards Collooney before turning left towards the Molloys' house along the Lisaneena road. She was cycling at a good pace, but out of the corner of her eye she spotted something shiny. It was the handlebars of a bike up four or five feet on an embankment. She didn't think anything of it and continued on to the Molloys'. When she arrived there she first thought Mrs Molloy was joking when she said Bernadette hadn't arrived for the fish; but she quickly realised something was wrong. She asked Ellen Molloy's thirteen-year-old daughter, Patricia, to come with her and help look for Bernadette.

The two girls retraced the journey along the Lisaneena road until they reached the bike up on the embankment. Ann then recognised it as Bernadette's, and knew there was no possibility that the ten-year-old could have put the bike up where it was.

Then she spotted her mother's purse lying in a small hole in the ground, the ten shillings and two pence still inside.

The following moments of panic and fear are forever etched on Ann's mind. She remembers how she and Patricia Molloy cycled as fast as they could back towards the Connollys' house and, out of breath from cycling, had met Ann's father. Gerry asked Ann where Bernadette was, and Ann then knew that her sister hadn't arrived home in the meantime.

Maureen Connolly had come out of the house to see what was going on, and when she realised Bernadette was missing she began to scream. Gerry and Ann drove back to where Bernadette's bike had been left, while Maureen began ringing everyone she could think of: gardaí, hospitals, doctors and neighbours.

Patricia Connolly was four when her sister was abducted. She can remember some things about that day.

> I remember I was in the house and I remember Tommy being in the house with me. Tommy would have been eight at the time. I can't remember Ann being sent to look for Bernie, but I can remember when Mum realised that Bernie was not with Ann. Mum went ballistic; she started screaming. I remember we had an elderly neighbour, Henry King, whose cottage was just next door. I can remember Mum standing outside the house and screaming at the top of her voice, and beating on Henry's chest as he tried to comfort her. She was screaming that her baby was gone. I don't remember much else, but Tommy says he remembers that when all the commotion started, Henry brought us over to his house to look at his little pups, to try and shield us from what was happening, but Tommy could hear people using the word 'kidnapped'.

When Ann and her father arrived at the spot where Bernadette's bike had been discarded, Gerry noticed a man's footprints and a child's in the mud.

In the meantime Maureen had phoned the local Garda sergeant, who drove immediately to the scene with another garda from

Collooney. As they drove down the lane they saw on the left-hand side that there were now about half a dozen people gathered where Bernadette's bike and her mother's purse had been found. Already fearing the worst, they moved people away from the bike and purse to preserve the scene. They then asked people to help them search surrounding fields, in case Bernadette was lying injured somewhere close. Within minutes it was clear that the little girl was nowhere in the vicinity. The Garda Sergeant went some distance up the lane to find the nearest house that had a phone, and he alerted Sligo station.

From early evening, while most of the country watched dramatic pictures of the three crew members of *Apollo 13* safely splashing down in the Pacific Ocean, extensive searches were beginning a few miles south of Collooney for Bernadette Connolly. Friends and neighbours helped the Gardaí to scour fields, rivers and lanes. Among those assisting were many of the twenty-two priests and brothers from Cloonamahon Monastery. Bernadette had disappeared within half a mile of the monastery. She was a familiar face to the priests and brothers there; she attended a youth club run by the monastery and was known as a champion Irish dancer.

Throughout the night, as the rain continued to fall, the searches continued for a number of miles around the Lisaneena road, but nothing was found. Bernadette Connolly was gone.

Gerry and Maureen Connolly had moved from England back to rural Ireland to provide their children with a safer environment in which to grow up. Birmingham had been good to the Connollys; they had many friends in Aston, including other Irish people who had been forced to leave Ireland to find work. Gerry and Maureen had become central figures in the Irish community in Birmingham in the late 1950s and early 60s. Gerry was the master of ceremonies at feiseanna that were held in the city, and the Connollys also played their part in organising St Patrick's Day celebrations. Ann and Bernadette were enrolled in an Irish dancing school in Aston and had many friends in school.

But Gerry and Maureen were also concerned about the safety of their children. Two children had been murdered in Birmingham in the early 1960s, including one who was killed across the road from where Ann and Bernadette went to school. The Connollys decided to move to Gerry's home county.

Gerry was a plumbing and heating contractor and had ambitions to set up a business south of Sligo, in the area around Collooney and Ballymote. It took a year before he was established in his business, and only then did Maureen move back to Ireland with their three children. Ann was eight years old, Bernadette was five, Tommy was three, and a year later Patricia was born.

In 1969 Maureen gave birth to her fifth child, a baby boy. Tragically, Gerard lived only for ten days before he died. By April 1970 Gerry and Maureen were naturally still grieving the loss of their baby son. The family was living in a comfortable cottage at Doorla, about three miles outside Collooney on the main road to Boyle. They had plans to move to a two-storey semi-detached house near the centre of Collooney but it was not yet complete.

A few weeks before she disappeared, Bernadette wrote in her copybook about where she lived. She wrote about Collooney being the nearest town and how there were pubs and drapery shops, butchers and a grocery shop. She wrote also about the five gardaí stationed in Collooney.

There is a barracks in Collooney. There are two houses that the guards live in. Some of the guards are married and they live in the houses. The guards that are not married have to get lodgings in some part of the town.

By the early morning of Saturday 18 April 1970 almost every garda in the Sligo district was being drafted in to help in searches for Bernadette. The local superintendent called Garda Headquarters, and within hours members of the Murder Squad had arrived in Co. Sligo to co-ordinate the investigation into Bernadette's disappearance.

There had never been an investigation like it before. There were many instances of children being attacked in random assaults, but in recent memory there was no case in Ireland of a child being abducted. Officially, detectives were classifying the case as that of a missing child, but privately many feared that Bernadette had been murdered.

The investigation into Bernadette Connolly's disappearance took place as an inquiry was continuing in Dublin into the murder of Garda Dick Fallon—the first murder of a garda in almost thirty years. Bank raiders at Arran Quay had shot the unarmed garda on 3 April 1970. Three men would later face trial for the killing but were found not guilty by a jury.

The murder of Garda Fallon and the sinister disappearance of ten-year-old Bernadette Connolly left many people shocked. Ireland was now clearly a much more dangerous place in which to live. Specialist Garda resources were split between the continuing murder investigation in Dublin and the case of the missing child in Co. Sligo. Frustratingly for the detectives involved in both cases, the unprecedented investigations into the murders of Dick Fallon and Bernadette Connolly would fail to catch those responsible.

When detectives from the Murder Squad arrived in Collooney to investigate Bernadette Connolly's disappearance they immediately arranged for her bicycle to be examined for fingerprints. They soon found a finger mark just below the saddle, which seemed to have been made in grease or oil. They then began a lengthy process of fingerprinting every person who might have had access to the bike, as well as more than five hundred other people who were living in the locality or were believed to have travelled close to where Bernadette disappeared on 17 April.

One thing that baffled the detectives was that the bike had been placed high up on the bank above the road. It had not been dumped in bushes but rather seemed to have been handled carefully. Did this suggest that Bernadette's abductor knew her and had offered to drive her the rest of her journey and to help her collect her bike in the lane afterwards? It had been raining at the time of Bernadette's disappearance, and perhaps she recognised the person who pulled up alongside her. Perhaps this person took Bernadette's bike with her permission and placed it up on the bank; perhaps he explained to Bernadette that it would be safe up there, while his real reason was that he planned to attack her but didn't want her bike to be found easily.

Is it possible that after placing the bike up on the embankment the man then turned back and immediately forced Bernadette into his car or van? Would this explain why the purse was dropped on the ground? Or did the attacker panic and drive off with Bernadette before she managed to scream for help, feeling he didn't have time to pick up the purse? Or perhaps he didn't notice the purse on the ground at all; or did Bernadette drop it deliberately?

As ten-year-olds go, Bernadette Connolly would have been more street-wise than most. Having lived in Birmingham until she was six, she knew a little more about the world than other children. Her parents had always told her not to talk to strangers in England and never to take sweets from strangers. If a stranger abducted Bernadette he had possibly driven up behind her and grabbed her without warning; it is not likely that she would have stopped cycling to engage in conversation with a stranger, and indeed it was raining, and Bernadette had an errand to run.

One thing that is without doubt is that the abduction of Bernadette Connolly took place within a matter of seconds. Nobody in the vicinity reported hearing any screams or cries for help. A number of men were working in fields in the area and would surely have heard a child crying, or the screeching of tyres. Is it possible that Bernadette was punched or otherwise knocked unconscious and then abducted? There are many possibilities that the Gardaí and Bernadette's family have considered over and over.

Detectives analysed the two routes that Bernadette could have taken to get to where her bike and purse were abandoned. She would first have cycled up the main road towards Collooney, as Kathleen Flynn and her son had seen her do. A short distance up the road she would have turned left to reach the Lisaneena road, but she would have had two options in doing so: she could have taken a short cut through Cloonamahon Monastery, or she could have bypassed the monastery and cycled further up the Collooney road before turning left onto the winding Lisaneena road. Her bicycle and purse were found half way down this quiet road with large trees dotted along the sides. Bernadette had less than half a mile to travel to the Molloys' house when she disappeared.

The Gardaí issued hundreds of questionnaires to try to establish what vehicles might have been in the area at the time of Bernadette's disappearance. Fourteen people came forward to say they had travelled the Collooney–Boyle road or other nearby roads at about the time of Bernadette's disappearance, but no-one had seen the ten-year-old girl. The last definite sighting of her was by the Flynns, more than a mile from where the bicycle and purse had been found.

Kerrie Connolly was born nearly two years after her sister was murdered. Growing up, she always knew something terrible had happened to Bernadette; she can't remember anyone telling her, it was just always there. She listens intently when Ann and Patricia talk about Bernie. On the walls of her home she has photographs of the sister she never knew. One shows Bernadette in her dancing costume, proudly holding a little trophy; another shows her smiling with her mother and their cheeks almost touching in a passport-type photograph. Bernadette normally wore glasses, round with pink rims, but in most of the photographs she has taken off her glasses to smile for the camera.

Kerrie told me how one day she found a box with Bernadette's precious belongings.

> I remember we had a wardrobe, and there was a box in it, and I took it out one day and was looking through it. There was a skipping-rope in it and copybooks. I had my back to the door and I was looking at all of Bernadette's stuff, and the next thing I sensed someone at my shoulder. I turned around and it was Mum. I remember thinking I was in trouble for taking out the box. Mum just bent down beside me and said, 'Kerrie, I don't want you looking at this on your own. If you ever want to look at this again, ask me and I'll show you; but it's very precious, and you can't tear anything, you have to be very careful.' And that's a very strong memory I have.

From some of the writings in her English copybook it is clear that Bernadette was a clever and imaginative pupil. Her book is neatly ruled with a small margin on the left, and she dated her essays. In an essay on 'Rain' she observed matter-of-factly:

> Only for rain we would be dead. We would not have anything to eat. Wheat and potatoes need water.

In an essay on 'School Play Time' she wrote:

> When the boys are playing football they get angry when the girls walk across the place where they are playing. The boys do not like to be disturbed … The girls sometimes play Mammies and Daddies. I like school play time, it is the best time of the whole day's school.

By May 1970 all lakes and rivers in the area around Collooney had been searched by the Garda Water Unit. All vacant houses, sandpits, septic tanks, sewerage systems, coal bunkers and other places had also been searched, but no trace of Bernadette had been found.

Maureen Connolly had given the detectives a detailed description of every piece of clothing that her daughter had been wearing. Detectives were also looking for Bernadette's glasses and the three medals that she wore pinned to her vest. Bernadette's description had been circulated to every Garda station in the country, and the RUC were also contacted. The police in Britain were also alerted, in case Bernadette had been abducted and taken out of the country on a ferry.

As the investigation continued, the questionnaires distributed by the Gardaí yielded reports of a number of vehicles seen on the day of Bernadette's disappearance. Some of these vehicles were never properly identified and remain lines of inquiry to this day.

A number of people reported seeing a dark-green Ford Escort van in the area on 17 April. A similar type of van was owned by Cloonamahon Monastery, which possessed some farmland and provided a local milk delivery service. The Gardaí questioned everyone at the monastery, but none of the priests, brothers or lay workers could say they were driving the van any time between 4:30 and 7:55 p.m. that evening. Other vehicles that remain unidentified or not adequately accounted for include a white Zephyr, a black Zephyr, a black Hillman Hunter and a Blue Anglia.

As the investigation moved into a second month and then a third, and with no leads emerging, detectives from the Murder Squad returned to Dublin to work on other cases. None of the fingerprints taken from more than five hundred people matched the print found on Bernadette's bike. And while the Gardaí believed some people were being evasive in their answers, there was nothing to indicate firmly who might be responsible for the ten-year-old's abduction.

In the weeks and months after Bernadette's disappearance there were constant visitors to the Connolly house. Neighbours brought biscuits and sandwiches and did whatever else they could to help. Gerry and Maureen also received countless letters and postcards of support from people throughout the country. The couple wrote a standard but heartfelt reply, thanking people for their consolation and encouragement following Bernadette's disappearance.

> We really don't know how we could have got through such a trying time had it not been for all the people who helped us or indeed suffered with us … Since Bernie is still not back with us and knowing how kind you have been in the past, we know we can ask you one more special favour—please remember her and us in your Masses and prayers. We will never forget you in our prayers.

On Tuesday 4 August 1970 Margaret O'Connor was loading turf at a bog in Limnagh on the border between Co. Roscommon and Co. Sligo. It was a warm, dry day, and Margaret was working close to a narrow sand road just north of the Curlew Mountains. As she paused for breath she suddenly got a very bad smell. She thought it was a dead animal, and she soon left the bog and headed home.

Two days later Margaret returned to the bog and again got a bad smell. She was standing on the roadside and knew by the smell that the source could not be far away. She decided to investigate and walked up onto a turf bank between the narrow road and surrounding bogland on her left-hand side. She walked along the embankment, studying the bog carefully as she went. She had travelled only a short distance when she looked into a bog drain and saw teeth and small bones.

For 112 days Bernadette Connolly's body lay hidden at Limnagh Bog, fifteen miles from the quiet lane where she had been abducted. For those sixteen weeks her body lay two hundred yards from a main road. Thousands of vehicles would have travelled along the Boyle–Ballymote road from the end of April until early August; but no-one except Bernadette's killer knew the little girl's remains were hidden a short distance away, up the narrow Limnagh road.

After making the shocking discovery, Margaret O'Connor ran to get her husband. When he arrived at the bog he agreed with his wife that the remains were almost certainly human, and they both thought of the missing Bernadette Connolly. Margaret phoned Boyle Garda station, and when Sergeant John Cuffe arrived at the scene he knew immediately that the remains were human. He cordoned off the area and rang his superiors.

Bernadette was still wearing her white vest with the three religious medals pinned to it. She was also wearing her brown anorak and blue blouse and her pinafore dress. Animals had tampered with Bernadette's body as it lay in Limnagh Bog. Her body would have been intact when her killer left her hidden at the bog, but by the time her remains were recovered Bernadette's legs and right arm were gone. Also missing were Bernadette's underwear, tights and slip. Her shoes and glasses were also not at the bog. A nine-carat gold signet ring she wore on her right middle finger was also never found.

A neighbour and a relative of the Connollys were asked to go to Limnagh bog to provisionally identify Bernadette's clothing. They confirmed that the anorak, white vest with medals and pinafore dress were similar to those worn by the missing ten-year-old.

Ann Connolly has vivid memories of the day Bernadette was found. A journalist had phoned the house from Dublin early that morning to ask if there were any developments in the case. The newspapers hadn't phoned in quite a while, and though the reporter made it seem like a routine call, with hindsight Ann believes the reporter had heard something.

> When the journalist phoned we had no idea that Bernie had been found. I remember that it seemed strange that he called like that. It put the hackles up my mother; she was saying maybe they knew something we didn't. I was helping Mam to get Patricia dressed and we were putting her hair back in a ponytail, and Mam got Tommy dressed. We were getting ready to cycle to Collooney, and then the phone rang again. It was another journalist, also ringing to see if there were any developments. Mam was now getting really concerned. We were about to leave the house when she looked out and saw Father Duffy and some neighbours and gardaí coming up the road. Mam stood at the front door and she started screaming, 'Oh, Jesus Christ, they've found her.' Mam knew they weren't coming with a priest with good news.

Gerry Connolly was working in Tobercurry that Thursday, and someone was sent to find him and break the news. Meanwhile people were trying to console his wife in Collooney. Ann remembers that her mother was hysterical.

> I was screaming and crying too, and I remember a garda slapped me on the face to try and stop me screaming. Mam was totally distraught, and she put her arms around me. I can remember her saying she was going to kill us all: she said she wanted us all to be with Bernie. And people were saying to her that she couldn't do that, that she had other children who needed her. But Mam just wanted to die. There was no such thing as counselling in those days; you were supposed to control your feelings.

At 9 a.m. on Saturday 7 August 1970 the assistant state pathologist, Dr R. B. O'Neill, visited Limnagh Bog and studied Bernadette's body as it lay in the turf. He noticed a pinkish stain on Bernadette's brown anorak, and he confirmed the belief of detectives that the body had been in the bog up to four months and that Bernadette's killer had brought her to Limnagh Bog a short time after she was abducted. Perhaps he had killed her here, or she may have been dead by the time her killer took her from his car or van and left her lying in the bog. Dr O'Neill and the detectives noted that all the items of Bernadette's clothing that were missing were from below the waist.

It was six or seven years after Bernadette was murdered before it dawned on her older sister that she may have been sexually assaulted. Ann was in Collooney when someone asked her if Bernadette had been raped.

> I was about eighteen or nineteen when someone asked me that question, just like that. It was only when this girl asked me one day that I thought about it. It was like a slap in the face. Bernie never even kissed a boy. We grew up knowing we should never take sweets from strangers or talk to them, because they might 'do nasty things to you.' But we thought those nasty things were that they might slap you or hit you, or shout at you, we were so innocent.

Bernadette's body was removed from Limnagh Bog and taken to Boyle District Hospital, where a post-mortem examination was carried out. Because of the length of time the body lay undiscovered it was not possible to give an exact cause of death. Without doubt she had been murdered, but it could not be established whether she had been beaten or attacked with any implement or whether she been strangled.

The three medals were removed from Bernadette's vest and placed in a small glass box. Detectives wanted to show her family the medals to further identify the little girl's remains. Bernadette had been a religious girl and never went anywhere without her

. Having shown Bernadette's family her medals, the Gardaí
them away again; they were still part of the evidence in a
m. ler inquiry.

While the post-mortem examination was being completed in
. Boyle, members of the Murder Squad arrived back in Co. Sligo.
Their inquiries had reached a brick wall in the weeks after
Bernadette disappeared. Now, with the discovery of her body,
detectives had a second crime scene to consider.

Considering the geography of the area, the Gardaí knew there
were three ways Bernadette's killer could have travelled from the
Lisaneena road to Limnagh Bog. If he had driven up behind
Bernadette as she cycled to the Molloys' house he could have
abducted her and continued driving past the Molloys' to the
junction with the road heading south for Ballymote. He could
have driven through Ballymote until he crossed the boundary
with Co. Roscommon and then turned left up the Limnagh road;
alternatively, having abducted Bernadette the killer could have
turned back towards the junction with the Collooney road and
turned right, travelling past the Connollys' house and driving
through Castlebaldwin and Ballinafad before turning right into
Limnagh Bog.

The third option, which has long been analysed by gardaí investigating the case, is that the killer could have travelled the fifteen
miles to Limnagh Bog without having to drive along any main
road at all. Assuming Bernadette was abducted at the spot where
her bicycle and her mother's purse were found, the killer could
have turned back and taken an immediate right turn down by the
back of Cloonamahon Monastery. He could then have driven
through a myriad of back roads, through the townlands of
Branchfield and Doobeg and through the village of Graniamore,
and then skirted around the Bricklieve Mountains before arriving
at Limnagh Bog. This isolated route may have been the journey
favoured by the killer if Bernadette was crying out or screaming
for help. If so, the killer had to be someone with local knowledge
of the back roads of south Co. Sligo.

Amid heartbreaking scenes, Bernadette Connolly was laid to

rest on Sunday 9 August 1970. Her youngest sister, Patricia, was only four years old and her brother Tommy was eight, and it was decided that they were too young to attend the funeral. Ann, who was thirteen, stood beside her distraught mother and father at Collooney cemetery. Girls from Bernadette's class led the funeral procession as the white coffin was carried through Collooney. At the graveside Gerry Connolly held his hand to his face as tears fell. Beside him, Maureen was doubled over in grief, a priest holding her tightly. Ann was also broken-hearted and stood at her mother's shoulder, her eyes fixed on the coffin containing her sister's body. A number of priests stood with the family at the graveside, along with local people, as children stood by silently, watching in sadness and bewilderment as Bernadette's coffin was lowered into the ground.

One of the local gardaí involved in the investigation was Seán Doherty, who would later become Minister for Justice. In a television interview shortly before his death he spoke about the immediate impact of Bernadette's murder on the north-west of the country. 'It was a horrific time,' he said. 'Homes were locked, doors were closed. Fear beset the totality of the population.'

Local detectives and members of the Murder Squad rapidly expanded their investigations in the days after Bernadette's body was found. The Murder Squad directed that every male over the age of fifteen within an area of 380 square miles was to be asked to account for their movements on 17 April. With the fingerprint on Bernadette's bicycle still not accounted for, detectives were directed to take fingerprints of teenagers or men who might have been near the place where Bernadette's bike was abandoned or the place where her body was found. By the end of August a total of 2,324 sets of fingerprints had been taken.

Then a chance conversation led to the Gardaí identifying the person whose finger mark was on the frame of Bernadette's bike. On 25 August, a garda met a man near Collooney, and during a general conversation the man referred to the mass taking of fingerprints and told the sergeant that he had previously handled the bike. The man's fingerprints had not yet been taken, and the next day he was asked to provide a fingerprint. Sure enough, his print was a match for the finger mark on the bike. This man told how he had once lifted up Bernadette's bicycle and put it in a car when his girl-friend had borrowed it from the Connolly family. The Gardaí eventually established that this man was nowhere near the Lisaneena road when Bernadette vanished; what they thought had been a crucial lead was now defunct.

Another line of inquiry that eventually led nowhere was the pinkish stain found on the right sleeve of Bernadette's anorak. When detectives had spotted the mark at Limnagh Bog they wondered whether it was some type of chemical that might lead them to Bernadette's attacker. This was a time before the Forensic Science Laboratory was in existence, and the anorak was sent to the Institute for Industrial Research and Standards in Dublin. Scientists analysed the pink stain and soon reported that it was caused by a fungal growth typically found in bogland.

With the fingerprint and anorak stain now adequately explained, the Gardaí were left with no real scientific evidence in the case. Detectives concentrated much of their subsequent inquiries on conflicts in evidence between people who completed questionnaires relating to the case. When such conflicts arose the Gardaí brought these people face to face in an effort to get to the truth. It would prove to be a futile exercise, and in the weeks and months after Bernadette Connolly's body was found there was simply no breakthrough.

One of the many conflicts related to whether or not the green van from Cloonamahon Monastery had been at a petrol station in a village near Collooney on the evening Bernadette disappeared. The owner of the shop and filling station was adamant that the van had pulled up outside the shop that night. The shopkeeper described how a man he recognised had been driving the van and had asked him to fill it up. The shopkeeper said he remembered it was the night Bernadette disappeared because the television was showing pictures of the *Apollo 13* space shuttle coming back to earth. When detectives spoke to the man who the shopkeeper said was driving the van he emphatically denied being at the service station that night. He told the Gardaí he had been at the shop on other occasions but not on the night of 17 April. The shopkeeper died in 1989 and maintained to his death that he had seen the man that night.

Another line of inquiry never adequately explained was a blue Anglia car spotted near Ballymote on the day of Bernadette's abduction. A witness came forward after Bernadette's body was found to say that four months previously they had seen a girl sitting in a blue Anglia car near a school close to Ballymote. A man was sitting in the driver's seat and the girl was in the passenger seat while the car was parked on a grass verge on a side road. The Gardaí tried to find every blue Anglia in Cos. Sligo, Leitrim, Roscommon and Mayo, but the blue Anglia in question was never identified.

In October 1970 the Connolly family moved out of the cottage in Doorla and moved into the centre of Collooney. Their newly built house was not fully ready for the move; the electricity was not even connected. But within weeks of laying her daughter to rest, Maureen Connolly could not stay in the old house any longer. One of the first things she said when the family arrived at their new home was, 'Wouldn't Bernie love this!'

In January 1972 Maureen gave birth to Kerrie, bringing more happiness into the house. Ann was now fifteen, Tommy was nine and Patricia was five. Maureen and Gerry never spoke to their remaining children about what had happened to Bernie. They would naturally talk about her and the happy times they had, but they never spoke about the evil that occurred in April 1970. Neither Gerry, Maureen nor their children ever had counselling; such a service didn't exist in the 1970s.

Twelve years after Bernadette's murder the Connolly family suffered a further tragedy. Maureen Connolly was only forty-eight when she died on 23 July 1982. She had overcome previous ill health when she had gallstones removed, but then she developed bowel cancer, and it was diagnosed too late. When Maureen died her eldest child, Ann, was twenty-five, while her youngest child, Kerrie, was only ten. Kerrie told me of the sadness the family have felt since then.

Even when I was out looking for my wedding dress I was thinking about how it was yet another day that neither Bernie nor Mum were here with us. Weddings and christenings and other family occasions have been robbed from them. And their presence has been robbed from us too. And just think what achievements might Bernie have had, what might she have done with her life. We've been completely robbed of all that.

Kerrie showed me a set of passport photographs that were taken of Bernadette and her mother. Bernadette was almost the image of Maureen. In one of the four pictures the two are smiling straight at the camera in a classic pose; in the other pictures they are pulling funny faces and making each other laugh.

Gerry Connolly was seventy-two when he died on 28 December 1999. He was deeply affected by the loss of his wife and by the loss of Bernadette. He could not and would not speak to his remaining daughters and son about the murder of their sister. He did speak to his friends who had been around at the time, and in his later years he spent many hours analysing and re-analysing things people had said and done at the time of Bernadette's disappearance.

In the absence of any clear answers about who was responsible for murdering his daughter, Gerry Connolly was tormented by trying to find out who killed his child. One person he often thought about was a student priest who had comforted the family in the weeks before Bernadette's body was found. This man had acted for a time as a buffer between the Connolly family and the outside world. Thousands of letters of support were being sent to the Connollys from people around the world, and this man would open their post, saying he wanted to make sure they didn't read upsetting material. He aroused curiosity when he suggested to the Gardaí that Bernadette might have been abducted by British forces in an attempt to ensure that IRA guns were discovered during searches for the little girl in Co. Sligo.

There was another unusual incident in the months before Bernadette's body was found when this man told of following a car that was driving suspiciously near the Connollys' house. He said the car drove towards Ballinafad but he then lost sight of it. Where Bernadette's body was later found is not very far from Ballinafad.

The student priest left Ireland in December 1970 and spent much of his subsequent life in Africa before he died some years ago. A fellow-priest who studied with him in 1970 subsequently met the sisters of Bernadette Connolly and told them it was his firm belief that this man had nothing to do with Bernadette's murder, that he simply would not have had the mentality to attack a young girl.

Gerry Connolly never publicly mentioned the name of any person he suspected of being involved in his daughter's killing. Before his death in 1999 he had spent three decades trying to piece together scraps of information and innuendo, but he died without the answers he longed for. In later years he confided in friends that even if he was 99 per cent certain he knew who killed his child he would still be more afraid of that 1 per cent of doubt.

———

Unknown at the time of Bernadette Connolly's abduction and murder, a dangerous paedophile from England was travelling through Ireland during part of 1970 and spent a considerable time in south Co. Sligo. The man, whose initials are R.R., was from Northampton and wrote for a fishing magazine in England. He was thirty-seven when he spent time in Ireland with another man in 1970, driving a dark-green van and sampling and reviewing a number of fishing lakes and rivers. At that time he had no convictions for sexual violence; his only conviction was for minor theft in England eight years previously. It was three years after the abduction and murder of Bernadette Connolly that this man emerged as a possible suspect after he abducted four young Irish girls in four counties.

In May 1973 R.R. abducted a nine-year-old girl in Co. Mayo as she was out cycling. He subjected the girl to a horrific sexual assault before bringing her back to where he had taken her. The girl was later able to give detectives a detailed description of her attacker and also of the van in which she had been abducted. It was some months before the English fishing journalist was arrested near a lake by alert gardaí who spotted his van and realised it matched the description of the one used in the attack in Co. Mayo. By the time he was arrested R.R. had also attacked young girls in Cos. Sligo, Cork and Cavan. He admitted the offences and was jailed for seven years.

When detectives investigating the murder of Bernadette Connolly interviewed the man he said he had not been in the country at the time of the killing. He told them he had arrived in Ireland eight days after Bernadette's abduction, arriving on 25 April 1970 to work on articles for the May edition of the magazine. With nothing to contradict the man's story, the detectives were never able to take the matter further.

In June 2003 two detectives from Co. Sligo travelled to England to meet this man. The then assistant commissioner for the north-west region, Kevin Carty, had directed a review of the investigation after Bernadette's sisters contacted the Gardaí with a number of questions about the case. One of their queries was about the extent of the original Garda investigation into the movements of R.R. throughout Ireland in the early 1970s. Their concern had been heightened by a newspaper report in 2003 suggesting that the convicted paedophile had in fact spent a considerable time in the area of Co. Sligo from where Bernadette was abducted. It was now suggested by a local man that in the early 1970s R.R. had visited Templehouse Lake, near Ballymote, and other places near where Bernadette had disappeared.

Two gardaí, assisted by Northampton police, called to R.R.'s door, and when the detectives introduced themselves and explained why they were there the man immediately recognised the name Bernadette Connolly. He agreed to meet the detectives voluntarily at the local police station later that day.

When he sat down with the detectives the man was able to recount the names of the two Irish detectives he said had interviewed him thirty years before. He told the new investigation team how he had provided the Gardaí at that time with documentary evidence from his employer to prove he had not arrived in Ireland until 25 April 1970, and said he had nothing further to add to what he had already said. The detectives travelled back to Ireland with little new information.

More recently this man, now in his seventies, was convicted in England of sexually assaulting another young girl and was given a lengthy prison sentence. The Gardaí have since made inquiries on a number of occasions through the English police about whether R.R. has anything further to tell them as he serves his sentence, and those inquiries continue.

When the fresh review of the murder file was undertaken in 2003, Bernadette's three sisters met Assistant Commissioner Carty and Detective-Inspector James Kearins on a number of occasions. The Connollys had many questions about the conduct of the original investigation; in particular they wanted to know what had happened to Bernadette's bike, her medals and their mother's purse, all of which had been kept by the Gardaí as evidence in the case.

Despite an extensive search of all possible sites, the gardaí involved in the fresh investigation were unable to find Bernadette's possessions. The materials had most probably been sent to Dublin in 1970 for safe keeping during the original murder investigation, but the relevant gardaí at the time or in later years did not have the foresight to keep them in safe storage. As with the loss of evidence from a number of major crimes in the 1970s, the Gardaí did not keep a proper chain of evidence relating to Bernadette's belongings, which greatly frustrated those involved in the fresh review of the case. It also annoyed the original Co. Sligo gardaí who had first worked on the case. With advances in forensic science it was conceivable that hairs or fibres undetectable by the human eye might have been found on Bernadette's bicycle or medals or on the purse. Even if that was not so and there was no prospect of a criminal trial, by rights the items should have been properly preserved and returned to the family.

Assistant Commissioner Carty and Detective-Inspector Kearins travelled to meet Bernadette's sisters to tell them in person that Bernadette's belongings could not be found. Ann, Patricia and Kerrie thanked the Gardaí for their efforts but insisted that searches and inquiries should continue to find out what exactly happened to their sister's medals and their mother's purse. Kerrie told me that this is the least the state should do.

> We're going to meet Bernie some day, and we have to do every-thing we can now to get justice for her, to get answers. At the very least we want her possessions back. Until then I'm not going to feel we have done what we could.

In Collooney, Ann goes back again in her mind to the time Bernadette disappeared. She has many memories but for years did not talk about things; it is only since her father died that she has spoken more. Because their father found it too upsetting to discuss Bernadette's murder, Ann is now an important source of inform-ation for her brother, Tommy, for her sisters and now for her own children, but she still sometimes finds it hard to talk. She remem-bers that a few days after Bernadette disappeared the Gardaí asked her to cycle the same route as Bernadette had done, to try to time the journey. Ann was so distressed by what was going on that she simply cycled as fast as she could to get it over and done with.

Another distinct memory is of a garda asking her detailed ques-tions designed to find out if anyone was interfering with her. It was a male garda who asked her the questions.

> I was only thirteen years old and still in a period of innocence. This garda was asking me if anyone ever grabbed my chest or grabbed me anywhere else. I was absolutely terrified. He was probably told to question me like this. I remember I ran to my Mam and I had to be sedated.

In recent times Ann has spoken about the feelings of guilt she had for many years. Naturally, when her little sister was taken away from her in such a violent way Ann was distraught. Ann and Bernadette had shared a bed and they were best friends. At times after Bernadette's murder Ann wished she could bring her sister back and take her place in that lane. Part of Ann's grieving involved feelings of regret for the times the two of them may have fought when growing up.

> You want to remember Bernie for all the happy memories and the way she was laughing and smiling and happy. It actually took me years to get like that. It still upsets me how when I was small there might have been times when I wasn't nice to her. We were great friends but, like all kids, we might have had rows. For a long time after Bernie was gone I would think a lot about how I might have been horrible to her about something. I couldn't remember how I was good to her, or how we'd have a laugh; I would just remember the times I'd be fighting with her.

In November 1969 a severe storm hit Ireland, and the pupils at Collooney Primary School were asked to describe it. Bernadette Connolly described how the electricity supply was disrupted as a result of the storm and how the Posts and Telegraphs men had to go out in lorries to fix telephone lines damaged by the storm.

> It was very wild on Sunday. The wind was blowing, the rain was falling, the thunder was rumbling. I do not think there was lightning at that time. It was wild after that too. But this time lightning fell. I never saw it but my sister Ann saw it.

If it wasn't for the chance discovery at Limnagh Bog in August 1970, Bernadette Connolly's would be the oldest continuing missing person investigation in the country. That sad label is now applied to Mary Boyle, who was only six when she vanished near Ballyshannon, Co. Donegal, on 18 March 1977. The Boyle and Connolly families have never met; a meeting was to be organised in the late 1970s but Maureen Connolly wasn't up to it. Instead she sent her heartfelt best wishes and prayers to Mary's parents and brother and sister.

While the family of Mary Boyle still suffer not knowing what happened to their little girl, or where she is, the family of Bernadette Connolly continue to suffer a different form of anguish. At least Bernadette's body was found and laid to rest, but her family are tormented every day, wondering who was responsible for her death and what exactly happened on the Lisaneena road on that Friday in 1970. It's the same type of anguish that the family of nine-year-old Jennifer Cardy in Co. Antrim suffer. Jennifer was also cycling when she was abducted near Ballinderry in 1981; her body was found a number of days later, but her killer remains at large.

Another girl who was abducted while cycling was Genette Tate, who was thirteen when she vanished in England in August 1978. Genette was doing a paper round in the village of Aylesbeare in Devon at the time, and whoever abducted her left her bicycle and newspapers lying on the ground in the lane from where she was taken. No trace of Genette has been found in the last thirty years, and the Devon and Cornwall Police continue to actively investigate her murder.

The reality that there are serial killers who attack children was proved in England in 1994 when a Scottish man, Robert Black, was finally convicted of killing three girls over a period of five years in the 1980s. Black abducted and murdered eleven-year-old Susan Maxwell from Northumberland in 1982, five-year-old Caroline Hogg from Edinburgh in 1983 and ten-year-old Sarah Harper from Leeds in 1986. Black was a driver of a poster delivery van who travelled throughout Britain and Ireland during the 1970s and 80s. The bodies of his three known victims were buried within an area 26 miles wide encompassing parts of three English midland counties.

When Black was convicted the English police invited the Gardaí to a conference to investigate whether he might be linked to the murder of Bernadette Connolly or the disappearance of Mary Boyle. After some inquiries it was decided that Black was not a likely suspect for the murder of Bernadette Connolly, but he remains a possible suspect for the disappearance of Mary Boyle.

The Gardaí have long wondered whether the person who murdered Bernadette Connolly tried to commit other similar attacks. If Bernadette was attacked by a paedophile travelling throughout Ireland, what stopped the killer from murdering another child? Was the person jailed for other offences and therefore not able to commit any other crimes? Or did he leave the jurisdiction and attack children elsewhere? Was he killed in an accident or did he die of natural causes soon after murdering Bernadette, so taking his secrets to the grave? Did he continue to assault children in Ireland but somehow decide not to kill again?

Or is it that Bernadette Connolly was not the victim of a random abduction but knew her killer? Was the killer someone who set out that day to find a local child to murder, or did he act on impulse in taking a young girl's life? Had he later any remorse for what he did; indeed might he have confided in someone or confessed his evil deed? Is the killer someone who is still living in the north-west of Ireland who has never come to the attention of the Gardaí?

In 1999 a man contacted the Gardaí with interesting information. He described how in April 1970 he had been a young boy and had been cycling along a road in Co. Sligo. He described how, as he cycled past a parked car, the driver had made a lunge for him; the boy managed to evade the man and continued cycling to safety. The boy had memorised the registration number of the car, and almost thirty years later he could still recall it. From the number the Gardaí found it had belonged to a Scottish man who had worked in the Sligo area as a television repairman. Detectives got in touch with their counterparts in Scotland and soon discovered that the man had convictions for sexually abusing boys. One garda involved in the case says the information was very interesting but didn't lead anywhere.

It was amazing that this man who narrowly escaped being attacked in 1970 could remember the licence number, and it gave us an interesting lead. When we learnt that the driver was a paedophile we thought we might be on to something. But we checked him out as best we could and all his convictions relate to offences against boys. Some people put forward a theory that maybe with the hood of her anorak up that Bernadette might have been mistaken for a boy, but she was wearing a pinafore dress and I don't think such confusion would have been there. However, the man coming forward to assist us is clear evidence that people have clear recall of information relating to traumatic events in their lives going back decades. I am convinced there are people still around who know or strongly suspect exactly what happened to Bernadette—the vehicle she was abducted in, the location where she was murdered and manner of her death, and the route her killer took to Limnagh Bog.

Ann, Tommy, Patricia and Kerrie have never been to the spot where their sister's body lay undiscovered for four months. Any time they are driving from Sligo towards Boyle on the Dublin road they know the Limnagh road is off to the right near Ballinafad, but they have no desire to go near the isolated place where such evil occurred.

The old family home at Doorla is now gone, and the road where Bernadette cycled past Oliver Flynn on the horse and cart that Friday in 1970 is now a 100 km per hour stretch of the N4. The nearby Cloonamahon Monastery where Bernadette spent many happy hours attending a youth club is now a care facility run by the Health Service Executive.

There is nothing to mark the spot where Bernadette's bike was placed by her killer on the embankment above the Lisaneena road. Even today the road is quiet, with only a few houses set back off the road. It's a scenic drive, with the nearby Tobarscanavan Loughs visible through the trees.

Somewhere in Co. Sligo or beyond, Bernadette Connolly's round, pink-rimmed glasses are lying unclaimed. The gold signet ring she wore on her right hand is also still missing. Her tights, underwear and shoes were also never found.

Bernadette's three sisters and surviving brother are all now parents themselves. Some of Bernadette's nieces and nephews are young adults and know much of the detail of the pain that was visited on the family in 1970. While Tommy and his family live in Co. Cavan, the three sisters continue to live in the Collooney area. Kerrie lives in the house that the family first moved into in late 1970, while Patricia and Ann live nearby. Bernadette is laid to rest with her mother and father and younger brother, Gerard, in Collooney Cemetery.

In December 1971 an inquest was held into Bernadette's death, but the jury heard that because the girl's body lay undiscovered for four months it was not possible to establish the exact cause of her death. The coroner, P. K. Johnson, told the court:

> The fact that the inquest into the death of the late Bernadette Connolly has concluded does not mean that the exhaustive investigations by the Garda authorities into her death have concluded. These investigations will never cease until the mystery of the little girl's terrible and tragic death is solved.

In the months before her violent death Bernadette Connolly filled half her English copybook with school work, including spelling corrections, where she wrote the correct spelling of each word three times. By April 1970 she had used a ruler to draw margins on ten pages that she would never get to fill. One of the last things she wrote was a description of herself.

Myself—23rd February 1970
My name is Bernadette Connolly. My address is Doorla, Collooney, Co. Sligo, Éire. My age is ten. My birthday is on the first of August. I was born in the year nineteen fifty nine. I have two sisters. I have one brother. My sister's names are Ann and Patricia. My brother's name is Tommy. There are four children in our family. Me and Tommy go to Lackagh School. My teachers name is Mrs. Kearns. My sister Ann goes to the secondary school in Ballymote. My sister Patricia does not go to school at all. I was born in England and so was Tommy and Ann. But Patricia was born in Ireland. I have a lot of friends,

Mary Flynn is my best friend. Ann Kearns and Rita Sweeney and Ann Sweeney are good friends of mine. I want to be a teacher when I grow up. I have brown hair. I have curly hair. I have brown eyes. I have glasses. I sit beside Patsy Kerins.

02 | THE MURDER OF MARIE KILMARTIN

For 176 days Marie Kilmartin's body lay hidden in a watery grave. The large concrete block that lay on the left side of her chest ensured that Marie's body stayed rigid beneath the bog water. She lay on her back, with her head turned towards her right shoulder. She was still fully clothed, dressed in her matching jacket and skirt, double-breasted herringbone overcoat and lace-up boots. Whoever killed her had used their bare hands to strangle her before throwing her body into the bog drain and dumping debris on top of her.

This was no random abduction: it was a deliberate killing of a woman by someone she probably knew. Someone ringing her from a nearby phone box had tricked Marie into leaving her house in Port Laoise.

Marie suffered from her nerves and would rarely if ever venture outdoors in the dark by herself. She set the house alarm and left her home at half past four on the afternoon of Thursday 16 December 1993, and she would not be seen alive again. In the following hours she was murdered at some unknown place and her body taken twelve miles from Port Laoise to dark, isolated bogland.

As the following months became years, the killer would not be brought to justice and would come to believe he had got away with murder; but he never reckoned on the appearance of Marie's daughter—a woman who for the first twenty years of her life never knew that Marie was her mother, instead being told she was a distant relative, who found out the truth only seven years after the killing and who has now made it her life's work to seek justice for her murdered mother.

An off-duty prison officer found Marie's body. Tom Deegan was on a break from a shift at Port Laoise Prison when he decided to bring his two daughters, one of his sons and a friend to visit his other young son, who was cutting turf at a bog north of Mountmellick on the Laois-Offaly border. It was Friday 10 June 1994, and fourteen-year-old Trevor Deegan was making use of the dry weather. He was working at a bog at the end of a long lane known as Pim's Lane, off the main Mountmellick–Portarlington road. He stopped his work and chatted to his father and his sisters and brother, and he drank a flask of tea they had brought. Two-year-old Rebecca began to wander off around the surrounding bog, and Tom followed, holding his daughter's hand.

All around lay acres of bogland, as far as the eye could see. Over to his left Tom spotted what looked like the wheel of a pram sticking up from a bog drain. Only the wheel was visible, with the rest covered by water and ferns. Tom looked closer: he'd seen something else, or at least he thought he had. It looked like a black boot sticking up towards the top of the water, but not only that: he thought he could see a human leg attached to it.

Tom was shocked but he didn't want to upset his children and so didn't go any closer to the drain, and he didn't say what he thought he had seen. Instead he brought his children home and told his wife about it. They agreed he should go back and investigate further.

It was still bright at about 9 p.m. when Tom Deegan ventured back down the winding lane to the bog. As he approached the drain he again saw the boot and what looked like a leg beneath the water. He slowly moved closer and could now see a second boot and a second leg. He immediately went to raise the alarm.

Marie Kilmartin was thirty-five when she was murdered. She was the third-youngest of four children born to Fred and Rose

Kilmartin. Fred was a successful businessman in the Ballinasloe and Athlone areas, building up a multi-million-pound car dealership and garage business. It was in Ballinasloe that Marie grew up with her sister, Theresa, and brothers, Anthony and Noel. She later went to school at the Ursuline Convent in Sligo.

At an early age Marie was diagnosed as having a psychiatric condition. To this day the underlying cause of her mental illness has not been established, but by late 1979, when she was twenty years old and it was discovered that she was pregnant, Marie was in mental turmoil. Her family placed her under the care of Dr Liam Hanniffy at St Fintan's Hospital in Port Laoise. Nurses remember her early time there as stormy; while being assessed she was in the most secure locked part of the hospital. It was here that Marie met a nurse, Pat Doyle, who in time would become Marie's best friend. Pat told me it's still difficult to think of how Marie was at that time.

> My heart went out to her when I first saw her. She was such a frightened young woman, and on top of being in a psychiatric hospital here she was pregnant. She was very lonely and very distressed. I spent a good deal of time with her right from the start. At first it was a nurse-and-patient relationship. I was arrogant enough to think I could cure her, or get her well again, get her going again. Over time, as she became better and better, it was a friendship of equals, and we ended up sharing a house in Port Laoise for over a decade. But I'll always remember how helpless and sad Marie was when she first came to the hospital. She seemed very lost.

On the afternoon of 29 March 1980 Marie gave birth to a baby girl at Port Laoise General Hospital, having been transferred from the nearby St Fintan's to have her baby. She wanted to keep her child, but she couldn't. She was distraught. She said she wanted to call her baby Rosemarie, and her wish was duly noted in the hospital records, which also recorded that Marie's baby weighed six pounds and three ounces. Within days the baby girl was taken

from Marie and brought back to Co. Galway to be adopted within the wider family.

Two months later, as Marie remained in hospital, the infant was
baptised at a church in Dublin as Áine Mairéad under the sur-
name of her adoptive family. From then on the little girl was Áine;
the name Rosemarie Kilmartin existed only on a birth certificate,
which recorded the date and place of birth and the identity of the
mother. For the following twenty years Áine wouldn't even know
this birth certificate existed. She would be told at an early age that
she was adopted, but not that her real mother was part of the
wider family. For years Áine would believe she had a different date
of birth and that she had no birth certificate.

————

Garda Pat Lyne was the first garda at the murder scene. He was on
duty at Portarlington station when he was told of the emergency
call about a body being found in a bog. He drove to Pim's Lane,
where Tom Deegan was waiting. Together they went down the
lane and Tom pointed out the drain over towards the left. Garda
Lyne looked closely at the darkened water and saw the two feet. He
peered more closely and could see a body beneath the water. The
body was covered with an old pram and parts of a gas heater.
There was a fresh growth of furze and ferns on the water, and it
was clear that the body had been there for some time. He could
just make out that the head and shoulders of the body were much
lower down in the water than the legs.

He immediately preserved the scene. Tom Deegan went back to
the top of the lane to direct more gardaí down as they arrived. By
10 p.m. senior officers were arriving at the scene, cordoning it off.
As they looked at the woman's boots sticking up through the bog
water, a number of gardaí immediately thought of Marie
Kilmartin, who had been missing for almost six months. A call
was made to the state pathologist, Dr John Harbison, and he
arranged to travel to the bog the next day. With darkness falling it

was now too late to do anything except preserve the scene; the body would have to remain in the water for one more night.

The last definite sighting of Marie Kilmartin was by two of her friends and colleagues on the afternoon of Thursday 16 December 1993. She had spent the earlier part of the afternoon working at a day-care centre for the elderly in Port Laoise. She was a volunteer worker and was loved by the men and women she helped to look after. She served meals, played cards with them, and chatted for hours. She was comfortable in this environment: it was a form of sheltered employment for her as well as a social outlet that gave her a feeling of self-worth.

She was now many years out of St Fintan's Hospital. Every now and then she would get depressed, especially when she would think about her baby girl being raised away in Co. Galway. But she had a strong group of friends around her in Port Laoise, and with their support she was able to function in the community. She didn't have to work: her family in Ballinasloe were well off. Her father had bought her a house in Port Laoise, which she shared with Pat Doyle, her best friend, who had helped get her back on her feet.

Marie normally worked part-time at the care centre, starting at about 11 a.m. and finishing between 2 and 3 p.m. She didn't drive, and during the summer she would sometimes walk the mile or so to her home at Beladd on the Stradbally road. But Marie didn't like the dark, and during the winter months she would always take a lift home.

That day Marie took a lift home with Frances Bleach and Frances Conroy. It was 4:10 p.m. when the car pulled up outside 12 Beladd, one of a row of spacious bungalows set in off the Stradbally road. The three women were in great spirits; they'd had a Christmas party that lunchtime for staff members and those who attended the day centre. Marie invited her two friends in for a cup of coffee, but the two women said they would head on. Marie grabbed a bag of shopping she'd picked up earlier in the day and said goodbye. The two women saw Marie go in the door of her house, and they drove off.

Perhaps the killer was watching. Perhaps he had followed the car all or part of the distance from the day centre in the town; or perhaps he had been parked near Beladd, silently waiting until he saw Marie go into the house. It was only a short time later, at 4:25 p.m., that the mysterious phone call was made to the house from a coinbox phone back towards the town centre.

Áine was thirteen when Marie was murdered. Growing up in a town in Co. Galway, she knew from an early age that she was adopted but never knew the full truth. She met Marie a few times, always believing she was a distant relative. It was only in the last few years that she discovered that Marie was her mother. Now a young adult, Áine has combined college studies with the launch of a nationwide campaign to raise awareness about her mother's unsolved murder. She is passionate and dogmatic about getting to the truth in the case. She has suffered much emotional turmoil in recent times; she has many sad memories and is angry that she wasn't told the truth sooner. But amid the pain there is some happiness: memories of Marie that are now amplified in her mind and that with hindsight have a deeper meaning.

> I would have seen Marie once every few years, and I didn't really think twice about her; I didn't have a clue. I have one particular memory of her which is quite endearing in retrospect. My adopted mum was driving me one day in Galway. It was during the summer, and we saw Marie and a friend walking along. For some unknown reason I made Mum stop the car and I gave Marie a Wispa bar that I had, and I gave her a big hug. At the time I didn't know why I was doing that. I am so happy now that I gave her that Wispa bar! Such a simple thing, but it must have meant the world to her at the time.

Another time, when Áine was about seven, Marie watched as she played the piano.

> I was with my cousin, and we were both playing the piano. Marie had come to visit, and she was there with my aunt

watching the two of us play. I don't remember this particular occasion, but I've been told about it since. Just think about that: my aunt watching her daughter, and Marie watching hers. I find it so sad to think of that scene. Why couldn't Marie keep me? I know she wanted to. Why couldn't she?

At midday on Saturday 11 June 1994 Dr John Harbison arrived in Co. Laois, where he met Inspector Philip Lyons. The inspector brought Dr Harbison to the bog at the end of Pim's Lane. Detective-Garda Tony Byrne had already been at the scene for a number of hours, taking photographs of the body and the surrounding bogland. A local priest was also brought to the scene and gave the last rites.

Dr Harbison studied the body as it lay in the water. One of the first things he did was to remove the large concrete block lying on the victim's chest. The block was about twelve inches wide, six inches long and four inches deep. In order to remove the body a pram and parts of a gas canister had also to be taken from the water. It was a distressing scene, which left many of the gardaí present visibly shaken. Shortly after half past twelve the gardaí began assisting Dr Harbison in taking the body from the bog water. The remains were put on a plastic sheet and then into a coffin. Garda Lyne, who had been the first garda at the scene, and Detective-Garda Patrick Egan then accompanied the unidentified body to Tullamore General Hospital, where Dr Harbison would shortly begin a post-mortem examination.

By the time she was murdered Marie Kilmartin was at a stage where she could recognise and admit when she wasn't feeling well. She could manage her depression: she could cope. What got her down was not being able to see her little girl. She would especially get sad around Áine's birthday, and Christmas time would also be difficult. She would buy presents for Áine but simply put them in a cupboard, perhaps pretending that she was giving them to her. She thought about her daughter every day, and she often cried. Her housemate and best friend, Pat Doyle, and her many friends at the day centre would keep her going, help her to keep her chin up. And when Marie would eventually smile again, as she inevitably would, her friends would describe her as radiant.

Dr Harbison began the post-mortem examination at five o'clock on Saturday 11 June 1994. It was less than five hours since Marie's body had been taken from the bog drain and less than twenty-four hours since the alarm had been raised. The Gardaí strongly suspected that the body now laid out in the morgue in Tullamore was that of Marie Kilmartin, but it would only be through the post-mortem examination that this could be confirmed. The body was intact but because it had been in the water for so long it would not be possible to make a visual identification. The examination would also be crucial in establishing how the unidentified woman had been murdered. Was it the concrete block that had killed her, or had there been some other weapon?

It was already clear from the clothing that the body was that of a woman. Dr Harbison first looked at the victim's hands, removing four rings from her fingers. Two rings were removed from her right middle finger, including a Claddagh ring. He then removed a nine-carat gold cameo ring, and from her left hand he removed a sovereign ring. He looked at the left wrist and removed a 'Guess' watch with a beige leather strap. He removed a gold chain with a heart-shaped locket from around her neck. Marie Kilmartin was known to wear scapulars around her neck, and Dr Harbison was asked to see if he could find them. He found one shoelace-type cord.

He removed Marie's black lace-up boots; they were size 37 and had been made in Brazil. Her overcoat was still buttoned up. He removed the coat and then her discoloured jacket and skirt, which he placed in warm water and biological washing powder. When clean, the skirt and top would turn out to be blue with a large white floral design.

An examination of dental records would later confirm Marie Kilmartin's identity, but it was through her jewellery that she was provisionally identified. Detective-Garda Egan had taken possession of her rings, watch and necklace from Dr Harbison. At Portarlington Garda Station he showed them to Marie's best friend, Pat, and she immediately recognised everything. She herself had bought the Claddagh ring for Marie, and had also given her the sovereign ring as a present. Marie had bought the cameo ring for herself in Dublin. Pat recognised the heart-shaped locket as one she had bought for Marie in Droichead Nua in the late 1980s. The large 'Guess' watch, with mother-of-pearl surround and Roman numerals, was one Marie's father, Fred, had bought for her as a present from China some years before. The green scapular looked like one Marie had got in the Poor Clares Convent in Carlow the previous summer.

Pat was also shown her best friend's clothes. She recognised them all: her overcoat, her grey, red and black woollen scarf, her skirt and top, her black lace-up ankle boots. Pat confirmed to the Gardaí that all the clothing and jewellery were Marie's and would have been worn by her at the time of her disappearance.

The impact on Pat Doyle of losing her best friend in such horrific circumstances was evident when we met. Pat saw Marie on her worst days and on her best. She witnessed Marie struggling against mental demons and saw her winning that battle. She saw her bravery in leaving the hospital and standing on her own two feet. She knew how much Marie missed her little girl, how she pined for her. Pat told me that within hours of Marie going missing she knew something awful had happened.

I remember we had a cup of tea that morning. I was heading to work early and Marie was going to work at around eleven. Marie was talking about who might give her a lift home after work. And she mentioned that some of the girls might go out for a Christmas drink after work, and she was wondering if she might go. I arrived home from work just after six that evening, and when I saw Marie wasn't home I wasn't too surprised initially, because I thought she might have been with the girls somewhere. But as the evening wore on and there was no word I just got very concerned. It wasn't like Marie not to phone to say where she was. I paced around and smoked cigarettes for hours and hours. I remember it was spilling rain. I listened to the radio to see if there had been any accidents. I started ringing around to see if anyone had seen her. And as I sat there late that night I just knew she was dead. I remember feeling this presence in the house. A few weeks before that we'd had one of those silly conversations about death. One of the people from the day centre had died, and Marie was quite upset, and she was asking me if I thought there was anything after death. And she was wondering if one of us died how we'd let the other know if there was something else. And I had said, 'Sure I'll come back and hold your hand,' and Marie, being Marie, asked, 'Which hand, Pat?' and I said, 'The left hand.' Well, that night as I sat waiting for Marie to come home I could feel something at my left hand. I just knew from then on that Marie was dead.

Whoever murdered Marie Kilmartin planned her abduction carefully. At any other time of the year Pat Doyle would have known exactly where Marie might be; but that night she had first thought that Marie might be at a Christmas function. It is possible that the killer intentionally availed of the Christmas period as the most opportune time to abduct and murder. He may also have known that Pat would not be home from work until six that evening. The killer most probably saw the two hours between Marie's arrival home and Pat's arrival home as the window of opportunity for committing the attack. If this is so it would suggest a large degree of premeditation.

When Marie left St Fintan's Hospital in the early 1980s she and Pat moved into a flat on the Dublin Road in Port Laoise. The arrangement suited both of them perfectly. Marie's family did not want her living by herself and were happy that a nurse was living with her. Pat was looking for a place to live; she'd been commuting from her family home in Castlecomer but wanted to get a place in Port Laoise. She was also becoming good friends with Marie, and the decision to become flatmates came easily.

I was just a couple of years older than Marie and we had been getting on very well during her time in the hospital. We were being taught in psychiatric nursing that community care was the big thing. I thought patients should get a chance to live in the community if they wanted to and if they were up to it. Marie had got better and better and it was time for her to start living again. We decided to share a flat, and we found one almost in the centre of town, close to the prison.

It was from a phone box across the road from the flat where Marie and Pat once lived that an unidentified man made the call that led Marie to her death. The call, made at 4:25 p.m. on 16 December 1993, lasted about two-and-a-half minutes. Phone records have established that no other phone call was made from that box between 4:11 p.m. and 4:42 p.m. The phone box still stands on the footpath on the left-hand side of the Dublin Road heading out of Port Laoise towards the prison.

A woman who was hitchhiking on the road that day later came forward to tell the Gardaí she had seen a man in the phone box at about half past four. She described him as being possibly 5 feet 8 inches tall, and he looked about thirty years old. While the description is vague, this man has not yet been identified and could well be the killer.

Is there any significance in where this phone call was made from? Did the caller know of the phone box from the time Marie and Pat lived nearby in the early 1980s? Or did this phone box simply suit the caller as he either drove into Port Laoise or out of it? If the killer had watched Marie going into her house about a mile away up the Stradbally road he would have had ample time to drive down to the phone box to entice her back out. The phone box may have simply been the closest public phone the killer saw.

However, the degree of planning involved in the murder would suggest that this phone box was specifically chosen by the killer from which to make the call. Even if he was not from the area he knew where the phone box was, and he knew it would afford him anonymity as he rang Marie.

As the state pathologist finished his post-mortem examination at Tullamore General Hospital he had formed the view that Marie

Kilmartin had been manually strangled to death. Her laryngeal prominence (Adam's apple) had been fractured at the upper horns, suggesting that two hands squeezing tightly around her neck had caused her death. There was no sign of any other injuries to the body. Though the body had been fully clothed, Dr Harbison examined the possibility that she had been sexually assaulted but found no evidence that she had.

To this day detectives are trying to establish what possible motive there was for Marie's murder. The fact that she was fully clothed, and had no visible injuries except for the fatal injury to her neck, led the Gardaí away from the possibility that the motive was sexual. She was still wearing all her jewellery when she was found, so the robbery of personal effects did not appear to be a motive either.

Detectives have investigated many apparently motiveless murders, where a person had killed simply out of badness, or illness; but such killers usually left a trail leading to their doorstep. Whoever killed Marie Kilmartin had been meticulous, not only planning how to get her out of her house under false pretences but, with local knowledge, having an isolated spot earmarked twelve miles away for leaving her body.

While a clear motive was difficult to establish, the available evidence pointed to somebody who knew Marie well. One hypothesis is that Marie knew some incriminating piece of information about somebody. Perhaps she knew it directly or indirectly; perhaps she realised herself the significance of the information, or perhaps she didn't. But if neither rape nor robbery was the motive, and if the killing was not a random crime, a credible explanation is that Marie was murdered to silence her for ever, with the precise reason perhaps still known only to the killer.

When Marie left the house after receiving the phone call she left her bag of shopping hanging on the back of a chair in the kitchen. This suggests that she had been in the house only a short time before leaving again, not having time to unpack the shopping. She didn't leave a note for Pat, so she probably expected to be back in the house within a few minutes. She may not even have had time to take off her overcoat and put it back on. She did, however, set the alarm on the house, which suggests that she was not just walking out to meet someone at the roadside but was going some distance to meet the person or was being picked up to go somewhere. Whatever the reason for her leaving the house a short time after Frances Bleach and Frances Conroy had left her home, it appears that she did not sense danger.

Marie may have been strangled in a car, or at some place in the Port Laoise area. She may have been punched or disarmed in some way and taken closer to the bogland at Pim's Lane on the Laois-Offaly border before her life was ended. The Gardaí have been frustrated by the fact that there is no murder scene; there is only the spot where Marie's killer dumped her body after taking her life. It is here that, after throwing her body into the deep water of a bog drain, the killer threw a concrete block on top of her and then also the frame of a pram and parts of a Super-Ser gas heater.

In the dark winter months, very few people go near Pim's Lane and the surrounding bogland. Some hunters might venture down the lane, shooting pheasants, or a courting couple might visit the isolated spot. But it's only in the late spring or early summer that the turf-cutting begins. As warm weather hits the midlands the water in the many bog drains recedes; and in June 1994, as the sun shone and the land dried, Marie Kilmartin's body was finally found.

———

Áine was thirteen when Marie went missing and fourteen by the time her body was found. She clearly remembers attending Marie's funeral. Looking back now she can recall people looking strangely at her that day. She can remember Marie's mother, Rose, holding her hand tightly the day after Marie was laid to rest. It was, naturally, a heartbreaking day, but Áine was feeling something more, something she couldn't explain.

The funeral was so sad: it was the saddest day of my life ever. I remember Marie's best friend, Pat, put her hand out to the coffin at the funeral and said, 'Don't go.' It was just so sad! I remember at the funeral I cried and I cried. I've never cried as much in my life, and I couldn't understand why, because I didn't know her very well and didn't know she was my real mam. But from then on I started to wonder about things—the way people seemed to look at me, and people were coming up to me at the funeral saying how sorry they were, and people seemed to be hugging me a lot. I didn't say anything to anyone about it, but I remember the day after the funeral looking at my nose in the mirror and seeing it was just like Marie's and thinking that was a bit odd. But I just kept quiet about it. I used to watch programmes like 'Ricki Lake' or 'Oprah' about adopted kids being reunited with their mothers, but I think I knew in my heart from the age of fourteen that that wasn't going to happen. But it was another seven years before someone finally told me the truth.

In was in 2000 that Áine learnt for certain that she was Marie's daughter. A cousin confirmed it when they were out socialising. But even after she found out the truth it would take much more investigative work by Áine before she would discover that she had a birth certificate, and that she had been born as Rosemarie Kilmartin in Port Laoise in March 1980. Almost everything Áine has learnt has been through her own initiative and persistence. She told me it took some time before she could cope with the reality of finding out she was Marie's daughter.

I found out the truth in June 2000. I was a total mess for a while after that. I just felt numb; I didn't know how to feel, and I kept that numbness with me until I opened up about it with Marie's friend in 2003. I remember saying to Pat, 'I just don't know how to feel.'

Marie used to worry about what Áine would think of her. She spoke about Áine a lot to Pat and to her friends at the day centre in Port Laoise. She worried that Áine would think badly of her if she ever found out she was her mother. She asked Pat to help her, if ever Áine came looking for answers, in telling her that Marie loved her dearly and that she had wanted to keep her but knew in her heart that she couldn't.

Pat told me that Marie was an extremely strong person.

> If I had to go through half of what she went through I wouldn't have survived it. She tried so hard to get over everything she had been dealt in life. She was so adamant that she wouldn't let her illness best her. She was a real fighter; she had a persistence to get out of hospital and live as she did. I know how hard it was for her sometimes to just go out and face the day, and how hard it was with the stigma of having been in hospital, and how hard it was not knowing the child she loved so much. But she had reached a good stage in her life, and for someone to have taken that away is the cruellest thing imaginable.

On the night Marie disappeared Pat hoped she might be with Liz Donovan, one of her friends from the day centre. Marie and Liz had got to know each other well and often had lunch together. But Liz was in Kilkenny at a Christmas function the night Marie vanished. She remembers Marie as an endearing and lovable person.

> I was working as a social welfare officer for the blind at the centre, and Marie was a volunteer there. We loved to have a chat and a cup of tea. We both loved watching soaps, and a favourite one we had was an American programme, 'Another World'. We used to have cheese sandwiches for lunch. It was always cheese sandwiches: we never wanted anything else. We went to a flower-arranging class together and we went to the pictures. Marie had a lovely nature and was very expressive. When she was feeling down she might dress in dark clothes, and when she was feeling well she just glowed. She never wanted people pitying her. She wanted to be taken on her own terms with her illness. She was just a very special, lovely person. And

she would be just thrilled with Áine; she would be so proud of her.

Marie's murder was investigated as part of 'Operation Trace', which examined the disappearances of a number of women in the Leinster area in the 1990s. Marie was murdered nine months after an American woman, Annie McCarrick, was abducted and murdered in the Wicklow Mountains. Despite intensive inquiries, no trace of Annie McCarrick has yet been found. Two years later a Co. Kilkenny woman, Jo Jo Dullard, was abducted in Co. Kildare and murdered. Her body has also not yet been found. In 1996 Fiona Pender from Tullamore was murdered while seven months pregnant. Her body also has not yet been found.

The bodies of a number of teenagers have also not been found. Ciara Breen was seventeen when she disappeared from Dundalk in 1997, and Fiona Sinnott was nineteen when she was murdered in Co. Wexford in 1998.

Marie Kilmartin's murder was examined by detectives from Operation Trace for two reasons: to see if the murder might be linked to any of the disappearances in Leinster, and in an attempt to learn from a case where a killer had gone to extreme lengths to hide the victim's body. Marie's murder is one of three cases in recent memory where a woman's body lay undiscovered for many months in bogland before being discovered by chance. The two other murders occurred in Co. Dublin, and they also remain unsolved.

In April 1988 part of a bog subsided at Glendoo Mountain near Glencree in the Dublin Mountains, and the body of Antoinette Smith became visible. The mother of two from Clondalkin had last been seen in Dublin the previous July after returning from a David Bowie concert at Slane, Co. Meath. She and another woman had travelled back by bus from Slane and had gone to a night club, La Mirage, near Parnell Square. After leaving the night club Antoinette and her friend had a dispute about where they should go next, and they parted company near Westmorland Street. For the following nine months Antoinette was classified as a missing person. But in the spring of 1988 part of the bog at Glendoo

Mountain subsided, and Antoinette's body was found. Her killer or killers had buried her body in a gully about half a mile from the Military Road. The 29-year-old was provisionally identified by personal effects found at the scene. She was still wearing a T-shirt with the words *David Bowie, Slane '87, Big Country*. She was also wearing denim jeans and a denim jacket. A plastic bag had been tied tightly around her head.

In June 1992 a man stacking turf at the Feather Bed near Glassamucky Brakes on the Dublin-Wicklow border discovered the body of Patricia Doherty. The 29-year old prison officer and mother of two children was last seen alive on 23 December 1991. She had spent the early part of that day at the Square Shopping Centre in Tallaght, buying Santa hats for her children, and there were a number of sightings of her later that evening by family and friends. The alarm was raised by her husband, Patrick, early on Christmas morning. He had asked other family members and Patricia's friends, and no-one had seen her. He had also phoned Mountjoy Prison to learn that Patricia had failed to turn up for work the previous day. He went to Tallaght Garda Station to report his wife missing.

As in the case of Marie Kilmartin, for six months Patricia Doherty was officially listed as a missing person until her body was discovered by chance. James Kelly had finished cutting turf in the Feather Bed in the Dublin Mountains when he made the shocking discovery. He was walking back towards the bog road when he spotted a body at the base of a bank of turf. The killer or killers had buried her body a hundred feet in off the bog road, about a mile from the nearest main road. The body had become visible when the surrounding turf bank had collapsed outwards. The key to her house a few miles away in Allenton Lawns in Tallaght was still in her trench coat. She was also wearing a blue wool pullover with red and green stripes, a black skirt and a multicoloured scarf. She was identified by dental records and by her watch and her engagement and wedding rings.

While the bodies of Antoinette Smith and Patricia Doherty were found in the same general area, there is nothing else to suggest that they might be linked. Detectives with Operation Trace studied these two murders and the murder of Marie Kilmartin in an effort to find similarities. They were conscious that the killers of Antoinette Smith, Patricia Doherty or Marie Kilmartin may well have been responsible also for the disappearance of up to half a dozen women who had vanished in Leinster.

As the investigations continued, the detectives came to the view that, in at least the case of Marie Kilmartin, the killer was known to the victim. One detective says that that's not to say the same person hasn't killed before, or since.

> In many of the cases of women who've been murdered and their bodies later found buried, or indeed women who are still missing, believed murdered, there are strong indications that they were killed by people they somehow knew. But we've always feared that there are serial attackers involved in some of these cases. We always have to keep our minds open to all possibilities, however far-fetched they may seem. Looking at the absolute callousness of the way the killers of Antoinette Smith, Patricia Doherty and Marie Kilmartin buried their bodies, any psychologist will tell you such people are capable of killing again. And look at the added insult to Marie's body, where household debris was dumped on top of her. Whoever did that has no feeling, no humanity. They might well have known Marie personally, but they are still a definite danger. That's the type of person who can kill again.

The failure to solve the murder of Marie Kilmartin has frustrated many detectives. Those who saw her body as it lay in the bog drain will never forget that image. But there is an added frustration, as one detective explained.

> In cases of missing people believed murdered, we are always talking about how if we could only find the person's body we would not only bring some peace for a grieving family but we would have a much better chance of catching the killer.

Whenever we find a body we have a chance of getting forensic evidence, or using geographical or psychological profiling to catch a killer. But here we have a case where a body was found and we have a certain number of pieces of the puzzle, but we just need that extra bit of information. I'm convinced this case can be solved, and if it was solved it would give such impetus to other cold cases.

Áine is angry at the way the state has handled her mother's murder. She points to one simple example.

The information on Marie's death certificate is incorrect. The official cert states Marie was thirty-six and that she died on the 17th of December 1994. In fact Marie was thirty-five years old when she died, and she disappeared on the 16th of December 1993. So how can you trust that the bigger picture is being looked at properly when small but hurtful mistakes like those are being made? And nobody else seemed to notice those mistakes, or didn't seem to care, until I came along asking questions.

In December 2006 Áine began a public campaign to get justice for Marie. She set up a web site, www.imom1512.com, and spent days handing out thousands of leaflets in Port Laoise and neighbouring towns, appealing for the public's help in catching her mother's killer. Áine is studying to be a teacher and has combined her studies with the continuing campaign. Apart from the support of close friends she has fought a lonely but persistent battle to get answers.

As she stood at the spot where her mother's body lay hidden for six months, Áine told me she will never give up her fight for justice.

The person who murdered Marie and left her here with a brick on her chest and a pram covering her must have a very hard heart. I've been through a lot in my life, but there is nothing I could go through that could give me such a hard heart. This is such a sad place. It just makes me feel so cold inside. It's the laneway leading up to this spot that disturbs me the most. A long, narrow lane: it's the darkest, gloomiest, saddest place I've ever been.

A heart-shaped memorial stone marks the spot where Marie's body lay hidden. It originally rested at Marie's grave in Ballinasloe, but Marie's family asked her friend Pat to place the stone at Pim's Lane.

———

On 25 June 1994, two weeks after Marie Kilmartin's body was found, two men were arrested in Port Laoise and questioned about her murder. The two men were arrested at about 8 o'clock that morning; one was taken to Port Laoise Garda station, while the other was held in Abbeyleix. Both men were released without charge after being questioned for twelve hours, and no file was sent to the Director of Public Prosecutions. One of the men knew Marie, and his vehicle was thoroughly searched, but no incriminating evidence was found.

In October 2006 senior gardaí in Port Laoise met members of the National Bureau of Criminal Investigation to discuss the unsolved murder of Marie Kilmartin. A 'cold case' review of the murder was undertaken, with local detectives saying the case was still very much open. It was decided that a full re-investigation of the murder should be undertaken, with every person originally interviewed about the case being interviewed again if still alive. A team of eight detectives was assigned to work full-time on the unsolved killing, with an incident room being set up at Abbeyleix Garda station. A Garda source confirmed that all original suspects and all original lines of inquiry would be re-examined as part of the process of seeking to establish the motive and the identity of Marie Kilmartin's killer.

During the original murder investigation the Gardaí investigated whether Marie had been in a romantic relationship before her disappearance. Pat Doyle told detectives that Marie had not been seeing anyone and furthermore had not had any such relationship during her thirteen years in Port Laoise. She would sometimes joke about wanting to marry an architect or an accountant, and having a big house with a swimming pool, but that was make-believe. Marie's life centred on her friends, and her voluntary work at the day centre. Those friends are convinced that Marie did not leave her house that December day for any romantic liaison.

Hundreds of people attended Marie's funeral when she was finally laid to rest in Ballinasloe in the summer of 1994. Considering that Marie most probably knew her killer well, it is a sobering thought that this person may even have been among the mourners.

Marie didn't have a dog growing up, so when she and Pat got a little Jack Russell terrier Marie spoiled him terribly. They called him Buttons, and Marie would let him eat chocolate and run around the house. He was good company for Marie when she was at home alone. When Pat was going down to Ballinasloe for Marie's funeral she left Buttons down at her own family home in Castlecomer. But in a cruel twist, while Marie was being laid to rest in Co. Galway, someone stole Buttons from the Doyle home in Co. Kilkenny. The dog was never seen again.

As I sat with Pat Doyle in Port Laoise, she smiled as she remembered her best friend.

> Marie was always on a diet, a perpetual diet. Then of course she'd forget all about the diet and pig out—you know that way. She loved knitting and rug-making. She loved make-up and clothes. She used to say she didn't have a stitch, and she'd actually have three wardrobes full of clothes. She loved getting her hair done, and anything that came into fashion she'd have to have it. She was into lots of music, from Daniel O'Donnell to Tracey Chapman. And she watched all the soaps, 'Glenroe' and 'Home and Away' and 'A Country Practice'. We went on holidays all around Ireland, and we went to Fatima and Lourdes and to Jersey. Marie was always trying to get a tan.

Pat showed me some of the poetry she has written to express the anger she feels at the murder of her best friend. The writing is dark; Pat does not believe there is any justice in this world. As she showed me treasured photographs of Marie it was clear that she misses her best friend deeply. She told me how her own mother died a short time after Marie was laid to rest.

> Mammy used to come on holidays with Marie and myself. The two of them got on really well. Mammy didn't believe Marie was dead until her body was found. She cried bitter tears that night. She used to ask simply, 'Who would kill an innocent?'

In 2003 Áine finally came knocking on Pat's door in Port Laoise. The two had met many years before, when Pat accompanied Marie on visits home to Co. Galway. Áine was now twenty-three, and it was almost ten years since Pat had hugged her at Marie's funeral. Áine had never forgotten that hug but only now realised its significance.

Áine told Pat she now knew the truth. They began to talk, and Pat told Áine all about Marie and how Marie always worried about what Áine would think of her if this day ever came. Pat gave Áine the jewellery that Marie wore and showed her photographs of the mother she never got to know. As they talked, Pat noticed that Áine had the same laugh as Marie, and the same mannerisms. She already knew that the two looked remarkably alike, but Pat now also noticed the same doggedness, the same fighting spirit.

In December 2006 Áine also met Tom Deegan, the man who discovered Marie's body in 1994. She got Tom's address and called to his house in Mountmellick. She felt compelled to meet the man who had found her mother and to thank him in person. She was in the Deegans' kitchen chatting with Tom's wife, Colette, when he arrived home from work. She gave him a hug, and they had an emotional meeting. Tom recounted to Áine his memories of finding Marie's body.

June 1994 was a time of mixed emotions for the Deegans. Days after Tom found Marie's body, Colette gave birth to a baby girl, their fourth child. One comfort for Tom was that it was he and not any of his children who had seen Marie's body in the water. Now, twelve years later, here was Marie's daughter standing up and campaigning on behalf of her murdered mother. Tom told me he hopes Áine gets the justice she is seeking.

Before I met Áine I knew about her from reading the paper and seeing her on the television launching her campaign. She is a very nice person and a very strong person. We had a chat here in the house for a couple of hours. Naturally, Áine was emotional, and I told her I was glad she had come to meet me. She brought a box of chocolates for the family, and she texted us last New Year's Eve to wish us well. We all wish her well in what she is doing now. It is a fierce thing to think that the killer is still out there, walking around the streets. It's not right.

Not everyone in Áine's family is happy that she has gone public. For many years people kept secrets from Áine, and there is naturally a degree of tension as she comes to terms with this. Áine says some of her relations can't understand why she has gone public about her own upbringing, and she in turn can't understand why no other family member kept constant public pressure on the authorities to catch her mother's killer. Naturally, people grieve in different ways, and some family members wish to maintain their privacy, but Áine feels the exact opposite. She feels compelled to speak out and to publicly campaign for justice to be done.

I have to say that the whole involvement in setting up the web site dedicated to Marie has been such a good thing for me. Since I stood up and effectively told the world that I'm Marie's daughter my life has gone from strength to strength. I had all these feelings and things going on in my head; and just getting out and letting people know I exist was a very good thing. I don't think anyone should have to go through what I went through. But I want to turn something very negative into something positive. My life was at a standstill until I started working on the campaign.

One question examined by the Gardaí is whether more than one person was involved in Marie Kilmartin's murder. There's nothing to firmly indicate this, and it's entirely possible that one person murdered Marie, dragged her body to the bog drain and then threw in the concrete block, pram and gas heater. However, detectives still wonder if there was a second person keeping look-out, or who may have helped carry Marie's body and dump it in the drain. From early evening it would have been pitch-black in the lane leading to the bog, and there are no houses in the area and no street lights. Two people would have been much quicker at disposing of a body and, more importantly, ensuring that there were no witnesses in the area.

There are many questions for which detectives have yet to find answers. Was Marie brought to Pim's Lane in the boot of a car, or in the back of a van? Was she still alive when she reached this dark lane? What route did the killer take? Did he drive through Port Laoise and take the N80 road to Mountmellick, turning right towards Pim's Lane, or did he take the Stradbally road past Marie's house towards Portarlington and then turn left towards the lane? Whatever route the killer took from Port Laoise, there is only one way in and out of Pim's Lane. The killer would certainly have to have had local knowledge. Is he from Co. Laois or Co. Offaly, or is he from further afield but somehow knows this area well? Could he be from Co. Galway and know Marie from before she came to Port Laoise?

Pat Doyle doesn't like visiting the place where Marie's body lay for almost six months. She says the scene is simply too sad to revisit often.

> We tried to sow a snowball tree at the spot but it wouldn't grow. I don't like the place; it's a horrible spot. I hate to think of Marie lying there with all the dirt. Marie was so tidy and neat and so into her cleanliness, and to think someone put her in a bog drain, and to leave her on her own there for six months and everyone distraught. It's so evil.

Pat Doyle retired from nursing a couple of years ago. Since then she suffers from arthritis, but the physical discomfort is nothing compared with the sadness she feels at losing her best friend. She shows me more photographs: Marie cuddling little pups, Marie opening a present on her birthday. Despite all her suffering Marie always managed to smile for the camera.

Back at Pim's Lane, Áine told me she is fighting not only on behalf of her murdered mother but for all murder victims.

> As dreamy as it sounds, my wish is for every unsolved murder to be solved. I want to see a re-investigation of every murder that has not been solved. There are far too many cases that have not been solved. I want to see every unsolved murder being given adequate resources to catch those responsible. And, if necessary, private detectives should be used, or retired gardaí should be brought back if they are available. One objective of the IMOM web site is to assess the demand for a charity to be set up that might help fund fresh investigations. If you were in my position you would feel the exact same.

Áine's doggedness has seen her personally contact more than 130 TDs about her objectives. Her persistence is working; she's getting a good response. They recognise that she will keep fighting until every available resource is made available for catching her mother's killer.

Áine doesn't go home to Co. Galway very often. The bulk of her life is now in Dublin, where she is studying to become a teacher. There's a lot of pain in Co. Galway; however, in Dublin she is charting a new life and career. She told me of the last time she met Marie.

> I was around twelve or thirteen and I was doing crochet in my house in Co. Galway. Marie came in with her best friend, Pat, and she was taking photos of the family. I remember she was always smiling and seemed so happy whenever I met her. Looking back, I know why. On that last occasion she took a photo of my adopted mam and dad. Recently I got that photo from Marie's possessions and I framed it and gave it to my adopted parents as an anniversary present.

Áine has been affected in many ways by the murder of her mother. She has become particularly alert to things going on around her, and she is also now very wary of people.

> It's not so much paranoia, but if I'm walking down the road there's never a number plate of a car that passes by that I don't look at. I'm looking to see if it has LS on it, or WH, or G, or whatever, and that is always there. And I started the campaign because if I'm going to feel like this I might as well do something about it. Before I knew who my mother was I used to look at women, wondering if they might be my mam. And now I've found out who my mam is I've ended up looking at men in Port Laoise and in Galway and other places and wondering if any of them is the person responsible for my mam's murder.

It was only in August 2005, when she was twenty-five, that Áine finally got a copy of her birth certificate. Through her own inquiries she has also managed to obtain documents from the church where she was baptised in Dublin, and also hospital records relating to her birth in Port Laoise. Áine is on a journey of discovery; and while she continues to learn more and more about her mother she is determined that Marie's killer will never be allowed to rest easy.

> I just want as many answers as I can find, and I will do until the day I die. Put yourself in my shoes. Or put yourself in Marie's shoes. Think about how she must have felt all the times she saw me and couldn't hold me as her daughter. Not only did the person or persons responsible for her murder take away her life, they also took away her opportunities. The one thing she ever wanted to be was a mother, and they took that away from her. From what I hear about my mother we would have had great craic. My life is like a mirror image of hers. She loved dancing and fashion and she loved all types of music. I can't share those things with her. I can't share anything with her.

03 | THE MURDER OF EDDIE FITZMAURICE

For five days and nights Eddie Fitzmaurice lay on the floor, his wrists tied together tightly behind his back. His ankles were also bound, and he was gagged. His hands and feet were tied so tightly that his circulation was severely restricted.

Over a number of hours, if not days, the 82-year-old used his elbows, knees, buttocks and shoulders to slowly move himself along the ground towards a window in an attempt to summon help. By the time his body was found, five days after he was attacked, he had managed to move from one bedroom, across a hall and into another bedroom close to a window looking out on the street below; but having made it that far he simply had no more strength. Because his attackers had dragged him from his bed, Eddie was dressed only in his pyjamas. At some point during those five days and five nights, as he lay on his back with his hands tied behind him, Eddie Fitzmaurice froze to death.

The gang that broke into Eddie's house and left him bound hand and foot never raised the alarm after they made their escape. The motive for the attack was robbery: the criminals attacked Eddie Fitzmaurice because they believed he had money in his house. Having beaten him, ransacked his house and fled the scene, the raiders could have made an anonymous phone call that might have saved Eddie's life. Instead the widowed father of four spent his last hours in pain, frustration and distress.

A young neighbour, Andrew Marren, found Eddie's body shortly before seven o'clock on the evening of Wednesday 6 May 1998. He had gone to the back of Eddie's house and found that a window was open. Andrew's mother had been concerned because Eddie's drapery shop was closed and she hadn't seen Eddie for some days. Andrew called out Eddie's name through the back window but there was no response, so he decided to go into the house.

For more than fifty years Eddie Fitzmaurice ran a drapery business in Bellaghy, Co. Sligo, beside the border with Co. Mayo. Bellaghy is a historic town dating from the 1500s but today is in effect part of a larger town of Charlestown and Bellaghy, which crosses the county boundary. Charlestown in Co. Mayo now forms the bulk of the businesses and houses in the area, while a simple walk across a now disused railway track on the N17 road brings you into the older town of Bellaghy, Co. Sligo. Eddie was a Mayo man, originally from Ballyhaunis, but he had settled in Charlestown early in life, where he and his brother Pat ran a butcher's shop in Church Street.

In 1947 Eddie married Rita Gavaghan from Bellaghy, and the two moved into Rita's original two-storey family home a few hundred yards on the Sligo side of town. The couple ran a drapery shop in the downstairs part of the house, and business thrived. They also had a grocery business next door, where they sold everything from oil to eggs. Rita and Eddie were familiar faces at fairs throughout Cos. Mayo, Sligo and Roscommon, where they sold bedding, clothes and footwear. The industrious couple also had some farm-land at the back of the house where they kept some cattle. They reared two girls, Valerie and Collette, and two boys, Billy and Oliver.

Rita was seventy-nine when she died suddenly in June 1990. In the years after her death local people in Charlestown and Bellaghy knew how much Eddie missed his wife; they had been inseparable for forty-three years. Their four children had by now all moved away from the area to make their own way in the world. Oliver moved to Limerick, while Billy, Valerie and Collette had all settled in London. They all had children of their own, and Eddie loved when his children and grandchildren came to visit. After his wife's death he continued living in the house in Bellaghy's main street and running the drapery shop downstairs.

By May 1998 Eddie was one month away from his eighty-third birthday, but everyone who knew him said he was the youngest man for his eighties they had ever known. Though he had been drawing his pension for almost eighteen years and was by far the oldest businessman in the town, Eddie was a fit and healthy man who had no intention of retiring. He worked hours to suit himself, rising at about eight in the morning and opening up his shop for a few hours in mid-morning. He ran the shop by himself and usually closed in the afternoon and then reopened in the evening. During the day he might go to a local pub for a drink and a chat with friends. He would also go to visit his wife's grave in the nearby cemetery. Always smartly dressed and wearing a cap, Eddie was a familiar face in Charlestown and Bellaghy. Though he lived alone, he was a sociable man and liked nothing better than meeting people while out and about, or having a good chat with a customer in his shop.

Eddie's shop was popular with many people, including farmers who wanted hard-wearing boots, trousers and shirts. Eddie also sold caps, socks, coats, wellington boots and shoes. He didn't have to advertise: he'd been doing his job for more than five decades, and many of his customers had grown up in clothes bought in his shop.

The last people Eddie would ever serve were two local women who went into the shop shortly after 8 p.m. on the holiday weekend of Friday 1 May 1998. The two women had a chat with Eddie as he sold them some pillowcases, and he was in his usual good form. At approximately 8:20 p.m. the two women left the shop and Eddie bade them good night as he prepared to lock up.

There are no further definite sightings of Eddie after the two women left the shop. It's believed that, rather than go out for a drink, Eddie decided to stay in, perhaps watching the 'Late Late

Show' on television, as he would sometimes do; or he may have gone to bed earlier that night. Either way, at some point Eddie headed upstairs, changed into his pyjamas and got into bed.

Were Eddie's killers watching as he locked up his premises? Did they wait to see him turn off the lights downstairs and then turn off the lights upstairs?

The killers approached his premises from the fields at the back of the house. Eddie's home fronted onto Bellaghy's main street, which is part of the N17 road linking Galway and Sligo, but at the back of the house there is open space. The killers may have parked in the centre of the town and walked from the main street around to the fields at the back of the house. They may have driven into Bellaghy and parked down a side road or at the back of Eddie's house. Or they may have approached the house entirely from the rear, perhaps walking through a number of fields to reach Eddie's house and perhaps leaving a getaway driver waiting for a signal to come and collect them.

Some time on the night of Friday 1 May 1998 or the early hours of the Saturday morning the criminals entered Eddie's house and shop by forcing open a window at the back. The number of raiders has yet to be firmly established, but it's thought there may have been at least two or three involved.

Eddie was lying in his bed when the raiders burst into his room. He may have been asleep or about to go asleep, but he was certainly taken by surprise to the extent that he was unable to raise the alarm. The 82-year-old was beaten about the head, he was gagged, and his wrists and ankles were tied so tightly that, had he lived, his hands and feet might have been permanently damaged.

Some time before 10 a.m. on the Saturday morning a young woman was standing on the road in Bellaghy thumbing a lift to Sligo. She was standing opposite Fitzmaurice's drapery shop when she heard the muffled voice of an elderly man calling out three times. She knocked on the doors of a number of houses nearby but didn't get any reply. A short time later a motorist stopped to give the woman a lift, and during the journey she mentioned the noises she had heard in Bellaghy. It would only be after Eddie's body was found four days later that the Gardaí would learn about what is now thought to have been Eddie crying for help.

Similarly, detectives are now aware that on the evening of Sunday 3 May a man heard a muffled male voice in the vicinity of Eddie's home. However, at the time the noise did not raise the man's suspicions. It is possible that this voice was Eddie still trying to call for help; certainly the evidence of the state pathologist, Dr Marie Cassidy, would be that Eddie may have lived for a number of days before dying as a result of hypothermia.

Andrew Marren entered Eddie's house at 6:40 p.m. on Wednesday 6 May. He walked upstairs while still calling out Eddie's name but heard no reply. In a bedroom at the front of the house he found Eddie's body.

In Charlestown and Bellaghy many people have fond memories of the late Eddie Fitzmaurice. They smile when they think of the man they knew, but each memory is tinged with sadness. What upsets so many people is the thought that Eddie was trying to call out for help over a period of hours, if not days, and was trying to reach a front window to somehow raise the alarm. People reflect on the sheer frustration he must have felt in trying to move his body slowly along the carpet with his hands tightly bound behind his back and his feet also tied together. How many hours did he lie helpless on his back while still alive? How many times did he manage to call out for help through his gag, or were there occasions when he tried to call out but his voice failed him or he simply couldn't muster the energy any more?

Angie Casey remembers seeing Eddie hours before the attack. He had walked down the town that Friday afternoon and was carrying a blue plastic bag for his messages.

He was wearing his cap, as always, that day. Eddie was a jolly, happy man, who always had time for a chat. He really missed his wife when she passed away. They were great buddies. Rita was always immaculate, with lovely earrings and her hair nicely done.

John Finn told me that Eddie would slowly sip a pint of Guinness while passing the afternoon or evening with friends in the town. Paddy Colleran smiled as he remembered getting his first pair of long trousers at Fitzmaurice's when he was a youngster.

> Eddie's shop was a great place for getting hard-wearing clothes and for boots as well. Eddie loved to knock something off the price for customers; he loved that kind of banter. The price tag might say five bob for something, and he'd give it to you for four.

Everyone is agreed that for eighty-two years of age Eddie Fitzmaurice was an active and vibrant man. He never thought for a moment about closing his shop for good: his whole life had been about selling, whether it was from his premises in Bellaghy or going from door to door in the area or to fairs, from Belmullet to Ballaghaderreen. Another local man, John Finan, told me:

> He was a great man for his age, very well regarded and a good character. It's very sad what happened. The people who did that are very sick. I can't understand the mentality of anyone who would leave a man like that.

Maura Durcan remembers her uncle with great affection. Eddie was one of six brothers and two sisters. In May 1998 he was the last of his siblings still alive. Maura works in the centre of Charlestown, and every day she travels past where Eddie and Rita ran their shop for so long.

> Eddie was my father's brother, and he was a very nice, obliging man and was always at the door of his shop, waving at people passing by. He was a very active man and a great churchgoer. He loved meeting people. There wasn't a person in Charlestown that Eddie didn't know. He was very well liked, and everybody had a good word to say about him.

Within minutes of Andrew Marren discovering Eddie's body the Gardaí had been alerted and were sealing off the house. Chief Superintendent John Carey and Superintendent Oliver Hanley soon arrived at the scene, and a full murder investigation was begun, with members of the National Bureau of Criminal Investigation being asked to assist the local detectives. Both Eddie's home and shop had been ransacked. The preservation of any potential evidence was uppermost in the minds of everyone, and this meant that Eddie's body had to remain in his bedroom until the following morning, when a full scientific examination of the house was completed and the state pathologist had studied the scene.

Dr Marie Cassidy later carried out a post-mortem examination at Castlebar General Hospital. She concluded that Eddie Fitzmaurice died as a result of hypothermia because of an inability to protect himself against low temperature, which in turn was due to the fact that he was tied at the wrists and ankles, and had also suffered exposure to cold because of lack of clothing. The pattern of marks and injuries showed that he had been bound and gagged while he was alive. His larynx had been fractured, suggesting that one of his attackers had gripped him around the neck, possibly in an attempt to force him to divulge whether he had money in the house. He had also suffered a number of minor blows to his head. Dr Cassidy said it was possible that he had lived for a number of days after being left bound and gagged.

To this day it is not known how much money Eddie might have had in his premises the night his killers struck. Certainly he was a man of means. He had spent more than sixty years of his life working solidly and successfully as a shopkeeper; but he was also a practical man and kept much of his money in the bank. He would definitely have had some cash on his premises as a float for the drapery business, but whether or not he had more money in his home is at this moment only known to the gang that attacked and killed him.

Detectives have long wondered if the killers had been in Eddie's shop in the days or weeks before the attack. Did they go into the shop under the pretext of buying something while trying to study the premises and guess where Eddie might keep money? Did they try to use a large-denomination note to pay for something so as to see if Eddie might go to a certain part of the shop to get change?

It's unlikely, however, that the raiders were simply looking for the shop takings. Having entered the house from the rear, the thieves could have simply searched the shop looking for cash. They took a decision instead to go upstairs and attack Eddie in his bed, beating him on the head and gagging him and tying his hands and feet. Did they beat him simply in order to subdue him, or was it part of a torture technique to find out where he had cash hidden in the house?

Within hours of Eddie's body being discovered an incident room was set up at nearby Charlestown Garda station. In time the investigation would become so extensive that the incident room was moved to the larger Swinford station some miles away.

As the Gardaí began their inquiries it was established that Eddie Fitzmaurice had last been seen five days before his body was found. They knew that the gang responsible for the attack had five full days to cover their tracks before the alarm was raised.

In May 1998 the population of Charlestown and Bellaghy was less than a thousand people. The community was stunned by the brutality of the death of one its oldest and most respected residents. Naturally there was a hope that the people responsible for tying up an elderly man and leaving him to die such a harrowing death would be quickly caught and brought to justice. But detectives knew that the gang responsible had almost a week to begin rehearsing stories or concocting alibis before a full murder investigation was established. As they examined Eddie's body in the bedroom of his home, and as a full scientific examination of his house and shop was undertaken, senior gardaí knew the investigation would be a long and methodical process.

One of the first things considered was the possible escape route used by the gang. Charlestown and Bellaghy served in effect as a crossroads between two major roads. The centre of the town was where the N17 from Sligo to Galway intersected with the N5

Dublin–Castlebar road. Each direction opened up the possibility that the gang had fled the scene of the crime in that direction.

Did the gang travel west along the N5 towards Swinford, Foxford or Castlebar? Even if the criminals did not live in that direction, did they travel that way to try to hide any money they had stolen from Eddie, or indeed had they planned to commit further attacks on elderly people that night? Alternatively, did they travel east on the N5 road towards Ballaghaderreen and Frenchpark and on towards Longford? If they went in that direction they could have continued on towards Dublin. But isn't it more likely that the attackers were from the west of Ireland, with detailed knowledge of the main roads and the back roads of Cos. Mayo and Sligo?

Had the gang of travelling criminals come from the Galway direction that night, driving along the N17 road through Charlestown and over the disused railway track towards Eddie's house on the right-hand side of the road? If they did come from Galway they could have travelled the full journey on the N17, passing through Tuam and Claremorris, or they could have driven along the N83 through Ballyhaunis, which then joins the N17 a few miles south of Charlestown and Bellaghy.

Or is it more likely that they had come south from the Sligo area, driving through Tobercurry and into Bellaghy, parking near Eddie's house? If they drove into Bellaghy from the Sligo direction they would have avoided travelling through the busy centre of Charlestown, a few hundred yards south of Eddie's shop and house. Perhaps the getaway driver parked close to Eddie's house in Bellaghy's main street and turned the car so that it was facing north towards Sligo, ready for a quick exit. Wouldn't this road from Sligo into Bellaghy be the preferred entry and exit point for a criminal gang who wanted to leave the area as quickly and quietly as possible without arousing suspicion?

Within two weeks of Eddie's murder the Gardaí had a list of more than sixty separate groups of people considered likely suspects for the murder. The list included people responsible for previous attacks on elderly people throughout the Republic as well as in Northern Ireland. Although it seemed more likely that the gang might have come from the Galway or Sligo areas, rather than travelling to the north-west from Cork or Dublin, for example, the Gardaí cast their net wide in a search for the killers. Detectives began a lengthy process of establishing the whereabouts of hundreds of known or suspected violent people for 1 and 2 May 1998. It is a detailed and laborious process, which continues to this day.

If the gang that attacked Eddie Fitzmaurice travelled some considerable distance to commit their attack they must have had a tip-off that Eddie might have money on his premises and that he lived alone. This opened up a distressing possibility that has long been considered both by the Gardaí and the community of Charlestown and Bellaghy. Was there a man or woman who had lived in the general area, or who had travelled through the area for a time, who pointed Eddie's shop out to the thieves? If there was such a person they may have thought the gang was merely going to rob the premises: they may not have known that Eddie would be brutally attacked and left to die. It is possible that such a person, or someone close to them, is tormented every day by what they have done.

———

The murder of Eddie Fitzmaurice was one of a number of killings of elderly men by criminal gangs in the late 1990s and early 2000s. A spate of attacks on elderly people who were beaten, tortured and killed in their own home left the country stunned. What was also shocking was that none of the murders were apparently linked: there were in fact a number of gangs roaming the countryside who were attacking and robbing elderly people and who didn't care whether their victims lived or died.

At the time Eddie Fitzmaurice was murdered in his own home a 68-year-old man was in a coma in Limerick after being found bound, gagged and freezing in his house in Co. Clare. Paud Skehan was a bachelor farmer who lived alone in his farmhouse at O'Brien's Bridge in the south-east of the county. On the night of

Thursday 9 April 1998 he was dragged from his bed by a gang of thieves from Limerick who had broken into his home. His hands and feet were bound with a tie and a television cable, he was flung downstairs and his feet were tied to the banisters. Over the following hours, as he lay on the concrete floor of his house, he developed bronchial pneumonia. When a neighbour found him on the Friday morning he was rushed to hospital, but he never regained consciousness, and after fifty-four days his life-support machine was switched off.

In time there would be some solace when one of Paud Skehan's killers was caught. A career criminal from Moyross in Limerick was one member of the gang who entered Paud's home and left him with the injuries that claimed his life. This criminal was caught because of the runners he wore on the night he beat Paud Skehan. During the attack he stepped in Paud's blood and left a clear mark of his shoe on the floorboards of the landing of his victim's house. When the killer was later arrested in Ennis on a separate matter he was wearing the black runners he wore on the night he murdered Paud Skehan. He pleaded not guilty to the murder and refused to divulge the names of his accomplices; today he is serving a life sentence for murder.

Two years before Eddie Fitzmaurice was murdered another gang of travelling criminals attacked a 68-year-old man, Tommy Casey, at his home at Oranmore, Co. Galway. Tommy Casey was attacked on 15 January 1996 but his body was not found until eight days later. His hands had been tied behind his back with a length of clothes line, and the cord had been tied around his ankles. He had suffered a severe beating, including injuries to his chest, which, combined with the way he had been left lying on his kitchen floor, contributed to his death from asphyxia. A 37-year-old man originally from Clonmel, Co. Tipperary, was later jailed for six years after admitting the manslaughter of Tommy Casey. A mother and daughter who were part of the gang had waited outside the house during the robbery. The two women later gave evidence for the prosecution after pleading guilty to the charge of trespassing with intent to steal. A second man is still wanted by the

Gardaí investigating the violent death of Tommy Casey and is believed to be on the run in England.

As with the separate murders of Eddie Fitzmaurice and Paud Skehan, nobody involved in the attack on Tommy Casey later raised the alarm. No-one made an anonymous phone call to the Gardaí or the Samaritans or any other group that could have saved a life.

Two years after the murder of Eddie Fitzmaurice, two criminal brothers from Dublin attacked two elderly brothers in their isolated farmhouse at Castlejordan on the Meath-Offaly border. 81-year-old Paddy Logan and his 85-year-old brother Peter were listening to a GAA match on the radio when two men broke in and attacked them. During the attack Paddy Logan's blood pressure rose significantly, and he suffered a fatal heart attack. The criminals had picked on Peter and Paddy Logan after a contact gave them a tip-off that the Logan brothers did not use banks and kept money at their home. While the criminal brothers entered the Logan farm-house and attacked their elderly victims, a woman kept watch out-side the house. The two criminals were later jailed for fifteen and twelve years, respectively, after admitting to manslaughter. It was the second time that the older of the criminals admitted taking the life of an elderly man. In June 1984, when aged seventeen, he had stabbed an 84-year-old man to death in an unprovoked attack in a field near Clondalkin, Co. Dublin. On that occasion he pleaded guilty to manslaughter and had been jailed for three years.

While the violent deaths of Tommy Casey, Paud Skehan and Paddy Logan devastated their families and local communities, there was at least some comfort in seeing some of their killers being caught and jailed. Three extremely violent criminal gangs were broken up by three separate investigations into those deaths. The gardaí investigating the murder of Eddie Fitzmaurice soon realised that hopes for a similar quick breakthrough in their inquiries would not be realised.

The solving of other violent crimes against elderly people brought to attention a number of hypotheses that should be con-sidered in the case of Eddie Fitzmaurice. While it is most probable that a group of men entered Eddie's house to rob him, were there also women involved—perhaps keeping watch outside the house as the attack occurred? Did the gang think that a woman parked in a car in Bellaghy or Charlestown would not arouse as much suspicion as a man? Had a woman or women entered Eddie's shop in the days or weeks before he was attacked in order to give the gang a description of the layout inside the premises? Be they men or women, are there people who assisted the gang but who had no knowledge or intention that Eddie Fitzmaurice would be physically harmed and who now want to clear their conscience?

In May 2005, on the seventh anniversary of the unsolved murder of Eddie Fitzmaurice, the Gardaí renewed their appeal for information about the case. During the previous seven years more than two hundred people had been nominated as suspects in the murder, and Garda investigations had brought detectives to every county in the country, as well as to Britain. By a careful analysis of alibi witnesses and documentary evidence many people originally nominated as suspects were eliminated from inquiries. The investigation by Mayo gardaí and the National Bureau of Criminal Investigation had been massive. More than 850 leads had been pursued, more than 800 statements had been taken, and countless questionnaires had been completed. But still the breakthrough the Gardaí were hoping for had not come.

Naturally, during their extensive investigations and searches the detectives had unearthed evidence of other crimes, as well as recovering suspected stolen property. Information on a number of suspected criminals had also been forwarded to the Criminal Assets Bureau. But, frustratingly, the core objective of solving the murder of Eddie Fitzmaurice had not been achieved.

On the May public holiday in 2005 the Gardaí took to the streets of Charlestown, handing out leaflets in a renewed appeal for information. The leaflet featured a photograph of Eddie Fitzmaurice wearing a shirt, tie and jacket and smiling at the camera. The picture had been taken when he was socialising in a pub with friends, and the arm of one man could be seen around Eddie's shoulder. The leaflets had been printed by Crimestoppers, who had joined forces with local business people to offer a reward for information leading to the prosecution of any person involved in the murder of Eddie Fitzmaurice. The leaflet stressed that the free Crimestoppers number—1800 250025—could be contacted anonymously, and that callers did not have to leave their name in order to give information.

The Gardaí also held a press conference at Swinford Garda station, where Superintendent Ken Brennan told reporters that the Charlestown community had never got over the murder of Eddie Fitzmaurice. The conference was also attended by Inspector Tom Fitzmaurice, Garda Pádraic Frain and Garda Seán Mulligan. Superintendent Brennan told reporters that the investigation into Eddie's murder would continue until those responsible were brought to justice.

> Perhaps the conscience of the perpetrator or perpetrators has got the better of them in the past seven years. We are confident that there are witnesses who could help the investigation team. People's circumstances may have changed, and I appeal to those people to contact us. People may think it is too late to come forward. It is never too late.

Superintendent Brennan also spoke on the television programme 'Crimecall' to appeal to the conscience of people who had not yet come forward. Detective-Inspector John O'Mahony of the National Bureau of Criminal Investigation, who had been one of the detectives to work on the case from the start, also made an appeal.

> In my experience it was one of the most callous murders I have investigated. Eddie Fitzmaurice was left to die a slow and lingering death. I am satisfied that there are people who still have information that could help solve Eddie's murder. There may be people who did not come forward because of their circumstances, and I would appeal to those people to come forward. They should not assume that the Gardaí already have

particular information, and people should not assume that any information they have is insignificant.

As part of the extensive fresh appeal the 'Crimecall' programme also filmed a reconstruction of Eddie Fitzmaurice's last movements and the type of attack he had suffered. The film crew interviewed Eddie's niece Maura Durcan and also Eddie's friend James Casey, who spoke fondly of a man who had been one of Charlestown's most familiar faces.

> Eddie was a great man to talk, he was a lovely man, a gentleman. He was a character. Every town has its characters, and Eddie was one of them, a real character. We were all devastated that Eddie would end up dying like that. We couldn't believe it.

In October 2005 detectives from Cos. Mayo and Galway, assisted by the National Bureau of Criminal Investigation, arrested seven people at places in Cos. Sligo and Galway. The six men and one woman included a husband and wife, and the seven were taken to Garda stations in Galway, Ballina, Swinford and Westport and questioned about the murder of Eddie Fitzmaurice. Three of those arrested were held under section 30 of the Offences Against the State Act, and four were held under section 4 of the Criminal Justice Act. All were later released without charge. Two weeks later a man was arrested in Cork and taken to Togher Garda station, where he was questioned about the murder. He was also later released without charge, and Garda investigations into Eddie's murder continue to this day.

In Charlestown a local businessman, George Craig, who is chairperson of Charlestown, Bellaghy and District Chamber of Commerce, told me of his memories of Eddie.

> I can remember Eddie unloading the goods from his car and putting them into the shop. And he was very good to the young people who grew up in the area. There were eighteen children in one family that grew up near him, and he always kept an eye out for them.

The population of Charlestown is a little over 1,200 at the moment but is likely to quadruple within a few years. With Knock International Airport only four miles away, the town is going from strength to strength. If he was still alive Eddie Fitzmaurice would be in his nineties. There is nothing to say that he wouldn't have continued to run his business in an even bigger and more successful Charlestown and Bellaghy. He was already the oldest businessman in the town, and by rights he should still hold that title.

As I sat with George Craig and other local people—Angie Casey, J. J. Finan, John Finn and Paddy Colleran—they all had precious and fond memories of Eddie, and they all had a clear message that, no matter how long it takes, his killers must be brought to justice.

Gardaí who have investigated the murder share that desire, including the Mayo and Sligo gardaí, for whom the attack on Eddie was also an attack on their own community. Gardaí who have been transferred into the area at various times have also seen the depth of sadness and anger that the murder of a defenceless man caused. Thinking of Eddie bound hand and foot, slowly crawling along the ground trying to summon help, leaves many gardaí simply lost for words. They are determined to pursue this case until it is resolved.

The desire for justice by the Fitzmaurice family remains as strong as it was in the days and weeks after their father and grandfather was taken from them so violently. Two months after Eddie Fitzmaurice was murdered an inquest into his death was opened and adjourned. Because the murder occurred on the Bellaghy side of town, the proceedings were held by the Sligo County Coroner. As proceedings were being adjourned, in July 1998, a solicitor for Eddie's four children appealed for anyone with information to come forward.

Eddie is now laid to rest with his wife, Rita, in the local cemetery. After his murder his shop and house lay derelict for several years. In recent times the premises were sold and turned into offices and apartments.

Eddie's niece Maura says the Fitzmaurice family and the community of Charlestown have suffered greatly. She appeals to those with information about those responsible for taking her uncle's life to give that information in confidence to the Gardaí.

> We still think of Eddie every single day. We are all so upset by what happened. I pass Eddie's shop every single day coming into town and going home. It's very hard passing by the place. You think you should still see Eddie there. You think he should still be at the door, chatting with people, or waving at passers-by.

04 | THE MURDER OF EILEEN COSTELLO O'SHAUGHNESSY

It's believed that Eileen Costello O'Shaughnessy was still alive when her killer pulled her from the driver's seat of her car and left her lying in the mud. Minutes earlier she had been subjected to a ferocious attack as she sat in her taxi. The heavy weapon her attacker used to repeatedly beat her on the head had fractured her skull, and she was bleeding heavily.

Eileen's injuries were irreversible, and it was inevitable that she would die. Her brain had suffered multiple lacerations and had swollen considerably. However, evidence suggests that as she lay alone in the dark and isolated boreen the 47-year-old woman managed to move the upper part of her body a couple of inches in a final struggle for life. But within a short time she fell into a deep state of unconsciousness, and soon afterwards she was dead.

For fifteen hours Eileen's body lay undiscovered near Tinkers' Lane, off the N17 Tuam road close to the town of Claregalway. For the last twelve of those lonely hours extensive searches for Eileen were being conducted many miles away, closer to Galway, after her bloodstained taxi had been found on the outskirts of the city.

From an initial examination of the car the Gardaí were seriously concerned for the missing woman. Blood was spattered around the driver's area: on the seat, the steering wheel, hand brake, seat belt, interior ceiling and rear-view mirror. There were also clumps of hair on the driver's seat and on the floor of the car. Eileen was nowhere in the immediate vicinity of her taxi, but detectives could tell from the state of the car that she had been the victim of a vicious and unrelenting attack. No-one, except her killer, yet knew that she lay dead seven miles away.

Three bakery workers found the blood-stained taxi and first raised the alarm. It was 11:44 p.m. on Sunday 30 November 1997. The three men were working a shift at Lydon's bakery outside Galway. They spotted a silver Toyota Carina taxi parked at an odd angle in the middle of a car park off the N17 road. The car lights were off and there was no-one inside, but the driver's window was open and the keys were in the ignition.

The three men were worried that the car might be vandalised or stolen if left where it was, and they decided to move it to another spot in the car park. One of them opened the driver's door and reached inside. The driver's seat had been moved fully forward against the steering wheel. The man reached down and put his right hand on the lever to release the seat and put his left hand against the driver's seat. He immediately felt something cold and wet. He quickly turned on the interior light and saw that he had blood on his hand and that there was blood all over the driver's section of the car. He and his two colleagues quickly moved away from the car and phoned Mill Street Garda station.

Eileen's son, Damien, was in Dublin for the weekend when he got a phone call from his cousin Kenny Costello in Galway. Kenny sounded alarmed; he told Damien his mother's taxi had been found abandoned, there was blood inside it and there was no sign of Eileen.

Damien was twenty-four and his sister Susan was twenty-six when their mother was murdered. Eileen doted on her two children, and her loss continues to affect both of them deeply. Damien remembers how he had the worst possible feeling when he got that phone call.

I was staying with a friend of mine at a house near Croke Park, and it was some time after midnight when my cousin Kenny rang me. He told me Mam was missing and there was blood in her taxi. I knew straight away by what Kenny told me: I just had a gut feeling, I had a feeling Mam was dead. I also had a feeling straight away—why I don't know—that no-one would be got for it. And unfortunately, to this day, it is still true.

Damien drove through the night to get back to Galway, arriving at first light. He went straight to Mill Street Garda station, only to be told that his mother had still not been found. Extensive searches had begun shortly after her taxi had been found, but the initial searches were concentrated on the area around the industrial estate where her car was abandoned in the north-east of the city. A large number of people had searched all night, but to no avail. Gardaí were joined in their searches by dozens of taxi-drivers as word spread that one of their colleagues had been attacked while working.

Eileen's husband, Tom, was staying with friends in Leixlip, Co. Kildare, on the night Eileen was murdered. Eileen and Tom had separated many years before. The period of the break-up had naturally been difficult for both, but they remained on good terms and kept in touch to talk about their children. They were both proud of how Susan and Damien had turned out: Susan was working in child care in London, and Damien was working in the Digital Equipment plant in Galway. Tom and Eileen were from the same parish in Corrofin, a quiet village a few miles outside Galway. Tom told me that he and Eileen had known each other almost all their lives.

I was three years older than Eileen and we knew each other since we were teenagers. We started going out in the late 60s. I became a garda in 1969 and was posted to Fitzgibbon Street in Dublin. Eileen was already living in Dublin and working in a coffee shop in Grafton Street, and we got married in 1971. We lived in a flat in Drumcondra, and later we got a house in Raheny. Both Susan and Damien were born in Dublin. In July of 77 the family moved back to Co. Galway when I was transferred to Woodford, outside Portumna. I was later moved to Galway city, ending up in the Traffic Corps in Mill Street. When we moved back home to Galway we built our own house out in Corrofin and had it built by the end of the 70s. Eileen and I separated in the early 90s, but we would still keep in touch, discussing our children. Eileen was always a very good mother to Damien and Susan.

Tom had been staying in Leixlip that Sunday in order to travel on to the High Court in Dublin the following day. He had been injured in the early 1990s while working with the Galway Traffic Corps, and his compensation claim was due to be heard on the Monday morning. However, Tom's nephew Kenny made contact with him and gave him the same distressing news he'd given Damien: Eileen was missing, and there was blood in her car.

Like his son, Tom knew from what Kenny was saying that the situation looked extremely bad. As he drove to Galway he tried to work out how to reach his daughter. Susan was living in London but just then was on holiday, travelling around Australia.

In the early hours of Monday 1 December 1997 hundreds of people were out searching for Eileen. The drivers of many of the 140 taxis in Galway met at a restaurant near where Eileen's car had been found to gather into search parties and assist the Gardaí. Eileen's brother Martin was rounding up all the drivers who worked for his bus company to help too. A spotter plane was also used to try to find Eileen. Despite the intensive search, Eileen's body was eventually found by chance by a young farmer at about midday.

Pádraic O'Connell was moving silage to a shed and was driving his tractor down Tinkers' Lane near the town of Claregalway when he spotted something out of the corner of his eye. He reversed his tractor towards the entrance to a narrow muddy boreen that separates two fields. A short distance inside the mud track he saw what looked like a body. He walked to within ten or fifteen feet of the shape and could immediately tell it was a woman's body. He ran to the tractor and drove home to raise the alarm.

Eileen lay on her back with her legs slightly bent at the knee and turned to her left. One of her arms lay outstretched, and the other arm was at a right angle, bent at the elbow. She was fully clothed and was still wearing a watch on her left wrist and a ring on her right hand. Her face was covered in blood and her eyes were closed. She lay across the boreen, with her head towards the centre and her feet towards the side. The boreen was seven feet wide and bordered on both sides by an old stone wall four feet high, which was covered with overgrown grass and hedgerow. An area of mud beside the body was flattened in line with it, suggesting that she had moved slightly while lying on the ground.

A short time after Eileen's body was found a local priest, Father Michael Mulkerrins, arrived at the scene and gave her the last rites. Gardaí covered the body with a black tarpaulin, and some were visibly shaken by what they had seen.

Many of Eileen's taxi colleagues soon arrived at Tinkers' Lane as word spread of the discovery. The Gardaí asked a friend of the family, Tom Byrnes, to provisionally identify Eileen, saving her family at least the trauma of seeing her lying dead in the lane.

———

Twelve hours before Eileen was beaten to death she began her shift with Galway Taxis. She didn't own her own taxi but was a nominated driver of cab 34, a silver Toyota Carina, 97-G-6663. At 8 a.m. on Sunday 30 November she parked her own green Volkswagen Polo at the Dyke Road car park in Galway and took control of cab 34. She had a thirteen-hour shift ahead of her and was due to arrive back at Dyke Road at 9 p.m. to hand over the keys to the owner of the car, who would then do the night shift.

Her colleague would later arrive at the Dyke Road at 9 p.m. as arranged, but Eileen never showed up. He contacted the taxi office and waited at the car park for several hours as he and Eileen's other colleagues grew more and more concerned.

Eileen loved being active and especially loved her work as a taxi-driver. She was a sociable person and loved to chat to passengers. She had developed Crohn's disease many years before and would occasionally become tired and run down, but she never let her illness get the better of her. Her family describe her as someone who could do ten things at once and do them all well. Before her children were born she had worked in Dublin in a busy restaurant. When the children were growing up she had set up a hairdressing business in Tuam with her cousin. Later she had worked from door to door selling aerial photographs of people's houses and had then got a job as a taxi-driver in Galway.

After separating from Tom in the early 1990s Eileen had moved back in with her mother, Nora, who also lived in Corrofin. Eileen would get up early every morning and have a fire set for her mother before heading to Galway to begin her thirteen-hour shift. She lived for her family, her work and her nights out with friends. Damien remembers the last time he saw his mother.

> I last saw Mam on the Wednesday before she was murdered. It was in the evening and I called to see her and Gran. Mam was after doing her day's work and she had her money out on the table and she was counting her float and was getting ready for the next day. When I was heading out she was still counting out the money. She was sitting at a big table in the sitting-room. I put my two hands on her shoulders and gave her a kiss on the head, and I said, 'I'll see you later on in the week.' That was the last time I saw her.

Eileen had been working as a taxi-driver for about four years. She had started with Big O Taxis, doing a night shift, and later moved to another company, Galway Taxis, where she got a day shift, which suited her better. She was universally liked by her fellow-drivers. One of her friends was Francis Churm, who helped Eileen get into the taxi business.

> I know Eileen's husband and I know her brother, Martin, for many years, but I didn't get to know Eileen until she came

looking for advice on becoming a taxi-driver. She knew my wife's cousin, and I helped her get her first job with Big O Taxis, where I was working at the time. I remember she told me how she knew the east of the city very well but not the west side. I brought her out to brush up on the west side, from Salthill to Knocknacarra and Rahoon. She was able to pick up the nuts and bolts of the whole business within only two weeks. I was amazed at that: she knew how the meter worked, and how the radio worked, and she knew every part of Galway. I got to know Eileen well during the following four years or so. We'd meet for a cup of tea in town or have a chat while on the rank. Eileen was a very honest, sincere, family-orientated woman. She cared greatly about her family. She was also very street-wise in her work. Before that awful night she had never been the victim of any type of crime while driving her taxi.

In the hours before Eileen was beaten to death she worked solidly, having more than a dozen fares throughout the day. Her first job took her from the western suburb of Rahoon into the city. Her next fare brought her from the Headford road to the train station. Then she drove out past the university to collect a fare at Supermac's in Newcastle, who she brought to Supermac's in Eyre Square. She then went back to Newcastle for another pick-up, also heading for the city centre. She next got fares at Knocknacarra and the Huntsman, a pub in the city centre.

At about midday she found herself in the Corrofin direction and called in to see a friend, Claire Rowe. They had a chat, and Eileen mentioned that her nephew Kenny was coming home from Australia that day, after being away for a year. Her daughter, Susan, was also in Australia on holiday and would be back in Galway for Christmas. After saying goodbye to Claire, Eileen dropped home to see her mother before travelling the sixteen miles back into Galway at about 1 p.m.

Her next fare took her from Tirellan, north of the city, into Eglinton Street. She then got a job that brought her from the

Claddagh into Eyre Square. At 2:30 p.m. she rang another taxi-driver, Noreen Mallon, on her car phone, and they arranged to go to the Skeffington Arms for a cup of coffee. Eileen told Noreen that she was looking forward to seeing her daughter at Christmas. Noreen would later describe Eileen as being in 'excellent form'. The two women remained chatting until 3:30 p.m., when they both went back to work.

In the late afternoon Eileen took fares from Salthill, Crestwood and the railway station. All were relatively local drops; she hadn't been outside the city except at lunchtime, when she had travelled the sixteen miles home to Corrofin.

At 6:10 p.m. Eileen went into Supermac's in Eyre Square to have a cup of tea and also to use the women's toilets. This timing is precise because she can be seen on CCTV entering the restaurant and leaving sixteen minutes later. Like the accounts given by everyone who met Eileen during the day, the CCTV shows her as a contented person going about her daily business. She is wearing a smart suit and her trademark tinted glasses.

After leaving Supermac's Eileen brought a fare from Eyre Square to Ballybane. On the way back into the city she picked up a fare at Mervue and dropped them off at Eyre Square. She met another taxi-driver, Martin Fitzpatrick, and gave him £6 for the Turloughmore lotto draw. Some time about 7 p.m. she picked up a man and a woman; she dropped the woman at Renmore, east of the city centre, and then left the man at the Tirellan estate. As she drove back alone towards the city she had about an hour and a half left before she was due to finish her shift.

The Gardaí are still trying to piece together Eileen's movements after she headed back into the city. One of the difficulties is that there are conflicting reports about where her car was spotted, and where she picked up the fatal fare.

One taxi-driver says he spoke to Eileen near the arcades in Salthill at about 7:30 p.m. and she was alone in her cab. Another driver says he spoke to her in the Francis Street area at about 7:45 p.m., while two other drivers say they saw her on the taxi rank in Eyre Square at about 7:50 p.m. and that she left the rank without a fare. However, another taxi-driver describes seeing a man getting into Eileen's taxi on the square before it pulled away. He told the Gardaí that the memory stuck with him because he had been first in line to take a customer but that a man wearing a baseball cap had passed by his cab and got into Eileen's car.

One piece of information that is not in doubt is that at precisely 7:59 p.m. Eileen phoned home to her mother in Corrofin. The call did not connect but was logged with the 088 Eircell network. There are many possible explanations for why Eileen did not complete her intended call. Perhaps she couldn't get a good signal where she was, or perhaps her phone battery was just about to cut out. Perhaps she was stopped in traffic somewhere or pulled in off the road and was about to ring home when a passenger hailed her or knocked on the door of her car.

It was some time about 8:15 p.m. that Eileen last spoke to the despatcher with Galway Taxis, Bernard Boyle. He was working at the taxi office in the centre of Galway when Eileen rang in on the car's CB radio. It was a short conversation, with Eileen saying she was going to Claregalway, a town six miles north of Galway on the N17 road to Tuam. Bernard assumed that Eileen had a fare in the taxi. About twenty minutes later he tried to contact Eileen on the radio. He had a customer wishing to be picked up in Claregalway, and he thought Eileen would by now have dropped off her fare and would be free, but she didn't answer her radio.

Eileen left one particular clue that detectives have analysed again and again. Taxi-drivers log the mileage travelled on every journey. The Gardaí know from an analysis of Eileen's car that the last fare she took travelled a distance of seventeen miles. Seven of those miles are accounted for by the journey the killer took from Tinkers' Lane back towards Galway after leaving Eileen lying fatally injured in the boreen; the other ten miles could be accounted for by a journey beginning at various points around Galway and ending up at Tinkers' Lane. Detectives have studied dozens of places on maps of the city, trying to decide whether Eileen left Eyre Square with a fare at about 8 p.m. that night or whether she got a pick-up off the street somewhere else in the city. There are suggestions, for example, that she picked up a fare at Cross Street, or perhaps Quay Street.

What is without any doubt is that some time between 8 and 9 p.m. on Sunday 30 November 1997 Eileen Costello O'Shaughnessy was beaten to death, and the attack began as she sat in the driver's seat of her taxi. What is still not clear is where exactly the taxi was when the attack began. Was Eileen forced to drive the taxi up Tinkers' Lane and then turn into the boreen before she was attacked? Or did she willingly drive up Tinkers' Lane before she was attacked without warning?

The assault on Eileen lasted a number of minutes and was relentless. As she sat trapped in her taxi she suffered more than a dozen injuries to her head from a heavy blunt instrument. She had bruising to one of her arms, consistent with someone holding her roughly. Most of the injuries were to the left side of her head, towards the back, but she was also struck on the forehead. She lost a lot of blood in the taxi before her killer left her lying on the ground in the boreen. One person who later saw her body said it appeared that her head had been 'smashed in'. She had a superficial injury to her chin, which might have been caused by her mobile phone, or perhaps her car radio. Was she trying to raise the alarm when the phone was snatched from her?

It is most likely that whoever attacked Eileen was sitting in the front passenger seat. This is clear from an analysis of the blood in the car. There was blood on the divide between the front seats and on the dashboard and interior roof but little if any on the front passenger seat, implying that a considerable quantity of blood from Eileen's multiple head wounds fell on the attacker's clothes rather than on the seat.

There is also a possibility that two or more people were involved in the attack. Perhaps the person holding the hammer or similar weapon was sitting in the back and caught Eileen by surprise by hitting her without any warning. Or perhaps someone sitting in the back seat held her by the hair as the front-seat passenger struck her with the weapon. This might account for the clumps of Eileen's hair found in the car after the attack.

Detectives have also considered whether the clumps of hair pulled from Eileen's head mean that a woman was involved in the attack. The experience of the Gardaí is that pulling hair during an assault is more a female trait than a male one.

While all possibilities are still considered, the one given most credence is that a man sitting in the front passenger seat, and acting alone, attacked Eileen. He may have been carrying a bag to hide the hammer or similar object; he may have suddenly pulled out the weapon and begun beating Eileen while pulling her hair and hitting her repeatedly on the head.

Though Eileen's taxi was not found until close to midnight, subsequent investigations led the Gardaí to believe that Eileen was attacked at least three hours beforehand. At about 9 p.m. there were a number of sightings of her silver-coloured taxi being driven by a man in an erratic manner on the N17 road, heading back towards Galway. One learner-driver told detectives he had to pull in to the hard shoulder as a taxi came bearing down behind him. The speed limit at the time on the road was 30 miles per hour, and the silver taxi was doing more than this. The learner-driver clearly remembered the incident because his car had cut out when he pulled over.

Another important witness is a woman who was driving along the same stretch of road who also saw a taxi being driven by a strange-looking man. She got a look at the driver and described him as having a beard and 'looking rough'. A third potentially crucial witness is a shop worker who was locking up for the night about 9 p.m. This man was in a shop across the road from the industrial estate where Eileen's taxi was later found abandoned. He saw a man getting down off a three-foot wall at the industrial estate, turning left and walking towards Galway. The man appeared to be in his twenties and of average height, with short red hair. He was wearing a waist-length jacket or top, possibly green. This man has never been positively identified.

Even before Eileen's body was found the Gardaí were studying the abandoned taxi to try to establish what the motive was for the attack that had obviously occurred in the car. In time the taxi would undergo a full scientific examination, but in the early hours of that Monday morning detectives were studying the car to see what was still there and what was missing.

It was noted that Eileen's black leather bum-bag, in which she would normally keep her money, was still in the car. A small container with loose change was also there, as was a plastic bottle of Club Lemon. A number of cards for Galway Taxis were lying on the floor of the car. Apart from some coins still in the car, there was no other money. According to the work Eileen had done that day, she should have had about £70 as her day's takings, but the money was not in the car. Eileen's mobile phone was also missing. The front dashboard had been badly damaged, and it was clear that an attempt had been made to pull out the two-way radio. It was not clear whether this was an attempt to steal the radio or merely to disable it; perhaps it had been done to try to stop Eileen raising the alarm.

As the Gardaí began their investigations they didn't yet know that the crime scene had already been tampered with. It would be weeks before detectives discovered that shortly after Eileen's car was abandoned by her killer it had been broken into by a gang of teenagers. The six boys who robbed the taxi didn't know they were stealing from a woman who lay dead six miles away. They had seen the car in the car park of the industrial estate off the N17 road. They noticed that the driver's window was open and that there was no-one inside. While the others kept a look-out, one of the teenagers reached into the car and grabbed whatever he could find. He managed to steal Eileen's black Nokia mobile phone and her cigarettes—a twenty pack of Silk Cut Purple. He would later tell the Gardaí he spent only a few seconds in the car, and that he never saw the blood all around him.

The youths ran from the taxi and tried to use Eileen's phone, but the battery was dead. They decided to smash the phone, and they dumped it in a laneway about six hundred yards from the abandoned car. They then left, oblivious of the fact that they had stolen from a murdered woman and had tampered with a murder scene.

A few days before Christmas 1997 the teenagers confessed to detectives about what had happened. Over previous days the

Gardaí had received confidential information about the six youths, and when they were questioned they quickly admitted what they had done. While confirming that he had taken Eileen's mobile phone and cigarettes, the main thief swore he had not taken any money or anything else from the taxi. His story was supported by the other youths, all of whom were also remorseful for their actions. They were all cautioned and released.

One motive for Eileen's murder that was quickly ruled out was any form of sexual assault. Eileen was fully clothed when she was found and had not been raped. While robbery was a likely motive, detectives noted that the killer had not stolen Eileen's mobile phone nor taken her leather bum-bag, which contained loose coins. If the killer had stolen the £70 or so that Eileen should have had as her day's takings, why not take other valuables from the car as well? If the killer did steal money, was it as an afterthought rather than a real motive? Indeed, was there a clear motive for the attack, or was Eileen's murder a random and motiveless crime?

The Gardaí have long wondered whether Eileen knew her killer. Having worked as a taxi-driver for four years she would have come into contact with thousands of people in Galway and the surrounding towns and villages. She may have known the person only to say hello to, or perhaps she had driven the person previously. Is it possible that as she drove her passenger through Claregalway and on towards Tinkers' Lane she recognised or knew the person as a familiar face and so didn't realise the imminent danger? There is nothing to firmly substantiate such a possibility: it is only one of several possibilities that detectives consider over and over.

Was Eileen suddenly attacked as she drove her passenger or passengers along the N17 road, and did the killer then somehow sit on top of Eileen so as to drive the car down Tinkers' Lane? It's an unusual possibility but cannot be ruled out. Or is it more likely that Eileen willingly turned down Tinkers' Lane before she was suddenly attacked close to the boreen a couple of hundred yards down the dark lane? One taxi-driver said he doesn't believe Eileen felt danger until it was too late.

I think she willingly drove down Tinkers' Lane and wasn't being threatened in any way at the time. I feel that if Eileen had sensed any danger before turning down the lane there's no way she would have left the N17. She would have driven into a ditch or into a wall rather than turn off a main road and go down that isolated lane. She would have tried to signal other motorists. I think the attack began and ended very close to where her body was found.

Assuming the likelihood that Eileen's fare was a random pick-up from Eyre Square or elsewhere in Galway, the killer was walking around Galway already armed with a hammer or similar weapon. Was he travelling home from some type of lawful work that involved the use of heavy hand tools, or was he simply carrying the weapon in his jacket or his bag and waiting for the opportunity to attack someone?

Damien O'Shaughnessy had to formally identify his mother's body. He went with his father to the morgue, the white sheet was pulled back and he confirmed that it was his mother.

In the years since her murder Eileen's family have tried to come to terms with what has happened. Damien says one of the worst people affected was his grandmother.

It's hard to put into words, but the first time I saw Gran after we knew Mam was dead, it was just they way Gran was sitting there in the house. She was so sad. It is one of my biggest memories, going to see Gran. She was in her late seventies at that time. How do you explain how a woman feels when she loses her daughter like that? Gran's world ended that day. It's very hard to bury a child, even if she is in her forties. Immediately after Mam was murdered I moved back from Galway to live with Gran in Corrofin, and I stayed there for the next six years. Eventually Gran went to live in a local nursing home.

Eileen was the youngest of four children born to Frank and Nora Costello. Their eldest child, a girl, died when she was eight months old. Nora later gave birth to P.J., Martin and Eileen, all of whom grew up in Corrofin. Eileen was close to her brothers. P.J. later emigrated to Canada, while Martin set up a transport business and raised his family in Corrofin as well. He told me that he misses his younger sister very much.

> Eileen was a powerful woman. She was a great worker, and she loved to play cards and she loved country and western music. I'll never forget everyone out searching for Eileen in the early hours of that morning. My son Kenny had just come home from Australia after a year and he had to make the calls to Damien and Tom in Dublin to say Eileen's taxi was found and it didn't look good at all. My wife, Mary, and my children, Kenny, Sinéad and Martina, all miss Eileen so much too. She never did anybody any wrong. It is so sad that this has happened.

On Friday 5 December 1997 Eileen was laid to rest at Kilmoylan Cemetery in Corrofin, following funeral mass at St Colman's Church. Contact had finally been made with Eileen's daughter, Susan, in Australia, and she had endured a long and sad flight home, arriving on the Thursday.

The church was packed, and many more mourners gathered outside, where the mass was relayed on loudspeakers. Susan and Damien stood beside their father at the front of the church, behind Eileen's coffin, which was bedecked with red roses. The altar was a sea of flowers, with some soft toys dotted among them. Senior gardaí who had seen Eileen lying in the boreen attended the mass. Many of her fellow taxi-drivers were there too. Over previous days Galway's taxi community had put black ribbons on their cabs in a simple expression of grief and solidarity. Hundreds of people from near and far gathered to pay their respects, as they had done the previous night when Eileen's body was brought from a funeral home in Tuam to St Colman's.

Father Paddy Williams was the chief celebrant at the funeral mass. He told those gathered that 'it could only be described as a tragedy of the highest proportions that a vibrant, hard-working

Bernadette Connolly, who was ten years old when she was abducted and murdered in Co. Sligo on Friday 17 April 1970.

Bernadette and her mother, Maureen.

Bernadette was a champion Irish dancer.

Bernadette (*on right*) with her older sister Ann and younger brother Tommy.

Marie Kilmartin, who was abducted and murdered in December 1993.

Marie Kilmartin *(on left)* with her best friend, Patricia Doyle.

A delighted Marie, at her home in Port Laoise, opening presents on her birthday.

Marie cradling pups after her dog Buttons gave birth.

Eddie McCabe, a father of four young boys, was shot dead at Cookstown Road in Tallaght in the early hours of 24 November 1995.

Galway taxi driver Eileen Costello O'Shaughnessy, who was beaten to death in November 1997.

Eileen and her children, Damien and Susan, enjoying a meal.

Eileen in earlier years.

lady from our parish who never did any harm to anybody but only wanted the best for her family and her work, that she should be brutally and heartlessly murdered. When a working mother is deliberately and cruelly done to death, then her family and the whole community are wounded to the core.'

He spoke of a time when murders were a rare occurrence in Ireland and how people might talk about that rare murder for years afterwards. 'Nowadays there seems to be a murder every other day, such is the state of our society.' The entire community had a strong desire that 'the perpetrator of this heinous crime will be brought to book. We pray for a successful outcome to the Garda investigation.'

Eileen's niece Martina read a tribute to her aunt. The mourners knew of Eileen's courage in coping with illness, they knew of her devotion to her family. They also knew of her love of a bit of fun on a night out and of her love of country and western music, from Daniel O'Donnell to Mick Flavin. Martina's words brought home to many the enormity of Eileen's loss.

Happy, peaceful days at last, struck by a vicious journey. Visions of brisk hands in a well-fought struggle flash through all minds. Her hearty laugh, her friendly chat, her warm, positive approach. She was unique, successful in doing ten things at once. She will always be remembered but never replaced. The taxi rank is minus cab number 34 and will never be the same again. Nobody will ever equal Eileen. Her dedication to her family and her career left no room for improvement. Her unacceptable death has placed a quilt of silence over the entire population of Corrofin, and of Ireland.

After the mass Eileen's coffin was brought from the church by Damien and his father and Eileen's brothers, Martin and P.J. Eileen was laid to rest alongside her father, Frank, who had died twenty years before.

As the Gardaí began their investigation into Eileen's murder, detectives in the county were also beginning a second murder inquiry following the discovery of the body of a 53-year-old

bachelor at his home at Indreabhán. Tom Clisham was found
lying on his bed with his hands tied behind his back. He had been
dead for a number of days. A Galway man was subsequently
charged with murder, but a jury at the Central Criminal Court
later found the accused not guilty.

As the Gardaí continued their investigation into Eileen's murder
it soon became apparent that any hope of an early breakthrough
in the case was unlikely. Eileen's taxi had to undergo an extensive
scientific examination, with every part of it examined for trace
evidence, including fingerprints. What made this line of inquiry
very difficult was that because the car was a public-service vehicle
there were many fingerprints or part-prints to be found, and every
person, including the killer, could argue that they had merely been
a passenger at some time in the past. Eventually six hundred
fingerprints would be taken during the Garda investigation.

Meanwhile some detectives turned their minds to the blood that
the killer would have had on his clothes. One garda says this is still
a definite line of inquiry.

> Whoever sat in that front passenger seat would have had a lot
> of blood on their clothes. The leather passenger seat did not
> have blood on it, so whoever was sitting there got Eileen's
> blood on their coat or jacket and their trousers. This opens up
> two very real lines of inquiry for us. One is that some people
> may have seen someone with blood on their clothes and have
> not yet told us. Maybe someone saw a man walking in a
> strange fashion in Galway that night, walking while trying to
> cover part of his jacket, or turning his body away from people
> as if to shield a leg of his trousers from view. It's something like
> that that we believe people still have in their minds and for
> some reason haven't come forward yet.
>
> The second scenario is when you consider, what did this
> man do with his bloodstained clothes? Did somebody see
> bloodstained clothes thrown away somewhere, or did anybody
> notice an unusual fire in a back garden or the like? Is there
> someone covering up for the killer? Did somebody help to

wash the blood-stained clothes and has kept quiet about it? Is there a woman who noticed her boy-friend or husband or father or brother doing his own washing when he normally wouldn't go near a washing machine? The answer is out there; the bloody clothes remain a very real line of inquiry.

Detectives considered whether the killer might have been a visitor to Galway. The city has always had a bohemian air, where tourists from the rest of the country and abroad come to sample the music, theatre and culture the city has to offer. While most visitors are law-abiding citizens, occasionally there are criminal elements who try to blend in. The Gardaí considered the possibility that a visitor to Galway might have killed Eileen and then fled the city. Could the killer or killers have left Galway on an early-morning train and have been back home in Dublin or elsewhere before Eileen's body was discovered that Monday lunchtime? One detective says such possibilities have not been ruled out but believes the killer is more likely to be local.

It's certainly possible that someone came to Galway with the intention of committing a robbery and that they came armed with a hammer. And it's possible they waited all day until they could hail a cab being driven by a woman, thinking they would meet less resistance as they tried to steal her takings. But maybe it's a little too far-fetched. We can't rule it out, but what leads me to believe that the killer is from Galway city or the county is the type of area where Eileen's body was left. There is no way her killer just happened upon that dark boreen where he left her body. He knew Tinkers' Lane; if not by name he knew where it was located. I just have a feeling that the killer knew the N17 road and he knew Claregalway and he knew where the sharp turn right was when you go past Claregalway that brings you down Tinkers' Lane. There was a degree of local knowledge involved. Whatever the motive for the attack, be it robbery or something else, I just don't believe it was a day visitor to Galway who killed Eileen.

One year after Eileen's murder two detectives travelled from
Galway to England after the London Metropolitan Police had
contacted them with some interesting information. An extremely
violent thirty-year-old man from Derry had been arrested in
London in September 1998 after beating a man to death with a
frying-pan. The man was also suspected of strangling a teenage
woman to death in Glasgow only days before his arrest. Among his
possessions was a phone number for Galway Taxis. A quick check
on the man revealed that he had indeed spent time living in
Galway, and had been a suspect for a rape in the locality.

The gardaí investigating Eileen O'Shaughnessy's murder met
the man in a London police station, and he spoke freely to them.
He told them he had worked as a chef in a pub in Galway, but he
denied any knowledge of Eileen's murder. Soon afterwards the
Gardaí were able to rule him out as a suspect when it was established that he had been in Cork on the night Eileen was murdered.

One detective remembers how this man originally seemed a
likely suspect.

This man readily admitted to police in London that he had
very violent thoughts and that he attacked people at random.
When he was first arrested in London he said he had been
planning to attack two shop workers with a hammer. He later
confessed to strangling a young woman he had befriended in
Glasgow in August 98, and he also told of how he killed a man
in a flat after fleeing to London. This man was later given two
life sentences in Britain for those two murders. He killed
people without any motive and spent time in psychiatric care
as well as prison. We knew he had lived in Galway before
travelling to Britain, and now here he was emerging as a random recidivist killer. But our investigations later established
[that] he was not anywhere near Galway at the time Eileen was
murdered. He went from being very prominent on our suspect
list to being marked off it. Somebody of his ilk would naturally
be a prime suspect in Eileen's case, but it wasn't him.

In 2001 a 37-year-old man was arrested in Castlerea, Co. Roscommon, by gardaí investigating Eileen O'Shaughnessy's murder. This man was originally from a village in Co. Galway and had been living in Ballybane in Galway at the time of Eileen's murder. He was lodging with a couple and had worked on building sites in Mervue and Merlin Park. He was arrested following a review of the murder investigation over the previous months. He was questioned by detectives at Roscommon Garda station over a period of twelve hours before being released without charge. So far this man is the only person arrested in connection with the murder, and he remains a suspect.

Before that fateful night Eileen O'Shaughnessy had never been physically attacked during the course of her taxi work. Once or twice she had witnessed men indecently exposing themselves on the street, and on one occasion she had to call the Gardaí when a customer refused to pay. Those were her only experiences of unsavoury characters before a murderer sat into her cab some time between 8 and 9 p.m. on 30 November 1997.

In the wake of Eileen's murder, taxi-drivers in Galway and beyond were fearful that the attacker would strike again. If it was someone stealing from taxi-drivers to finance a drug habit, there was a likelihood that the killer would attack again soon. But no other taxi-driver was attacked in the same fashion in Galway or elsewhere. The only other serious attack on a taxi-driver in Galway had occurred many years before Eileen's murder when a man was left blindfolded and badly beaten by a gang who stole his car.

The Gardaí have studied ten thousand questionnaires filled out by people in Galway and beyond relating to their whereabouts on the night of Eileen's murder. During the investigation detectives took 1,800 statements from potential witnesses. More than 2,000 'jobs' were issued—lines of inquiry that gardaí must follow up. Among the extensive file are statements by people who spotted what they believed was a silver Toyota Carina taxi during that crucial period of 8 to 9 p.m. To this day the Gardaí are trying to establish whether or not each sighting was of Eileen's car.

A mother and daughter were driving on the N17 Tuam road between 8 and 8:20 p.m. when they spotted a car parked on the hard shoulder a short distance from the Corinthians rugby ground a few miles outside Galway. They noted that it was a taxi and seemed a bright colour. A short distance away in the direction of Claregalway a group of people also reported seeing a taxi. The group had been at 7:30 p.m. mass in Galway and were heading home when they saw a taxi at the junction of the N17 and Cloon Road. These witnesses say they saw the car at about 8:20 p.m.

These sightings could well have been Eileen's taxi as it travelled towards Claregalway. The timings would seem to tally with Eileen's call to the Galway Taxis office to say she was en route to Claregalway. The car would have continued on through the town, staying on the N17 road and heading for Tinkers' Lane.

The turn for Tinkers' Lane is quite sharp, and any turning car would have to slow down considerably. A number of witnesses did come forward to say they had seen a taxi turning into Tinkers' Lane that night. One witness said the taxi did not use its indicator, while another believed the indicator was showing. One man said he saw the taxi turning into the lane at 8 p.m., and he said he could be specific about the time because he had been making a phone call at the time.

If all these sightings are of Eileen O'Shaughnessy's taxi, not all the timings can be correct. The taxi could hardly have turned down the lane at 8 p.m. and then be sighted on the other side of Claregalway towards the city at 8:20 p.m. However, no other taxi-driver could be found who was either pulled in on the hard shoulder on the N17 some time between 8 and 8:20 p.m. or who turned into Tinkers' Lane at 8 p.m.

Another line of inquiry that has never been resolved concerns a red car that was seen coming out of Tinkers' Lane at 2:20 a.m. on the morning of Monday 1 December. This car was spotted more than five hours after Eileen O'Shaughnessy had been murdered and her body left in the boreen a few hundred yards away. Detectives have often wondered if the occupants of this car saw Eileen's body or noticed anything suspicious as they drove down Tinkers' Lane, which links the road for Tuam with the road for Mountbellew. What is particularly unusual about this car is that it came out onto the N17 without its lights on, and the driver turned on the lights only when flashed at by a driver. The Gardaí have considered whether the occupants might have been a couple having a relationship who didn't want to be seen. The driver of this car, and anyone who was with him or her, has never come forward to be eliminated from inquiries.

Two months before his mother was murdered Damien O'Shaughnessy met his future wife, Jennifer. The couple met while on holiday in the Canaries and immediately hit if off. They made arrangements to meet again back in Ireland, and on the October holiday weekend Jennifer travelled to Galway. She was from Firhouse, Co. Dublin, and so they made an arrangement to meet again in Dublin at the end of November. The weekend that Eileen was murdered Damien had travelled to Dublin to meet Jennifer, but they got their wires crossed about where they were due to meet in the city centre and missed each other. Then Damien got the phone call from his cousin Kenny to say that his mother was missing. Eileen never got to meet Jennifer, but Damien had told the family about her. The plan was that they'd all get to meet Jennifer that Christmas.

Damien and Jennifer now live in Kinnegad, Co. Westmeath, with their two young children, Dillon and Kayleigh. As we sat in his kitchen Damien told me that his mother's loss affects everyone in the family.

> It's a real pity that Mam never got to meet Jennifer. And we also have two young children now who are without one of their grandmothers. Dillon and Kayleigh are really missing out, and Mam is missing out too. She never got the chance to be a grandmother. Whenever our children start asking questions we'll tell them about Granny in Heaven and explain more to them as they get older. But it's times like this that you really miss Mam. Jennifer and I are going out tonight for the first time in months. Jennifer's sister is minding the kids, but you think Mam could be here, should be here minding Dillon and Kayleigh.

Tom O'Shaughnessy still lives in the family home in Corrofin. After Eileen's murder he tried to go back to work at Mill Street Garda station but found it difficult to be working in the station where his wife's murder was being investigated. As a garda he had been able to explain to his children and other family members why detectives seemed to be asking the same questions on many different occasions and in many different ways: it was all designed to try to get every conceivable piece of information that could help the investigation.

Tom retired in 1999, having completed thirty years' service. He told me that his one wish, for his children's sake and his own, is that Eileen's murderer will be brought to justice.

After such a long time I don't really hold out much hope at this stage, but it hasn't been for want of trying. The investigation team in Galway left no stone unturned as they went about the case, but if it hasn't been solved yet, I don't hold out much hope, unless something happens out of the blue, and we all hope it does. I would dearly love for the case to be solved for everyone's sake, especially Damien and Susan. I beseech anyone with information to come forward.

Following Eileen's murder Susan returned to London, where she continues to work in child care. Damien and herself were always close but are even more so since their mother was taken from them. Damien says that their father helped both of them come through an extremely difficult time.

Mam's murder had a very big effect on Dad. Even though they had separated there was no ill feeling between them. They were still on friendly terms. Only for Dad I think I would have gone crazy. He was brilliant; he was a rock for Susan and me, especially with them being separated. I think Susan and I are the only ones who will know what Dad did for us. No money could compare to what he did for us, the support he gave us, especially in the year or two afterwards, and even to this day.

Eileen's family placed a memorial plaque at the spot where her body was found. The boreen is still there, separating two large fields. The hedge along the stone walls is not nearly as overgrown as it was when Eileen's killer left her lying in the mud. Driving down Tinkers' Lane from the N17 road one can see a number of newly built detached houses on the left. A couple of hundred yards down on the right-hand side is the boreen where Eileen's body lay. The plaque at the entrance to the boreen has a photograph of Eileen and reads:

Cherished memories of Eileen Costello O'Shaughnessy, Corrofin, Tuam, Co. Galway, who died tragically here on 30th November 1997 aged 47 years. Gone forever but never forgotten. Rest in Peace. Always remembered by your family.

Damien doesn't go to the spot where his mother was murdered. He says he gets too angry.

I go to Kilmoylan Cemetery, because that is where Mam is laid to rest. I haven't really been to where Mam was found. I get too vexed when I go to the spot. I would like to catch the person who attacked Mam and do the same to that person or persons. That's how I feel. They are cowards that do that type of thing. I don't think the killing was pre-planned. It could have been a robbery that went wrong, but I had asked Mam if she was ever robbed would she hand over the money and she said she would. If the killer were brought to justice it would mean a huge amount to our family, especially for Gran, who is in her eighties now. But you need the help of the public.

The weapon used to murder Eileen O'Shaughnessy has never been found. A wheel brace that she had in the car was examined but was ruled out as the weapon used to hit her more than a dozen times and fracture her skull. Detectives have long believed that the murder weapon was either a hammer or something very similar. It would have been small enough for an attacker to swing in the confined space of a car but heavy enough to cause catastrophic injuries to Eileen's head.

Detectives have considered various explanations for where the mysterious man was heading after leaving Eileen's car abandoned on the outskirts of Galway. The sighting of this man by a shop worker opposite Lydon's bakery at about 9 p.m. is crucial. The shopkeeper described how this man, with fair to red hair cut short and about 5 feet 9 to 5 feet 11 in height, was walking in the direction of the city. This journey would have brought the man to the Font Roundabout, also known as Fleming's Roundabout. He then had three options: he could have turned right towards Glenburren and on towards Tirellan; he could have kept going straight, bringing him through Mervue and into Wellpark or Renmore or on into the city centre; or he could have turned right along Bóthar na dTreabh into the Ballybane estate.

The possibility that the man intended going in the Ballybane direction gains more credence when one considers that until a few weeks before Eileen's murder it was possible to drive towards Ballybane from the car park where the car was abandoned. A set of bollards had only recently been erected, and perhaps the killer did not know this. Perhaps he planned to drive further towards Ballybane and then panicked when he could drive no further. Was this person living in the general Ballybane area, or did he park his own car near here, or was he going to Ballybane in an effort to throw the Gardaí off the scent completely? The 'Ballybane theory' is only one of hundreds that the Gardaí continue to analyse.

Co. Galway has been the scene of a number of acts of violence in recent times, in particular the murder of an eighty-year-old woman in the hallway of her home in Ballygar in the east of the county in February 2000. Nancy Nolan, a widowed mother of six, was murdered by a local man who was on day release from prison while he was serving a life sentence for another murder. Thomas Murray was only seventeen when he took his first life in 1981, stabbing a 73-year-old local farmer, Willie Mannion, to death. Like the killing of Nancy Nolan nineteen years later, the murder of Willie Mannion was a random, motiveless attack. Chillingly, Murray told the Gardaí at that time: 'I killed Willie Mannion ... I had it planned, but I hadn't it planned too long ... I wouldn't do it again in a million years.' Murray served eleven years of a life sentence before being granted his first day release in 1992. By mid-1997 he was granted full temporary release, and this continued until he was caught indecently exposing himself to children in Galway in July 1998. Despite this, the state saw fit to give him further periods of release until he murdered Nancy Nolan.

In the west of the county the community of Leitir Móir was shocked by the murder of seventeen-year-old Siobhán Hynes in 1998. The Leaving Cert pupil disappeared after going dancing one Saturday night in nearby Ceathrú Rua. Her body was found at an isolated rocky foreshore at Tismeáin Beach, south of An Cheathrú Rua, the following afternoon; she had been raped and murdered. Her killer was a local man who is now serving a life sentence for murder and a concurrent ten-year sentence for rape. Siobhán's parents, Aindí and Bríd, and her two sisters hope Siobhán's killer spends the rest of his life in prison and never has an opportunity to cause such hurt again. Indeed they would wish that he first serve the ten-year sentence for rape and only when that is completed begin a life sentence for murder.

Off the north-west Galway coast the community on the island of Inishbofin still mourn the loss of three elderly sisters killed by a man who set fire to their house in a motiveless attack in 1999. The killer was originally from Co. Down and had arrived on the island only hours beforehand. A jury at Galway Circuit Criminal Court later convicted him of arson and manslaughter, and he is now serving a fourteen-year jail sentence.

Apart from the murder of Eileen Costello O'Shaughnessy, the Gardaí have made significant progress in investigating almost every other killing in Co. Galway in recent times. Some trials have led to convictions, while others have led to acquittal, but at least a jury has had an opportunity to decide on each of those cases of murder or manslaughter. The failure to make similar progress in the murder of Eileen Costello O'Shaughnessy has left many gardaí frustrated. In that case no file has ever been sent to the Director of

Public Prosecutions. One garda who has worked on the case from the start says that solving Eileen's murder remains uppermost in everyone's mind.

> This was a hard-working woman out making a few bob, and she was battered to death. Rest assured that we will not rest until this case is solved. But we need the public's help.

Every year Eileen's friends from the taxi business and elsewhere get together for Eileen Costello O'Shaughnessy Memorial Night. The event is organised by a six-person committee from Galway's taxi community. It's a simple idea, where her friends have a table quiz or a race night and raise money for local charities. So far the fund has raised about €50,000. Her friends are also seeking approval from the city council to erect a sculpture of their murdered colleague in Eyre Square, close to the taxi rank.

On the night that his mother was murdered, Damien O'Shaughnessy had a feeling the killer would not be caught. He would dearly love to be proved wrong. He told me of happy memories of growing up, and he smiled as he remembered a family holiday to the Isle of Man and times when he would drop in to see his mother and grandmother.

> It's the ordinary things that I miss most, everyday, simple things, like meeting her for a cup of coffee in Supermac's in Galway city—ordinary things that we will never do together again. I used to really enjoy calling in to Mam and Gran for a chat in Corrofin. Mam had a little rug or throw, and you'd often go in and Mam would have that over her as she sat on the couch. After she was murdered and I was living with Gran, you could still pick up the rug and get Mam's scent.

05 | THE DISAPPEARANCE OF CATHAL O'BRIEN AND KEVIN BALL AND THE MURDER OF PATRICK O'DRISCOLL

Cathal and Kevin were the first to disappear. Cathal O'Brien lived in a flat at 9 Wellington Terrace on the north side of Cork. The three-storey house comprised six self-contained flats; Cathal's flat was at the top of the house. The 22-year-old was a socially conscious young man who had befriended a homeless man, Kevin Ball, while working as a volunteer with the Simon Community. He had been advised by other volunteers not to socialise too much with those they were trying to help, but he didn't agree. He had now parted company with the Simon Community and was helping Kevin and other homeless men by occasionally letting them stay in his flat.

Cathal was a computer graduate and had moved to Cork in the summer of 1993 seeking work. However, the computer industry was still in its infancy and jobs were scarce, and by April 1994 he was signing on for unemployment assistance. In mid-April the two men collected their social welfare benefits from separate post offices in the city. The woman who served Cathal would later remember how polite he was.

Investigations suggest that whatever sinister events befell Cathal O'Brien and Kevin Ball took place some time around 18 April 1994. There is little firm information about the specific time or date of their disappearance, but the last definite sighting of Cathal was about this time. What is without doubt is that Cathal and Kevin failed to collect their next payments, and no trace of either man has since been found.

Patrick O'Driscoll was the next to vanish. It was now December 1994, and Cathal O'Brien and Kevin Ball had been missing for eight months. During that time Cathal's family had been actively looking for him and had called to Wellington Terrace on a number of occasions, but they were told by another resident of the house, Fred Flannery, that Cathal and Kevin had gone to England on a ferry. None of Cathal's friends had heard from him. His disappearance was out of character and his family were deeply concerned. His father contacted the Gardaí, but in the absence of evidence of anything sinister having occurred the authorities did not at first treat his disappearance with any great alarm.

No-one was asking about Kevin Ball's whereabouts. Originally from England, he was forty-one and had spent most of his life on the streets, sleeping rough. He had a family in Wales, but he visited only occasionally. When he vanished from Cork in April 1994 nobody even reported him as a missing person.

It is now believed that Patrick O'Driscoll may either have known or have strongly suspected what happened to Cathal and Kevin. Patrick was a gentle person, and there is no suggestion that he was responsible for the attack on the two men, but investigations suggest that he may have known who the culprits were. He was not living at Wellington Terrace when the two disappeared but was a regular visitor to friends at the house.

In the months before Patrick himself disappeared, his family could sense there was something preying on his mind. He had spoken to one person about the disappearances of Cathal and Kevin and was clearly troubled by whatever he knew or suspected. However, he did not make any report to the Gardaí. On 10 December he moved out of his parents' house at Mahon and into a flat at 9 Wellington Terrace. Five days later he failed to turn up for a family dinner. By that time he was dead.

A garda at Mayfield station took the phone call that would spark the most intense murder investigation ever undertaken in Cork. It was 2 January 1995 and one of Patrick O'Driscoll's brothers was expressing concern about the welfare of his brother. Patrick had been expected at a family dinner in Cork on Sunday 15 December but had not shown up. His brother told the garda that the 32-year-old had not made contact with any member of his family over Christmas or the New Year. His family were particularly concerned because Patrick was an epileptic and was prone to having fits if he didn't take his medicine. He was also vulnerable because he had the sight only of his right eye, having lost his left eye in a traffic accident sixteen years before.

Patrick's brother told the garda that something else was now deeply troubling the family. He described how the family had now learnt that Patrick had spoken about two men who had disappeared from Wellington Terrace some months before. Patrick had seemed troubled by the disappearances, and now he was missing too, and his family feared this was too much of a coincidence. The Gardaí immediately put out a description of Patrick O'Driscoll, including his distinctive white eye patch. They also began investigating whether anyone had been reported missing from Wellington Terrace in previous months.

Six months before Patrick O'Driscoll disappeared, Cathal O'Brien's father, Séamus, called to 9 Wellington Terrace to look for his missing son. Today the three-storey building still stands at the end of a row of similar houses in the hilly suburbs high above Kent Station. The house faces south, taking in an impressive view of Cork's docklands and the River Lee. The person who owned the house in 1994 and rented it out as flats later sold it. He did not live at the house, and there is no suggestion that he knew of anything untoward happening there at the time.

As he knocked on the door in July 1994 Séamus O'Brien was by now very concerned for his son. It was not unusual for Cathal to be out of contact for a couple of weeks, but it was now more than two months since any of his family or friends had heard from him. What had really alarmed the family was the fact that Cathal had missed his mother's birthday at the end of June. This was really unusual: Cathal was close to his mother and would phone her regularly, and he would certainly never forget her birthday.

Fred Flannery answered the door to Séamus. He lived in Flat C on the second floor and was in effect the live-in caretaker of the building. A slight man, about 5 foot 3 or 4, he knew all the occupants of the other five flats. Most were unemployed, like himself, and happy to pay the £35 per week that gave each of them a one-bedroom flat with communal bathroom and shower. Fred had been living at Wellington Terrace since August 1993, one month before Cathal arrived there.

Séamus O'Brien will never forget his first meeting with Fred Flannery. He didn't know it at the time, but he was face to face with the man who in time would be charged with the murder of Patrick O'Driscoll. From that first meeting Flannery appeared odd to Séamus: it was certain things he said and particular mannerisms he had. Over the coming years Séamus would confront Flannery a number of times to try to get information about Cathal's whereabouts. He would come to believe that the odd things that Flannery said during their first meeting had an intended sinister undertone to them.

> Flannery told me that Cathal was gone away. He said Cathal and Kevin Ball had gone to Swansea on a ferry. He said something like Cathal 'wasn't himself when he came down that stairs.' I remember standing at the hallway of Wellington Terrace and looking inside. The place was in the process of being done up, and in one room I could see part of a ceiling had been removed and there was the remains of the base of a shower visible, and Flannery made some comment about how easy it would be to electrocute someone. And he was saying these odd things to a perfect stranger.

Séamus O'Brien spoke to other people who lived in Wellington Terrace, and they all said they had not seen Cathal for months. At first Séamus thought it was possible that his son might indeed have gone to England or elsewhere. Cathal was very socially conscious and often spoke about the need to help those less fortunate in the world. Séamus contacted aid agencies in Ireland and abroad to see if Cathal had signed up with them. He asked Jim Sullivan, the local garda in Kilmore, Co. Wexford, to look at the ferry lists to see if Cathal had in fact travelled with Kevin Ball to England. He spent days speaking to workers with the Simon Community in Cork and to homeless people in the city. He went to soup kitchens for the homeless, and he walked the streets of Cork looking for his son. But everywhere he went he got the same response: nobody had seen Cathal or Kevin for some time.

―――

By the time Cathal O'Brien disappeared in April 1994 he was at a crossroads in his life. It was two years since he had graduated from Waterford RTC with a diploma in commercial computing, but he was finding it tough to get a job in the industry. He had arrived in Cork in mid-1993 after moving from the family home in Co. Wexford. Coming to Cork seemed a natural choice: many of his college friends were there, including his best friend, Niall O'Neill. Cathal soon saw an advertisement for a vacant flat at a house in Wellington Terrace, and on 29 September he moved into Flat E at the house. The small attic room was very basic, but it gave him a view of the docklands, and he was only a ten-minute walk from the city centre. He began working with the Simon Community at its hostel in John Street.

Niall O'Neill first met Cathal when they began studying together at Waterford RTC in 1989. They became best friends and lived together for the second year of their course. After college their friendship continued, and they were best friends right up to Cathal's disappearance. When Cathal arrived in Cork, Niall was already living in the city and looking forward to the birth of his first child. He was doing volunteer work with the Simon Community, and Cathal joined him as an evening volunteer. Niall has many treasured memories of Cathal as someone who loved life and was always in good humour.

When we first met in college we hit it off immediately. Like most first-year students, Cathal was initially fairly quiet, but he was immediately very likeable and we quickly became friends. We had separate digs in first year, but in second year we moved into a rented house with other friends at Peter Street in Waterford. It was typical student accommodation, and Cathal and I shared a small attic room. Cathal evolved through our years in college. He grew his hair, his circle of friends and his confidence. At the core was always the same reliable, kind, considerate and fun-loving Cathal. We spent two great summers working in Holland during our college holidays. I remember Cathal had a number of girl-friends during our college years, and each time he fell in love it was 'for ever.' He was always totally committed to any relationship he was in. He was very easy to live with and was never in bad humour. He was a big David Bowie fan. I'd often wake in the mornings to the sound of him blaring a Bowie song and singing along.

When Cathal joined Niall as a volunteer with the Simon Community in Cork his empathy and compassion for those less fortunate was apparent. As he became friendly with the staff at the John Street shelter he also befriended some of the residents. He did soup runs in the evening, and with his easy manner he quickly gained the respect of both volunteers and residents at the hostel. Along with Niall he did a sponsored sleep-out in the city to raise awareness about homelessness.

In September 1993 Niall's baby daughter was born, and soon Niall would spend less and less time as a volunteer. He and Cathal would still meet regularly, and Cathal especially loved to visit and to hold the newborn baby.

As Cathal continued working with the Simon Community he maintained that he saw everyone on an equal level, and he treated his homeless friends just as he treated his other friends. Eventually this would bring him into conflict with the management of the local Simon Community. They told him they did not think it appropriate that he should socialise to such an extent with those he was trying to help. Cathal disagreed, and in early 1994 he parted company with the Simon Community. He still, however, maintained a friendship with some of the homeless people he had met through his work. One of those was the 41-year-old Englishman Kevin Ball.

Kevin was a drifter, a New Age traveller from England who never seemed able to settle in one place and live a steady life. Originally from the village of New Malden in Surrey, south of London, he was a strong man with a thick beard who often wore a knitted cap. He was also a heavy drinker. His life hadn't always been like this; in 1978, when he was twenty-three, he had been in a relationship with a woman and they had a baby girl. However, for some reason the relationship did not last and the little girl was eventually brought up by a relative of Kevin's in Wales. Over the following years Kevin travelled extensively around Britain and then travelled to the Continent before eventually ending up in Ireland and settling in Cork, where first he slept rough and then availed of the services of the Simon Community.

Kevin Ball seemed caught in an endless cycle of drinking and never settling down. Yet evidence would also suggest that he was seeking to re-establish contact and make amends with his daughter. In 1992, when she was fourteen, Kevin visited his daughter at her home. He told her about his travels to the Netherlands and beyond, and some of his life experiences. On that occasion he stayed only a short time before returning by ferry to Ireland. In late 1993 he sent her a postcard from Cork, and he rang her on a number of occasions. He last visited at the end of March 1994 and subsequently took the ferry from Swansea to Cork. He rang his daughter in Wales once more to say he was living in a caravan and working in a butcher's shop. However, there is no evidence that he had any job, and he was not living in a caravan but was in fact staying in Cathal O'Brien's flat whenever he could. Kevin may have told his daughter white lies to try to put her mind at rest or to try to gain her approval. Whatever prospect there was of strengthening their relationship would soon be lost, however, when Kevin vanished without a trace.

Cathal O'Brien last saw his family a few weeks before he disappeared. He had travelled back to Kilmore for the Easter holiday period and spent ten days in the family home. While there he had a chat with a local man about becoming an actuary. He was still considering all options about where he would go next in life. He had been going out with a young English woman in Cork, but that relationship was now over. If he received the mature student's grant the following year he might go to study in Dublin or Galway. He might stick with computers or might study something else; he really hadn't made up his mind. In the meantime he was living in Cork, trying to work things out.

Cathal was in good form during his visit home that Easter. He told his family about some of the people he had met during his time working with the Simon Community and what had led them to homelessness. However, he didn't tell anyone that he was allowing some homeless people to stay with him in his flat.

On 9 April, Séamus O'Brien drove his son into Wexford to get the bus back to Cork. He would not see him again.

Cathal was the fourth of eight children born to Eileen and Séamus O'Brien. He grew up in the quiet village of Kilmore, south of Wexford. The family had originally settled in Co. Wexford when Séamus got his first job as a school principal, about the time Cathal was born in 1972. Today Séamus still works as a school principal in Castlebridge, just outside Wexford. But since 1994 his life, and that of his family, has changed dramatically. Since Cathal disappeared he has spent thousands of hours searching for his son. He has searched fields and forests using shovels and sometimes his bare hands. He has knocked on countless doors around Cork and beyond, pleading for anyone with information to help.

Over a period of five years in the late 1990s he would rise early every Saturday and drive the 120 miles to Cork. He would spend all Saturday and Sunday searching for his son, before returning to Wexford in time to prepare for the school week ahead. Sometimes family members and neighbours would travel with him; at other times he made the journey alone.

At the O'Brien family home in Kilmore, Séamus showed me

treasured photographs of his children graduating. Among them is a smiling Cathal.

> When Cathal graduated from Waterford he came home here to Kilmore for a while. It was a different Ireland in the early 90s, and jobs, especially in computers, weren't as plentiful as they are today. Cathal was marking his time back home, I suppose, biding his time. He was a well-intentioned and balanced young man. He was very close to his brothers and sisters and he was a very caring person. When he moved to Cork it didn't surprise us that he started working as a volunteer with the Simon Community. That was the type of young man he was. He was just beginning to mature and blossom into adulthood, and he never got that chance.

During January 1995 senior gardaí in Cork realised that something unusual and potentially sinister had happened during the previous year. The phone call from Patrick O'Driscoll's brother on 2 January had sparked intensive but low-key inquiries. These investigations had established not only that Patrick O'Driscoll had disappeared, failing to collect social welfare payments due to him, but that two other men, Cathal O'Brien and Kevin Ball, were also missing and had also failed to collect their benefits. What seemed to definitely link the cases was that Cathal O'Brien lived in the same block of flats as Patrick O'Driscoll; and further inquiries had established that Kevin Ball, though officially homeless, had also been living at Wellington Terrace.

 Both Cathal O'Brien's family and Patrick O'Driscoll's had repeatedly told the Gardaí that the disappearance of their loved ones was entirely out of character. In Patrick O'Driscoll's case the fact that his epilepsy medicine was still in his flat further increased concern for his well-being. The Gardaí had also made inquiries abroad to establish whether any of the men were claiming social welfare benefits somewhere, but this also drew a blank. By mid-February there were now fears that the three men had fallen victim to foul play. The local media were already beginning to ask questions. A decision was made to go public with an appeal for information on the three missing men.

On Monday 13 February 1995 the Gardaí held a press conference and issued a nationwide appeal for information. They issued photographs of the three missing men. Cathal O'Brien's photograph showed his distinctive long hair tied back in a loose ponytail, Kevin Ball's showed his thick beard, and Patrick O'Driscoll's showed the familiar white patch over his left eye. The case was featured on the television programme 'Crimeline' the same evening, and there was a large response from the public. The description of Patrick O'Driscoll's eye patch in particular was generating dozens of reported sightings. As the Gardaí followed up each of these leads it transpired that there was another man in Cork wearing a white patch, though his was over his right eye.

Most of the reported sightings were of Patrick O'Driscoll, and not of Cathal or Kevin. Their trail seemed to have run cold, but detectives hoped that one of the many lines of inquiry being followed in relation to Patrick O'Driscoll might also lead to the other missing men.

The last sighting of Patrick O'Driscoll by any of his family was on Wednesday 14 December 1994 when his brother-in-law Stuart Bailey called to Patrick's flat in Wellington Terrace. The two men made an arrangement for Patrick to come for dinner with the Bailey household the following Sunday, 18 December, but he never showed up.

That Sunday night Stuart and his wife, Jean—Patrick's sister—called to Wellington Terrace looking for Patrick but he wasn't at home. They met another resident of the house, Fred Flannery, who told them he had last seen Patrick the previous Thursday morning. The O'Driscoll family knew Fred Flannery well. He was from the same part of Cork. On 28 December he had phoned Patrick's family and offered to help look for him. They searched along a disused railway line and in some pubs and then searched a disused hut. Flannery had stopped outside this hut, and when they looked inside they found a box used to hold eye patches. It would later be alleged by the state that Flannery's offer of help was merely a smokescreen to divert attention away from Wellington Terrace. Prosecutors would claim that by the time Fred Flannery helped to search for Patrick O'Driscoll he had already been involved in murdering Patrick, dismembering his body and burying his remains in a field.

Those who knew Patrick O'Driscoll describe him as a likeable character who was always in good form, a chatterbox who wouldn't intentionally harm anyone. In 1978, when he was fifteen, he had been a passenger in a car that crashed and he had suffered severe facial disfigurement on the left side of his face, also losing his left eye. He was unconscious in hospital for several days and would later undergo painful reconstructive surgery using bone grafts. He also had titanium steel plates inserted in his head. By the time of his disappearance he was still awaiting an award of £184,000 that had been approved by the High Court. The award had been under appeal, so Patrick still hadn't seen a penny of the money. He was a single man and was close to his elderly parents, Eileen and Patrick, and his sisters, Jean, Bernie and Marie, and his brothers, Paul, Noel, William and Jim. Patrick had a son from a former relationship but did not get to see his child very often.

Patrick was on the dole and took pleasure in simple things. He was known to occasionally drink too much and then abstain for weeks because his drinking aggravated his epilepsy. With his white eye patch he was a familiar face in a number of pubs around the north side of the city, and a few days after his disappearance his ticket came up at a Christmas raffle at the Temple Inn. He would never get to claim his prize of a mountain bike.

———

Nuala Treacy was in a taxi heading to her mother-in-law's house when she first heard the Garda appeal about three missing men. When she got to the house she watched the television news and saw the three photographs. In particular she noticed Cathal O'Brien with his distinctive long brown hair tied in a ponytail. She was shocked. She hadn't seen Cathal since the previous April, and now it was being reported that he might have met with some harm. She contacted the Gardaí to say she had spoken to Cathal about ten months before. She was able to narrow it down to April 1994, because that was about the time that the couple who had been sharing a house with herself and her partner had moved out. Cathal had called to the house looking for his friend Niall, not knowing that he and his partner and daughter had just moved out.

During 1995 two detectives visited Nuala a number of times, and soon they told her that she most probably spoke to Cathal only a short time before he disappeared.

> I first met Cathal around September or October 1993. My husband, Jonathan, and I were sharing a house with another couple at Assumption Hill in Blackrock in Cork. I remember Cathal as a very easygoing person. He was Niall's friend more than a friend of my husband's or mine, but I was very fond of him. He often visited Niall and would stay for dinner. I remember the last time I saw Cathal was when he called to the house one day looking for Niall. He didn't know that Niall had just moved out a day or two beforehand. I remember Cathal seemed a little bit agitated or unsettled. I invited him in for a cup of tea and a slice of apple pie. He stayed for about an hour. He said he needed to speak to Niall, and he didn't seem himself. He didn't seem relaxed as we sat. He was quite talkative, and stressed that he wanted to get hold of Niall. He asked me to ask Niall to ring him and he eventually headed off.

Nuala described to the two detectives what Cathal had been wearing. She remembered that he was wearing a red-and-blue check lumber shirt, which he wore open. She believed he was wearing a blue T-shirt and blue jeans and perhaps desert-type boots. He was wearing his long hair loosely tied in a ponytail.

Detectives have long wondered if there was any significance in Cathal's demeanour when he visited Nuala Tracey's house. Was there something troubling him that might have something to do with his subsequent disappearance, or was it something more innocent? Had he overheard or seen something at Wellington Terrace that had caused him alarm, or was he merely looking for advice about something, perhaps job-related?

In May 1995 the Gardaí began a fingertip search of land between an industrial estate and St Joseph's Park housing estate in Mayfield on the north side of Cork. They were particularly interested in a long stretch of soil, about twenty feet by five feet, that seemed to have been added to an embankment in recent times. They had established that the mysterious soil had been left there without permission. It was now three months since detectives had gone public about the case, and they now had confidential information from a sixteen-year-old boy that Patrick O'Driscoll had been murdered and his body dismembered.

Dozens of people throughout the country and in Britain were still reporting sightings of a man with a white eye patch like Patrick's, but the Gardaí now believed the 32-year-old had been dead since the previous December. One of the murder suspects, Fred Flannery, was known to frequent the area that was now being searched.

The teenage boy who spoke with Gardaí would eventually become the main prosecution witness in relation to Patrick's murder. In the early months of 1995 the boy was deeply troubled; he spent time at a residential centre for drug treatment in Limerick before returning to Cork and meeting the Gardaí. He had a disturbing story that he was compelled to tell: he described seeing parts of a body at Fred Flannery's flat in Wellington Terrace.

The teenager described in detail how, about a month after he last saw Patrick O'Driscoll, he was in Patrick's flat one night with Fred and another man. He said the three of them were chatting and smoking cannabis. He said that after a while Fred and the other man went upstairs to Fred's flat, bringing with them a bow saw, a Stanley knife and blankets. The teenager remained in Patrick's flat listening to music. After about half an hour a woman called to the house, and the man who had been in the flat with Fred let her in.

The teenage boy said that Fred then called him upstairs and showed him part of a human arm and leg in a cupboard. He would later tell a jury at the Central Criminal Court that Fred 'showed me a bit of a hand ... a hand, wrist and about three inches of an arm.' He was also shown 'a leg with a stocking on it.' The limb part was a foot to just above the ankle. 'There was a black sock with diamonds on it. Fred said they were Pa's [Patrick's], and he was after killing him.'

The teenager described how Fred Flannery told him he had killed Patrick O'Driscoll about two to three weeks earlier in Patrick's own flat. He said Fred told him he had hit Patrick with a hammer and had then put a rope around his neck and choked him. He said Fred showed him a coal bag and said Patrick's body was in the bag. 'I was going to run ... but I was afraid,' he told the Gardaí.

Fred had asked him to carry a different heavy bag down to a car outside. Fred brought the coal bag downstairs and put it and a 'gear bag' into the boot of the car. The teenager said he and the woman and the other man then travelled in the car to a house, and Fred followed them on his motorbike. Later Fred drove him home and told him to keep quiet and that if he was ever worried about what he'd seen to come and talk to him.

Some days later the sixteen-year-old was with Fred and the other man and overheard them saying that Patrick O'Driscoll's body was buried in a field near Glanmire Wood, outside Mayfield. He told detectives he heard the men discuss digging up the body and reburying it in another field.

In early May 1995 the teenager brought gardaí to a place at Glanmire and pointed out a specific area of a 25-acre field where he believed Patrick's body might have been buried. On 12 May the Gardaí carried out an exploratory dig in the area and reached as far as solid subsoil without finding anything. They continued to concentrate their inquiries on sifting through the large mound of earth a mile away at the back of St Joseph's Park in Mayfield, with the intention of returning to the Glanmire site and conducting further digs later.

About two weeks later, on the night of Tuesday 23 May, two reporters with Cork 96FM, Barry O'Mahony and Paul Byrne, went to a section of the 25-acre field at Glanmire following a tip-off. This was only a couple of dozen feet from the part of the field that the teenage witness had originally pointed out to the Gardaí. At this second spot the two journalists found evidence of disturbance of the soil, and they were confronted by a putrid smell. The Gardaí were immediately called, and by dawn a team was back at the field in Glanmire. Within a short time they found evidence that a body had been buried in the ground but had since been moved. Garda forensic science experts found human tissue, hair and a fingernail. Because of the type of soil disturbance and the overpowering smell, it appeared that a body had been dug up in the previous few days. It seemed quite possible that a body had been brazenly removed from the ground under cover of darkness after the teenage boy had pointed out a nearby section of land to the Gardaí.

Based on the allegations against Fred Flannery, it was time for the detectives to arrest and question him.

Meanwhile the Gardaí began a search for another freshly dug grave in the fields around Glanmire, where the body might have been reburied, but none was found. The fingertip search of soil near St Joseph's Park would in time also yield nothing. In fact it would be more than a year before Patrick O'Driscoll's body was found elsewhere, purely by chance, and by that time Fred Flannery would be a free man once again.

Early on the morning of Saturday 27 May 1995 Fred Flannery was arrested at a flat where he was now living in the Mardyke area, just south of the River Lee. As investigations had intensified at Wellington Terrace over the previous weeks Flannery had decided to get away from the north side of the city.

At the same time that a team of detectives arrested Fred Flannery, a second man was also taken into custody. The two were held at separate Garda stations and questioned for twelve hours. As the time came for both men to be either charged or released, the Gardaí consulted the Director of Public Prosecutions. A decision was taken that Fred Flannery should be charged with the murder of Patrick O'Driscoll. The second man was released from custody.

Shortly before 11 p.m. that night Fred Flannery was brought

before a special sitting of Cork District Court and charged with the murder of Patrick O'Driscoll on a date between 15 and 31 December 1994 at 9 Wellington Terrace. A large crowd gathered as he was brought into court, his head covered with a brown jacket. Several times during the brief court hearing observers noted that Flannery held his head back and seemed to raise his eyes as if to prevent tears forming. He was remanded in custody and taken to Cork prison.

The family of Cathal O'Brien looked on in horror as these events unfolded in mid-1995. Over the previous year Cathal's father had said the family was still holding out hope that Cathal might have travelled to England or elsewhere and might yet make contact. Séamus went on radio and television to make an emotional appeal for information; but as the disappearance of Patrick O'Driscoll changed from a missing person's inquiry to a murder inquiry, Cathal's loved ones were faced with the awful realisation that he too had most probably met with violence.

Séamus now turned his attention to the man charged with murdering Patrick O'Driscoll. He told me he had confronted Fred Flannery on many occasions.

I met him in court on one of his appearances and I interrupted his passage back to the cells. The prison officers, in fairness, gave me an opportunity to speak to him, but it was only two minutes. I straight out asked him where Cathal was and what did he know about Cathal, but it was a total blank. I later went to see him when he was in Cork Jail. He agreed to meet me, and he sat down and he smoked his cigarettes, but he said he couldn't speak to me; he said the prison was wired. Later, in 1997, when he wasn't in prison any longer, I went down to Macroom and spoke to him. I thought because he wasn't facing a murder charge any longer that he might talk. But the meeting was very unsatisfactory. He got an opportunity then, as I saw it, of helping ease terrible suffering, but he flatly refused. He wasn't the sort of person for helping anyone really.

On Thursday 27 June 1996 Fred Flannery arrived in handcuffs at the Central Criminal Court in Green Street, Dublin. It was the second week of his murder trial. The first few days of the trial had led to much public interest. The case had then gone into legal arguments, and there had been little to report so far that second week. As Fred Flannery was brought back into court that Thursday another crime was dominating the headlines: the journalist Veronica Guerin had been shot dead on the Naas Road, Dublin, less than twenty-four hours before.

Three hours after arriving at court in a prison van that Thursday, Fred Flannery walked free, amid extraordinary scenes. Not only was the murder charge against him dropped but the judge hearing the case directed that Flannery never again face trial for the murder of Patrick O'Driscoll.

The trial had been in danger of collapse for days after it emerged that the Gardaí had made certain documents available to the defence and prosecution only after the trial had begun. The jury had already heard testimony from a number of people, including the teenage boy, the main prosecution witness. But in the absence of the jury the defence said it was deeply unhappy that documents were forthcoming only after the trial had begun. A superintendent entered the witness box and swore on oath that the documents had not been deliberately concealed. Among the documents were statements from people who claimed to have seen Patrick O'Driscoll after the date he was alleged to have been murdered. Most observers thought the jury might be discharged and a date for a retrial set. However, in a highly critical judgement Mr Justice Robert Barr said the trial was 'so tainted that it cannot be satisfactorily retrieved.' He told Fred Flannery he was free to leave the court and made an order for a permanent stay on the murder charge being brought against him again.

After thirteen months in custody, Fred Flannery was suddenly a free man. He walked out of court with his solicitor by his side and, besieged by reporters and photographers, walked down through Dublin's fruit and fish market towards the quays. He was wearing his familiar crew-neck wool jumper and carried a leather jacket in his right hand. He seemed bemused by the media presence and was no longer trying to cover his face. Asked repeatedly by reporters to give his reaction to the court ruling he would only say, 'It's grand to be free.'

The permanent stay on the murder charge deeply upset the gardaí who had been involved in preparing the case. An internal Garda inquiry was carried out to investigate Mr Justice Barr's criticisms. The gardaí involved in the case maintained that there had not been any deliberate suppression of documents: anything that had happened had been as a result of human error, they maintained, and Garda headquarters accepted this.

Patrick O'Driscoll's family were stunned by the development. To this day they cannot understand how a person charged with their brother's murder could walk free without a jury being given an opportunity to give a verdict in the case. The O'Driscolls still wonder why a new trial date could not have been set, with a new jury being sworn in.

In the immediate aftermath of the collapse of the murder trial the O'Driscoll family were still faced with not knowing where Patrick's body lay. Despite extensive searches in Glanmire Wood and surrounding fields in the months before Fred Flannery's trial, the Gardaí could not find the spot where they believed Patrick's body had been reburied shortly before Flannery had been arrested and charged in May 1995. Then, on 19 July 1996, three weeks after Fred Flannery walked free from court, Patrick O'Driscoll's body was found.

A man out walking his dog made the discovery in woodlands at Lotabeg, near Mayfield. He was walking through a heavily wooded area close to the Tivoli dual carriageway when his dog stopped at a particular section of ground. The man noticed a foul smell and immediately left the area and contacted the Gardaí. James Keane was the first garda on the scene. He looked at the section of ground and saw evidence that it had been disturbed. He poked the ground with a stick and he too noticed the foul smell.

Patrick's dismembered body had been buried in a shallow grave at the base of a sycamore tree. His skull and torso were found in a sports bag. Other bones were found in the earth, while others were still wrapped in the remnants of blankets. The upper arm, foot and hand bones were retrieved. Parts of the arm bones were still in the sleeves of a pink-and-green check shirt, and one of the feet still had a diamond-patterned sock on it.

At the National University of Ireland, Cork, Dr Margaret Bolster assembled Patrick's skeleton and established that only his breast bone was missing. Dr Robin O'Sullivan, a lecturer in anatomy at NUIC, also examined Patrick's skeleton. An analysis of the cut surfaces of the bones suggested that they had been cut with a handsaw.

Two surgeons who had operated on Patrick O'Driscoll soon confirmed his identity. Adrian Sugar and Michael John Earley had carried out four operations on Patrick in the mid-1980s to try to repair the injuries sustained in the road accident in 1978. They had used bone grafts to try to build up his collapsed left cheekbone and the area around his eye, in the hope of being able to insert an artificial eye. The two consultants studied the skull found at Lotabeg and confirmed that the remnants of steel wires attached over the surface of the skull exactly matched those that had been inserted in Patrick's skull. The doctors were in no doubt that the skull found at Lotabeg was Patrick's.

In the late summer of 1996 Patrick O'Driscoll's family were finally able to lay him to rest. From the moment they had reported him missing they knew something terrible had befallen him. In June 1996 the family had suffered the added trauma of seeing one of Patrick's alleged killers walk free from court. But now at least there was some solace in having Patrick's body and in giving him a proper burial.

There were heartbreaking scenes at the Church of the Holy Cross in Mahon as Patrick's funeral mass was celebrated. Many gathered outside and stood silently as Patrick's coffin was brought from the church for burial at St Michael's Cemetery, pausing on the way for a few silent moments outside his parents' home. Among those who attended the funeral was Cathal O'Brien's father, Séamus.

When I met Patrick's sister Jean in Mayfield she told me the family will never come to terms with the horrific nature of Patrick's death.

Patrick was a lovely, gentle person. He loved his pint and his tobacco. The type of man he was, if he saw a woman getting off the bus with heavy bags he'd offer to help her carry them. Patrick was a handsome young man before the accident when he lost his eye. He went through a lot of physical pain after the accident and a lot of operations; he went through hell. We were told at that time that he mightn't live, but he pulled through, and it is so cruel that he was later taken away from us so violently. I will never make sense of it. I don't hold anything against the Gardaí, but things can't just be left as they are. We have Patrick back, but we never got justice, never saw anyone convicted of murdering our brother. And what about the families of Cathal O'Brien and Kevin Ball, still waiting for answers to this day. I can't imagine what we would have gone through if we hadn't got Patrick back. I think about the O'Brien family in Wexford every single day.

As Patrick O'Driscoll was laid to rest, Séamus O'Brien intensified his efforts to find his son. He concentrated on the Glanmire Wood area and Lotabeg, and with the assistance of family and friends he thoroughly searched acres of open ground. It was a physically and emotionally draining procedure but one that he and others simply had to do.

We spent weekends upon weekends searching over years and years. We thoroughly searched Glanmire Wood. A line of us searched it; it's a narrow strip of woodland with a very steep incline, very difficult terrain. We did a big search in woods in north Cork at a big plantation. I myself spent many days searching on my own, looking at the area around Wellington Terrace and Grattan Hill, and also the fields around Lota. The Gardaí had done their own searches, and part of what we were doing was keeping the momentum going, to make sure the people involved knew we were active and that Cathal mattered. That is the one thing that I always want to get across. Cathal mattered; he still matters to us.

When Cathal disappeared he had four brothers living away from Kilmore—John, Cormac, Niall and Diarmuid—and two younger sisters and one younger brother still living at home—Ailse, Doireann and Ferdia. Cathal was close to all his brothers and sisters, and they helped support their parents, Eileen and Séamus, during the years that would follow. But five years after Cathal disappeared, the O'Brien family suffered another tragedy.

Cathal's brother Cormac was driving his Harley-Davidson motorbike near Frankfurt when he was struck by a van and suffered fatal injuries. Cormac had been in Germany working as an accountant and had brought his bike out for one last journey before he sold it. It was Saturday 3 July 1999 and he was travelling from Stuttgart to Frankfurt when the collision occurred. He was taken by helicopter to a hospital south of Frankfurt and placed on a life-support machine.

Séamus was searching a field at Lota in Cork when Eileen phoned him with the news. They immediately travelled to Germany to be by Cormac's bedside. Cormac lived for a number of weeks after the accident but never regained consciousness. He eventually got a chest infection and he died with his parents by his side. He is laid to rest at the cemetery in Kilmore.

It is a cruel coincidence that in the years before his death Cormac had not only helped search for the body of his younger brother but had also helped search for a friend who vanished in India in June 1996. Paul Roche from Co. Wexford was thirty when he disappeared while hiking through the Himalayas; he has still not been found. Paul and Cormac had known each other since secondary school and had been friends. When Paul disappeared, Cormac spent a month in India with Paul's family trying to find him.

———

Like other parts of Ireland, the south-east corner of Co. Wexford has suffered a number of missing-person tragedies in recent years. In February 1998 a nineteen-year-old mother, Fiona Sinnott, vanished in sinister circumstances from the house she was renting at Ballyhitt, a short distance from Kilmore. Detectives fear that Fiona was murdered and her body hidden at some unknown place. In recent years a number of excavations in the area have been carried out but without success. A number of people have been arrested, but no charges have been brought. The Gardaí believe there are people in Co. Wexford who hold crucial information about the case. Cathal O'Brien's father has spoken to members of Fiona's family to express solidarity and hope.

Apart from Cathal O'Brien and Kevin Ball, a number of other people have disappeared from Cork in recent years. In the northern suburb of Mayfield, close to where Patrick O'Driscoll's body lay undiscovered for eighteen months, the family of Frank MacCarthy still wonder what happened to the 23-year-old who vanished one February evening in 1993. He was last seen at Lotamore, near Mayfield, wearing a wine-coloured three-quarter-length coat.

Another person originally from this area vanished in July 1993. 23-year-old Michelle McCormick disappeared from Owenahincha Holiday Park in west Cork. When last seen she was wearing black cycling shorts, a black top and flip-flop shoes. Investigations have led the Gardaí to fear that Michelle was killed and her body thrown into the sea at Kinsale Harbour in a bag weighed down with stones. Almost ten years after her disappearance a man was charged with the manslaughter of Michelle McCormick, but the case was later withdrawn and the man walked free from court.

Detectives who investigated the disappearance of Cathal O'Brien and Kevin Ball continue to hope that someone will pass on anonymous information that will bring some comfort and closure for both families. Such hope is strengthened by examples of men who were murdered and whose bodies were found only as a result of confidential information being passed on to the Gardaí.

For three years the body of seventeen-year-old Patrick Lawlor lay undiscovered close to the ninth lock of the Grand Canal outside Dublin. Then, in January 2002, his body was found following a tip-off to the Gardaí. Detectives suspected all along that Patrick had been murdered and his body hidden, but it was only as a result of exact and confidential information that his remains were found. And in February 2002 the body of 22-year-old Neil Hanlon was found in a shallow grave on open ground close to Crumlin Vocational School in Dublin. He had been missing for five months, and the Gardaí privately feared he had been murdered. It was only with anonymous and precise details that Neil's body was found and he was finally laid to rest in Mount Jerome Cemetery in Harold's Cross.

———

If Cathal O'Brien and Kevin Ball were killed by the same people who killed Patrick O'Driscoll it is quite possible that their bodies were at first not taken very far out of Cork. But the land around Lota and Glanmire has been searched again and again, without result. Were their bodies brought to a different part of the city, or were they taken further away from Cork, and if so, how?

If Fred Flannery had any of the answers, he never confessed. After walking free from the Central Criminal Court in June 1996 he settled with his partner outside Cork and kept his head down, coming to the attention of the Gardaí on only one occasion for riding his motorbike without insurance. That he was odd was without doubt. There were a number of examples of bizarre behaviour, with threats of real or imaginary violence.

On one occasion while he was in custody awaiting trial for the murder of Patrick O'Driscoll, Flannery was refused bail when a judge heard that he had asked someone for the loan of a shotgun 'to take a few heads.' Years later he also asked Séamus O'Brien to get him a gun when Séamus visited Cork to implore Flannery to say what he knew about what had happened to Cathal. There were also reports of Flannery having thrown a gas canister through a door at Wellington Terrace when he had lived there.

But ultimately, a jury of his peers never got the opportunity to pass judgement on Fred Flannery or to weigh up the prosecution evidence that was to be brought against him for the murder of

Patrick O'Driscoll. When Patrick's body was found three weeks after Fred Flannery was set free from court, the ruling by the Central Criminal Court meant that the Gardaí could not charge Flannery again.

Séamus O'Brien told me of the immense frustration he still feels at the permanent stay imposed on Flannery facing trial for Patrick's murder.

> In fairness, Flannery never had to answer for anything, because he was effectively protected by that ruling. I would have expected as a citizen of this country that a case could simply have been withdrawn from the jury and a mistrial could have been declared. A new jury could have been sworn in and they could have started again. I do feel that a consequence of that ruling meant that Cathal was possibly lost to us for ever. I don't think the Gardaí deserved the criticism they got. They failed to submit a file relating to possible sightings of a man who three weeks after the trial collapsed was proven to be dead. If the case had been listed for a retrial the prosecution case would have been even stronger, because Patrick's body had then been found. But to see the case collapsing like that with so many unanswered questions was equally as savage as the thought of what had happened to Cathal, because I thought the whole justice system had abandoned us.

On Friday 16 May 2003 Fred Flannery took his own life. It was almost seven years since he had walked free from the Central Criminal Court and more than nine years since Cathal O'Brien and Kevin Ball had vanished from Wellington Terrace. In the months before his death Flannery had been living with his partner, Kathleen, and her young family at a farmhouse at Carrigaline, south of Cork. In the hours before his death he had been smoking cannabis. He was not depressed and did not appear agitated in any way. He did not leave a suicide note.

Séamus O'Brien remembers getting a call from Cork 96FM shortly after the news of Fred Flannery's death. Within moments he was on the air being asked how he felt about the news.

> Down through the years we had little sorrow for Flannery. He certainly showed us none. But I remember I was rung up by Neil Prendeville on Cork radio and asked about the news of Flannery's death, and I immediately said, 'He was somebody's son.' Looking back, maybe it was a curious thing to say, but revenge was never a factor with me. It isn't built in to my thinking. If you followed that road you'd end up in Cork Jail or the like, and then where would everybody be. Our feeling is that we will do everything within the law to honour Cathal and remember him. We value him so much, and miss him terribly.

The Gardaí privately hoped that Fred Flannery's death might lead to other people finally coming forward with information about Cathal O'Brien and Kevin Ball. Certainly the suspicion of detectives had always been that more than one person was involved in their disappearance. While Fred Flannery was one suspect, there was also another.

The man who was arrested along with Fred Flannery on the morning of Saturday 27 May 1995 has never been charged in connection with Patrick O'Driscoll's murder or with Cathal's and Kevin's disappearance. While the Director of Public Prosecutions felt there was enough evidence to charge Fred Flannery with Patrick's murder, he did not believe there was enough credible evidence to bring charges against the other man, who was in his mid-thirties at the time of his arrest. Even after Patrick's body was found, lending greater credibility to the state's case, the DPP did not direct charges to be brought. In recent years this man continued living in Cork. He was originally from Mayfield and was not living at Wellington Terrace at the time of the disappearances or of Patrick O'Driscoll's murder.

The prosecution case during Fred Flannery's murder trial had stated that a woman had also called to the house on the night Patrick's body was allegedly moved out of Wellington Terrace. The state's key witness, the teenage boy, said he heard Fred Flannery ask the woman if she might 'dump a bit of rubbish' for him. The jury had heard that the woman later drove the teenager and a man from Wellington Terrace to another house in Cork, while Fred Flannery followed them on his motorbike. However, the murder trial would be dramatically halted before the jury got to hear greater detail of what was alleged to have happened.

There are many unanswered questions. Were Cathal and Kevin attacked at the same time, or was one attacked when he started asking questions about the other? What was the motive for any such attack? Did Cathal and Kevin witness or overhear something that led to their deaths? What did their attackers later do to cover their tracks? Was anything such as carpet or furniture removed from the house, and what happened to Cathal's and Kevin's belongings? What about the reported fire at a flat in the house on 27 April 1994, which caused damage to flooring and a door? Was it just a coincidence? What about the reports that a settee was removed from a flat in the house in mid-1994, stripped down and re-covered by a person known to one of the suspects? Is this a red herring, or could there have been blood or fibres or other evidence of violence on the settee? Unfortunately, these potential leads were made known to the Gardaí only eight months later, when they began their investigations after Patrick O'Driscoll vanished from 9 Wellington Terrace.

Séamus O'Brien eventually stopped going to Cork every week. The physical and mental exhaustion was overpowering. By 2000 he and his family and friends had searched Lota and Glanmire as best they possibly could. The large-scale Garda searches had long finished. Séamus continued teaching in Castlebridge and watched as his youngest children also left the family home to study and work and make their own way in the world. The youngest son, Ferdia, followed Cathal's path and went to study in Waterford Institute of Technology. Their daughters, Ailse and Doireann, turned to teaching and the law, respectively. Of their remaining children the eldest, John, lives in Dublin, Niall lives in New Jersey, and Diarmuid is in Sweden. In 2006 Séamus and Eileen entered a new phase in their lives when they became grandparents for the first time.

Séamus and Eileen O'Brien have done everything physically possible in trying to find their son. They have met the families of other missing men and women to try to help others.

Séamus's relentless efforts saw him meet the men suspected of murdering his son. He also met elements of Cork's criminal underworld and travelled to Britain searching for answers.

> Eileen and myself and our sons and daughters are living our lives and getting on with our lives. We have made it through these awful times. You can stare right into the face of evil but you cannot let it take away your appreciation for what is good and what is right. We have suffered and have been scarred by Cathal's disappearance and the failure to find him, but, thanks be to God, it hasn't crippled us entirely. Cathal would be the last person in the world to want further damage to be caused.

On a sideboard in the O'Briens' living-room is another photograph of Cathal grinning at the camera. Perhaps today he'd still be working in computers, or maybe he would have continued his campaigning ways and be out in Africa or Asia with an aid agency. Or maybe he'd be doing something completely different. Séamus smiled as he described his son.

> Cathal was the type of person who would make you laugh, he'd make you smile. He was so enthusiastic about things, and he was a cerebral sort of fellow. He'd read a lot. I know that if he had managed to get himself out of the environment in which he was in Cork he would have adopted a fresh outlook or approach. He was only twenty-two, for God's sake. He was entitled to flounder around for a while, to take his time, to find his way and get life experience. Cathal would have continued leading a productive and fulfilling life.

Niall O'Neill still misses his friend greatly. A few days before Cathal disappeared in April 1994 Niall had moved out of Cork towards Kinsale. Nuala Treacy later told him that Cathal had called to the house looking for him, but Niall would never get to speak to Cathal again. He tried to reach him at Wellington Terrace but he wasn't there. Niall didn't become alarmed at first, thinking that perhaps Cathal had taken a notion to travel somewhere for a while.

Within months Niall got an offer of a job in the Netherlands, and he and his family moved there for a few years. As he left Ireland he was still optimistic that Cathal would turn up with a funny story to tell to explain his unexpected absence. Over time Niall, like Cathal's family, came to realise that his friend had not chosen to go away.

> I still think about Cathal very often. He was without doubt one of the kindest and most genuine people I've ever met. I still talk about Cathal a lot. I generally speak of him in the 'I wish you could have known him' sense. He set a benchmark for friendship for me. Cathal had so much potential, he truly had so much to offer the world. It's such a shame he never had the chance.

Niall has great memories of himself and Cathal going to the Netherlands for summer work during their college holidays. They stayed in a campsite south of Rotterdam and worked in an onion-processing plant. It was terrible work, but they had a great time. They cycled to work on old bikes and played chess at work, using different-coloured onions for the chess pieces. They bought cheap runners; Cathal's were green and Niall's red, and they swapped one runner each and for the entire summer wore mismatched shoes. Niall says that was the type of young man Cathal was, with his sense of fun, humour and happiness.

> One summer he arrived in Holland with just a spare pair of jeans and a toothbrush. He was fully confident anything else he needed would fall into place, and it did. He was a happy, carefree person who would do anything for family or friends. He often spoke about his family. He had great respect and fondness for his parents. Cathal delighted in simple pleasures:

loud music, new books, hot baths, cold pints and nonsense conversations. He loved to cook, and I remember he was delighted when I got him a set of saucepans when he moved into his flat in Cork. And he loved to read, especially science fiction.

For Cathal's twenty-first birthday Niall gave his friend a copy of *The Lord of the Rings*. During the investigations after Cathal's disappearance the Gardaí took away some of his books from the family home in Wexford, including this present. They were examining Cathal's possessions to get his fingerprints and DNA. The Gardaí still have the book.

In Kilmore, Séamus and Eileen continue to hold out hope that answers will come about the whereabouts of their fourth child. When Cormac was tragically killed in Germany in 1999 there was at least an explanation, and they could bring his remains back to Co. Wexford. But, as Séamus explained, grieving for Cathal is different: there is no explanation, no logic, no grave.

As the years continue and Cathal still hasn't been found you become more and more cynical. You would think that if he were to be found it would have happened sooner. But you can never give up, you never know what is going to happen. There is always hope; but if Cathal is to be found now it may be through an act of nature, or an act of God, rather than human intervention.

Outside the front door of the O'Brien family home in Kilmore is a camellia bush. At the beginning of every year it blossoms, blood red. Every February, to mark Cathal's birthday, his family travel from Co. Wexford to Cork and they bring flowers from the bush to leave at Wellington Terrace.

06 | THE MURDER OF CECILIA McEVOY

Cecilia McEvoy was on her way to the pictures when somebody strangled her to death on the evening of Monday 5 November 1962. The 21-year-old had left her home at Grange, near Stradbally, Co. Laois, with the intention of hitching a lift into Port Laoise. Her plan had been to cycle the six miles to the cinema, but the lamp on her bike wasn't working. Undeterred, shortly after 7 p.m. Cecilia put on her bottle-green overcoat, said goodnight to her family, and headed out the door.

Cecilia was only on a visit home to Co. Laois when her killer struck. She worked in Dublin as a domestic servant in a house in Drumcondra. She was happy living in Dublin; one of her sisters, Maureen, was also living in the city and they met regularly. Cecilia naturally missed her parents and other sisters and brothers and enjoyed getting back home whenever she could. In November 1962 she was back in Co. Laois for a couple of days to sort out legal issues surrounding a compensation payment she was due. She had been injured in a road accident when she was a girl and was entitled to a payment of £300 (about €6,500 in today's values) when she turned twenty-one. In fact she'd celebrated her birthday on 27 October and had already been to visit her solicitor in Port Laoise, but she hadn't yet collected her cheque.

Cecilia was in good form and happy to be back in the family home for a few weeks. Her mother had cooked a nice dinner that Monday night. After finishing her dinner Cecilia got ready to go to Port Laoise. There were two cinemas in the town; she might go to the Colysseum or maybe to Paul's.

Cecilia walked down to the main road that links Stradbally and Port Laoise. Because her intention was to hitch a lift, it's most probable that she willingly got into a car, not realising she was in danger. However, because there are no witnesses it remains a possibility that she was pulled into a car or van while she walked along the side of the road.

Two men found Cecilia's body three miles north of Port Laoise at 9:40 a.m. the following morning. Val O'Connor and Jerry Maher were driving through the open expanse of land known as the Heath when they made the shocking discovery. Cecilia lay on her back about fifteen yards in from the side of the road. She was fully clothed except for her shoes, which were missing. Her green overcoat was draped on top of her, covering part of her face. The two men knew immediately by looking at Cecilia that she had been dead for a number of hours. They ran to a nearby pub and rang the Gardaí.

Four gardaí arrived at the scene within minutes, and Superintendent James McLaughlin followed soon afterwards. He studied Cecilia's body and knew from the marks on her neck that she had been strangled. She was not carrying any identification, and neither the gardaí nor the two men who found the young woman recognised her.

As well as Cecilia's brown shoes, her brown handbag was also missing and would never be found. Similarly, the scarf she had been wearing when she left home would never be found. As she lay in the grass at the Heath she was still wearing her red-and-white dress and fawn cardigan. The green overcoat she had put on while heading out the door less than fifteen hours before was now covering most of her body. The right side of her face was visible, but the coat partly covered her left side. It had been draped sideways over Cecilia by her killer after he strangled her and left her lying in the grass.

In the Ireland of 1962 the random abduction and murder of a young woman was almost unheard of. Hitching a lift into a town or village was a common form of transport. As the Gardaí began a murder investigation in Co. Laois that Tuesday morning they didn't yet know who the victim was or indeed that she had been hitching a lift into Port Laoise. But with an average of one murder every month or two in the early 1960s, Garda headquarters immediately contacted the Department of Justice to keep them informed of an investigation that would dominate the news for weeks. Meanwhile a team of detectives from the Technical Bureau in Dublin, led by Superintendent Patrick McLoughlin, was en route to the scene.

One of the other phone calls made by gardaí that morning was to the news room of Radio Éireann. A description of the dead woman had already been relayed to all Garda stations—early twenties, 5 feet tall, brown hair, slim, round face—but there was no report of any missing woman matching the description. The Gardaí needed to establish the woman's identity as quickly as possible, to break the tragic news to her family but also to begin a process of establishing her last movements. They asked Radio Éireann to broadcast the description of the murdered woman on the lunchtime news.

Shortly after the 1:30 p.m. news the Gardaí discovered that Cecilia McEvoy from Grange, about six miles away, was missing. She had last been seen leaving her home between 7 and 7:15 p.m. the previous evening. It was only late on the Tuesday morning that her family had discovered that she had not returned home from the cinema. She hadn't been seen early that morning, but her family had thought she was most probably having a well-deserved lie-on. But by late morning they discovered that her bed had not been slept in.

While local people in Grange tried to comfort Cecilia's family, another neighbour, Ellen Maher, was brought to the Heath by gardaí, and she provisionally identified Cecilia. A Garda car brought Cecilia's mother, Kathleen, to the scene, and word was sent for her father, James, to return home from work urgently. Only when he returned to the house was he told that his daughter had been murdered.

Cecilia McEvoy was the sixth of ten children born to Kathleen and James McEvoy. She had six brothers and three sisters—Noel, Maureen, Kathleen, Peter, James, Joseph, Ellen, Kieran and Nicholas. James McEvoy was employed by the ESB, and he and his wife worked hard to provide for their family. The family were industrious, growing their own vegetables and even making their own butter. James was also a talented carpenter and made most of the furniture the family had in their thatched house. There were twenty-two years between the eldest child and the youngest; at the time of Cecilia's murder her siblings ranged in age from seven to twenty-nine. Two of her sisters were married—Maureen in Dublin and Kathleen in Switzerland. The eldest son, Noel, was married and living in Dublin, while Jim was working in England and Joseph was a soldier on UN peacekeeping duties in the Congo. Peter, Ellen, Kieran and Nicholas were all still living at home.

Each of Cecilia's brothers and sisters has memories of happy times they had with their murdered sister, and each has a distinct memory of how they learnt she was dead. Joseph remembers the frustration of trying to get home from the Congo.

> I was with C Company in Leopoldville and I remember clear-ly being summoned in to see the chaplain. He asked me my name and address and the names of my brothers and sisters. Then he said he was sorry but that he had bad news. He told me Cecilia had been murdered. I wanted to get home as soon as possible, and I came home with a battalion that was leaving the Congo. I came back on a Globemaster—a big aeroplane that was used to carry troops at the time. The journey home took two-and-a-half days. It was a really slow plane that flew direct to Dublin Airport. But by the time I got back to Ireland Cecilia had been laid to rest.

Jim discovered that his sister had been murdered by reading it on a newspaper poster.

I was working in Dorset in England at the time; I'd been there since 1957. I got a telegram from Dad saying, 'Come home immediately, very urgent.' I got a lift to Bristol and eventually managed to get a flight. I remember getting off the plane in Dublin and heading into the city, and I saw on a billboard a headline about a girl from Port Laoise found murdered. I got a taxi from Dublin to Port Laoise.

Superintendent McLaughlin studied the scene where Cecilia's body lay. She had obviously been brought to the open space by some form of vehicle. He looked closely at the grass nearer to the roadway and saw the tyre mark of what looked like a small car. From this spot he could see the drag mark where Cecilia's killer had pulled her body a short distance in off the roadway. It appeared that the young woman had most probably been dead when she was taken from a vehicle and left at the Heath. Whether she was murdered in a car close by or on open ground elsewhere would never be established.

Cecilia's body was examined at the scene by detectives and by the state pathologist, Dr Maurice Hickey. It was soon established that the young woman had not been sexually assaulted. Though her cardigan and dress were slightly disturbed and stained with mud and grass, this was as a result of being dragged from a vehicle and left lying on the ground. Cecilia's clothing was later sent for analysis to a laboratory in Dublin. However, no scientific leads emerged from this line of inquiry.

One thing that intrigued detectives and that was never explained was why Cecilia's overcoat was placed on top of her body. Was it simply a crude attempt to hide the body from view, or was it the work of someone who was overcome by remorse for what they had done and in their troubled state thought that by covering Cecilia they could somehow fix things?

Such questions have long been considered by Cecilia's family. The thought that a random killer attacked their sister has tormented the McEvoys for five decades. Joseph says the family are still deeply upset.

When you lose a member of your family like that, it is devastating for everyone. And it's hard to comprehend that something like that can happen to someone so innocent, and to think she was thrown there on the ground like that; to think such a quiet person was killed in such a brutal way. It caused us a lot of anguish, wondering what type of person might have done that.

Cecilia's sister Maureen spent many happy times with her in Dublin in the early 60s.

I was living in Berkeley Road on the north side of Dublin, and Cecilia was working and living a short distance away at a house at Grace Park Terrace in Drumcondra. Cecilia used to come around and visit myself and my husband and our young children. We used to meet up maybe two or three times a week and go shopping. The shoes she was wearing when she was murdered, I was with her when she bought those. And she was only after getting a new handbag, and she got a new little ring; she was wearing that ring when she died.

The woman who employed Cecilia at her home in Dublin, Helena King, told reporters at the time that the young woman had been a reliable and conscientious worker. 'Cecilia was a very good and very nice girl. She never went out to dances, but she liked TV,' she said.

As the Gardaí studied Cecilia's body they noticed that her long painted fingernails were bent and damaged, suggesting that she had fought for her life. Detectives believed that the person who strangled Cecilia might well have had scratch marks on his face or arms.

In the late 1940s Cecilia and Joseph were playing close to their home on the Stradbally road. Cecilia was six or seven at the time and Joseph was two years younger. Suddenly a car driven by a man from Co. Roscommon came hurtling towards them and struck Cecilia. She suffered serious injuries to her face and shoulder as she was dragged for a distance, but she survived the accident. However, she was left with a permanent injury to her eye and over the coming years would have to attend the Eye and Ear Hospital in Dublin. She had to wear glasses after the accident and would sometimes get headaches when the sun was particularly bright. The little girl was awarded £300 compensation, and the money was lodged in an account administered by the court, to be given to her when she reached her twenty-first birthday.

By November 1962 Cecilia had no real plans for spending her money. She might buy herself some nice things or get presents for her family, but that would not really eat into the sizeable compensation payment. Cecilia had left school at fourteen and worked at various jobs, firstly in Stradbally, then in Dublin, where she eventually took a job as a domestic servant in a house in Drumcondra. She had been working at her latest job for five weeks and got on well with her employer. She was content and secure in Dublin and would most probably have put her money in a bank until she decided where she was going next in life. It's quite probable, though, that her imminent payment gave her an extra spring in her step as she headed out to the cinema that November night in 1962. Life was good for Cecilia McEvoy; but some time on that Monday night a murderer shattered her dreams.

A wax imprint was taken of the tyre mark found at the Heath. It was identified as a well-known brand, but it was hoped that the individual worn tread recognisable in the imprint might single out a vehicle, if only the Gardaí could identify a particular suspect. Unfortunately, some journalists learnt about this piece of evidence and decided to print details of it. If he was reading the extensive newspaper reports on the murder investigation it's likely that the killer changed his tyres over the following days.

During initial investigations the Gardaí established that, along with Cecilia's missing shoes and handbag, a scarf that she normally wore was also missing. Despite extensive searches throughout Co. Laois these belongings were never found. Every report of clothing being found was followed up. When a pair of shoes with small block heels similar to Cecilia's were found by an alert member of the public in Bandon, Co. Cork, the Gardaí first thought they might have a new lead, but the shoes were not Cecilia's.

Cathal O'Brien was twenty-two years old when he disappeared in Cork in April 1994.

Cathal (*on right*) with friends Niall and John while on a working holiday in the Netherlands in the early 1990s.

Cecilia McEvoy (*on right*) with (*from left*) her brothers Jim, Nicholas and Kieran and her mother, Kathleen. Cecilia was twenty-one years old when she was murdered near Port Laoise in November 1962.

All set for school: Cecilia in younger years, with her brother Joseph.

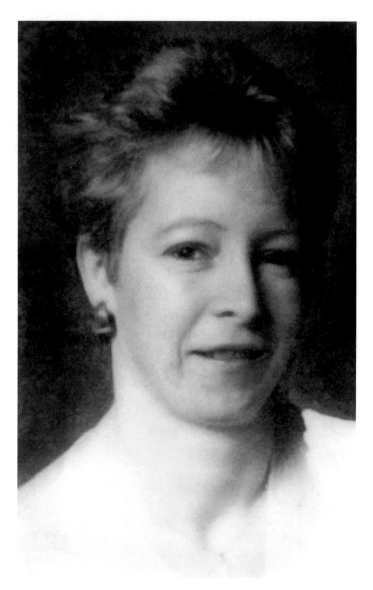

Catherine Brennan, who was shot dead in Tallaght in November 1995. Twenty-nine-year-old Catherine was a hard-working mother of two young children.

Brian Stack, Chief Prison Officer at Port Laoise Prison, was shot in the back of the neck in Dublin in March 1983. He was left paralysed and brain-damaged and died eighteen months later.

Brian with his three sons, Austin, Kieran and Oliver. This photograph was taken after Brian had been shot. He died on 29 September 1984.

A passionate sportsman, Brian in earlier years with his three sons (*from left*) Oliver, Austin and Kieran.

Brian was well known throughout the country for his dedication to amateur boxing.

A treasured family photo of Arlene Arkinson, taken many years before she was abducted and murdered in August 1994. Arlene's body has not yet been found.

Arlene pictured on a special day.

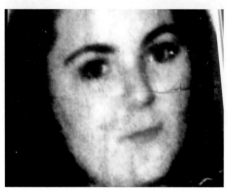

One of the last images of Arlene. She was fifteen years old when she was murdered.

The Gardaí interviewed people who attended both cinemas in Port Laoise on Monday 5 November. Nobody had seen Cecilia in town that night, and she had no ticket stub on her when her body was found. This merely confirmed what everyone already suspected: that Cecilia had been abducted within minutes of walking from her home to begin hitching a lift into Port Laoise and was most probably dead a short time after a motorist stopped for her.

Cecilia's family have treasured photographs of Cecilia from the 1940s, 50s and 60s. In one black-and-white picture she stands beside her younger brother, Joseph. Both of them are in their school uniforms.

> We used to sing songs going to school: 'The Isle of Inishfree' and 'The Forty Shades of Green' and also those come-all-ye songs. We walked the two-and-a-half miles to and from school in Ratheniska every day. And when we came home from school we had chores to do: we had potatoes to wash, sticks to cut, and we helped get things ready for dinner.

In mid-November 1962, having spent a short period back in Port Laoise with his grieving family, Cecilia's brother Joseph had to return to the Congo. In the wake of his sister's murder he had been given a few days' compassionate leave; but with tensions at their highest in the region where Irish troops were stationed, Joseph had no option but to go back to Africa.

When Cecilia left her home that Monday night she had only a few shillings on her to pay for the cinema. The Gardaí wondered whether robbery might have been a motive for the attack. Was that why Cecilia's handbag was never found? But Cecilia was still wearing her wristwatch on her left hand, so the killer was not likely to have attacked her with robbery in mind.

Investigators wondered whether there was any particular significance in the three items that were never found. If the killer chose to leave Cecilia's coat on top of her body, why did he decide to take her shoes, handbag and scarf away from the scene? Why, for example, had her shoes been removed from her feet? Could they simply have come off during the attack, or when she was being dragged along the grass to the spot where her body was left? Did they come off as Cecilia tried to kick her attacker? Did the killer make a conscious decision to keep Cecilia's shoes: had he picked them up off the ground and then realised he might have left fingerprints on them? Or did he find them later in his car? And what about Cecilia's handbag and scarf? After leaving her body at the Heath, had her killer not noticed that these items were still on the floor of his vehicle?

What did the killer then do with Cecilia's shoes, scarf and handbag? Did he simply burn them, or throw them out? Or did he give them to someone as a present, perhaps his girl-friend or his wife?

An early suspicion that Cecilia might have been strangled with her own missing scarf was soon ruled out. The state pathologist carried out a post-mortem examination of Cecilia's body at Port Laoise General Hospital and confirmed that she had died as a result of manual strangulation. The only other visible injuries were to her painted fingernails and an abrasion on her left cheek. Dr Hickey concluded that Cecilia died some time between 7:30 p.m. and 1:30 a.m. on the night she was thumbing a lift.

Cecilia was not in a romantic relationship when she was murdered. While fearing that she had fallen victim to a random attacker, the Gardaí could not rule out the possibility that she might have known her killer, even if they had met by chance that night. They investigated all the people Cecilia knew in Dublin and Co. Laois, but this line of inquiry led nowhere.

While Cecilia was most probably abducted and murdered in a random crime, it would never be established whether she was strangled by an opportunist killer who was travelling around Co. Laois looking for someone to attack. If she was attacked by a serial killer, the Gardaí wondered why the attacker did not try to strike again. In the years immediately after Cecilia's murder there were no similar killings of young women. If the killer had driven around that November night looking for a woman to attack, what happened to stop him doing the same thing again? Was he in prison for other offences, or was he dead? Or did he somehow manage to control his murderous impulse for years afterwards, perhaps living quietly, perhaps even married with a family? If Cecilia was killed in a premeditated act by a random killer, what was the motive? Was it simply a desire to cause hurt to another person?

One possibility long considered by the Gardaí and by Cecilia's family is that she was strangled by someone who did not set out that night to kill. Perhaps the killer was planning to attack Cecilia in some other way when he stopped beside her on the Stradbally road. Did he then make an inappropriate gesture or comment to Cecilia as she sat in the front seat and then panic about the situation he was in and kill the young woman to cover his tracks? Indeed, was the man someone that Cecilia recognised and who feared she would report him to the Gardaí because of strange or threatening behaviour? Is it a somewhat bizarre scenario like this that would best explain what is apparently a motiveless murder?

Another possibility is that Cecilia had planned to meet someone that night in Port Laoise. However, when she left her home she didn't say she was meeting anyone to go to the cinema. Having been back at the family home in Grange for more than a week before her death, Cecilia had not been out socialising at night. She had been into Port Laoise and Stradbally during the daytime, but her intended trip to the cinema was her first night out. Is it possible that she met someone on one of her earlier day trips to either town and arranged to meet and go to the cinema? Perhaps she met a friend who she hadn't seen in months, if not years. If so, that person has never come forward.

The McEvoy family have considered many possible explanations in a search for answers about the murder of their sister. Joseph recounted one possibility that was given to him by a woman who claims to read tarot cards.

This woman put the hair standing on the back of my neck with what she told me. She was here with my wife and myself one night, and the discussion came up about Cecilia. This woman recounted a vision of Cecilia having met a man in Port Laoise and arranging to meet again that night. The woman said the man picked Cecilia up and drove down onto the Heath. An argument happened, and this man had Cecilia's arm twisted up behind her back. The woman said Cecilia's death was not premeditated: it should not have happened. I remember clearly she told me Cecilia thanked me for the cardigan I had given her some months before she died. It was a white cardigan with gold buttons. No-one else could have known about that cardigan. The only other people who knew were my mother, my father and my wife.

If Cecilia was attacked by someone she had planned to meet, did she make it to Port Laoise before being attacked? Or if she planned to meet someone in Port Laoise, did that person happen to drive by the Stradbally road on his way to Port Laoise and come across Cecilia walking along the road?

Joseph had given the white cardigan to his sister on a visit to Dublin in mid-1962. It was the last time he would see her alive.

I was home on a break from the army and I hired a car in Kildare, and I had it out for a week. I brought my mother and father up to Dublin to see Cecilia. It was the first time I'd seen her in a good while. We had a great day.

At the time of Cecilia's murder her sister Maureen was pregnant with her fourth child.

I had great chats with Cecilia during the months that I was pregnant. She had asked me if I had a baby girl to call her Cecilia. A month after Cecilia was murdered I gave birth to my daughter, and I named her after Cecilia. It was only years later, when my children grew up, that I told them the detail of what happened to their aunt. When there was a write-up about it in a newspaper some years ago we had a good chat.

Joseph and his wife, Mary, also named one of their children Cecilia. She was their second child. Tragically, their little girl was only one-and-a-half years old when she died from meningitis.

During the first few days of the investigation into the murder of Cecilia McEvoy the Gardaí tried to identify every vehicle that had travelled along the Stradbally road or the Heath on the night Cecilia was attacked. At least ten people came forward to say they had seen a young woman hitchhiking on the Stradbally road. The descriptions tallied with Cecilia's height, hair and clothing. None of the witnesses had seen what car Cecilia might have got into.

In the absence of information about the precise spot where Cecilia accepted a lift from her killer, detectives decided to concentrate on the stretch of road at the Heath close to where Cecilia's body had been left. The tyre mark that had been spotted on the grass verge where Cecilia's body was found appeared to show that a car had driven from the Stradbally direction before pulling in onto the grass. If this was the killer's car, the Gardaí wondered whether he had then done a U-turn and headed back towards Stradbally or whether he had continued driving straight ahead to the nearby junction with the Dublin–Port Laoise road.

It was eventually established that at least twenty-nine vehicles had travelled along the Heath between 7 p.m. on Monday 5 November and 2 a.m. the following morning. Detectives had pieced together statements from people who had either directly seen one or more cars driving along the road or had heard cars driving in the area. Of the twenty-nine vehicles reported to the Gardaí, twenty-four drivers were eventually traced and accounted for their movements. This left a further five that were believed to have driven along the stretch of road only yards from where Cecilia's body was left. Those five vehicles were never identified.

One elderly man told the Gardaí about seeing two men pushing a car along the straight stretch of road at the Heath some time between 1:30 and 2 a.m. on the night of Cecilia's murder. This witness remembered that the men were pushing the car quite slowly. One had his hand in through the window so as to steer the car as they both pushed it along. Detectives wondered who the men might be. Had they merely broken down and were pushing their car quietly so as not to disturb people at such a late hour, or had they been involved in the attack on Cecilia and were trying to quietly make their escape? Indeed, this raised another question, which is purely speculative: could more than one person have been involved in the murder?

Some detectives believed that a credible suspect was a man who was one of three hundred people to give a statement to the Gardaí. This man denied any knowledge of Cecilia's death and gave a full account of his movements. Some hours after leaving a Garda station he was found dead on open ground. Subsequently the Gardaí received information about this man's whereabouts on the night of Monday 5 November that apparently conflicted with his statement. However, because of the man's death this line of inquiry could go no further.

Cecilia was murdered more than thirty years before a number of women vanished in sinister circumstances in the Leinster area. It's feared that a number of those women were abducted and murdered by a serial killer. Unlike the disappearance of women in the 1990s, however, Cecilia's killer did not go to great lengths to hide her body; and her killing has never been linked to any other violent incidents in the 1960s. One detective says that the lack of a motive for the murder of Cecilia McEvoy has baffled the Gardaí.

Cecilia was a young woman who had no enemies. She was only home in Co. Laois for a couple of days, and we know that she was very well regarded in Dublin as well. Everything about the killing suggests a chance encounter on the road between Stradbally and Port Laoise. But the lack of a motive for strangling this woman to death is difficult to explain. If Cecilia was the victim of someone who killed for no reason, you might expect such a person to attack again. But no other women fell victim to such an assault in the years after Cecilia. Perhaps the killer was dead or in prison by that time. Or could such a person make a conscious decision not to attack again? Were they almost caught on the night of the murder and narrowly escaped being identified by a passing motorist, and did this scare them away from doing the same thing again?

Cecilia's mother and father were distraught at the circumstances of their daughter's violent death. In the years after the murder they still held out hope that they would get answers about who was responsible for taking the life of their child.

A few weeks after Cecilia's murder gardaí came to their door in the early hours of the morning. They had a pair of shoes and a green scarf and asked whether Kathleen and James could identify them. However, the shoes were a pair of high heels; Cecilia had been wearing small heels. And the scarf was not Cecilia's either.

Both James and Kathleen McEvoy died without ever knowing who killed their daughter. James died in 1982 and Kathleen died twenty years later. The couple had often thought about what Cecilia must have suffered in the moments before her death. When she had seen her daughter's body at the morgue in November 1962, Kathleen had to be sedated. Over the following years she would often express the wish that whoever had killed her child might 'die roaring.'

During the extensive newspaper coverage of the murder in November and December 1962 there were a number of inaccuracies in certain reports on the investigation. One of the most glaring mistakes was when a photograph of one of Cecilia's sisters was published in some papers with the statement that it was a picture of the young woman murdered at the Heath. This caused a great deal of upset for Cecilia's family, who had given the Gardaí a photograph of Cecilia to pass on to newspapers.

In March 1972 a 52-year-old woman was strangled on open ground at Little Curragh, Co. Kildare. Kathleen Farrell, a single woman from Blackmillershill, near Naas, worked as a cashier in the Tower Cinema in Kildare. She was fully clothed and still wearing her sheepskin jacket, gloves and boots. She was found lying on her back in furze; she had bruising to her head and neck, and a post-mortem examination established that she had most probably been strangled. A man from the midlands was subsequently charged with her murder, but the state case was later withdrawn. The murder of Kathleen Farrell was similar to that of Cecilia McEvoy in a number of respects: both women were strangled, both were still clothed and had not been sexually assaulted, both were killed close to their home, and little real attempt was made to hide their bodies. However, the crimes were ten years apart, and most detectives who investigated Kathleen Farrell's murder found no credible link with the unsolved murder of Cecilia McEvoy.

As the years went by and with no news emerging about the identity of the killer, Cecilia's family sought to honour her memory in other ways. They erected a plaque at the spot where for hours her body lay before being discovered that Tuesday morning. The plaque was four feet high and read:

> Erected to the memory of Cecilia McEvoy, Grange Upper, Stradbally, believed murdered in this area, November 5, 1962.

But in the late 1960s the plaque was vandalised when someone smeared it with tar. The memorial was later destroyed when it was smashed under cover of darkness and taken a number of miles away by someone who threw it into a river near Athy. A man was questioned about the incident by the Gardaí, but no charges were brought. The McEvoys replaced the plaque with another memorial stone with different wording, and to this day the new plaque remains at the spot. It reads:

> In Loving Memory of Cecilia McEvoy. Died 5th November 1962. Aged 21 years.

When Cecilia was laid to rest the funeral procession was a mile long. She is buried at the cemetery in Ratheniska, and her parents now rest close to her.

In Port Laoise, Cecilia's brother Joseph tells me there is a credible hypothesis that his sister's murder was not premeditated.

> Cecilia may have been attacked during something that got out of hand. It could have been a married man that she knew and who she didn't want anything to do with. He might have said or done something that he regretted and he attacked her then. That would be my reading of it.

Joseph believes there are people still alive who know or strongly suspect who the culprit is.

> Anybody who commits that type of crime, it stays in their mind. I don't care who they are or what they are; I'm sure the person who killed our sister has spoken to someone at some stage. I'm sure maybe more than one or two people know who the killer is. Cecilia didn't deserve the death she got. She wasn't causing anybody any trouble. Our family was devastated by her killing. And in the years after her murder we were very upset at the failure to see the person responsible being brought to justice. We were upset at the failure to get justice for Cecilia.

Ireland in the 1960s was a less violent country than it is today, but there were still murders that shocked the country. Less than nine months after Cecilia McEvoy was murdered a sixteen-year-old Dublin girl, Hazel Mullen, was killed in the basement of the Green Tureen restaurant in Harcourt Street on 17 August 1963. Her killer was Shan Mohangi, a 22-year-old medical student from South Africa, with whom she had been in a relationship. In a particularly shocking aspect of the case, Mohangi dismembered Hazel's body. He later confessed to the killing and was found guilty of murder and sentenced to death before a retrial was ordered and a jury convicted him instead of manslaughter.

In April 1964 a Co. Cork farmer was beaten to death as he lay in bed with his wife. His killer was a former employee, Jimmy Ennis, who had only recently been released from Port Laoise Prison, having served a sentence for another random attack. Ennis broke into the farmhouse and stole some cash before going upstairs and killing the farmer by beating him on the head with an iron bar. He also struck the man's wife, causing three deep wounds to her forehead, but she survived. Ennis was later convicted of murdering the man and jailed for life.

The difference between Cecilia McEvoy's case and those of Hazel Mullen and the Cork farmer is that the killers in those two cases were caught. Shan Mohangi was given a seven-year sentence for manslaughter and was subsequently deported to South Africa, having served less than half his sentence. Jimmy Ennis is now by far Ireland's longest-serving life prisoner. He continues serving his sentence in the minimum-security Shelton Abbey Prison in Co. Wicklow and has declined the opportunity of applying for parole.

At least in those tragic cases there was some form of justice in the killers being identified and prosecuted. Cecilia McEvoy's family longed for the same progress in the investigation into her killing, but it wasn't to be.

Two weeks after the murder of Cecilia McEvoy in November 1962 the Minister for Justice, Charles Haughey, was interviewed on television about the fear that existed with such a killer at large. He acknowledged the concern and upset felt by the public at the fact that a 21-year-old woman thumbing a lift to the cinema could be murdered in such a fashion. He sought to reassure people that the Gardaí were doing everything in their power to bring the killer to justice, and pointed out that of fifty murders that had occurred in Ireland in the 1950s, forty-five had been solved. There had been two murders in 1960, both of which were solved. Of eleven violent deaths in 1961, nine were solved.

However, despite the best efforts of the Gardaí the murder of Cecilia McEvoy would never be placed in the 'solved' category. And over the following five decades, as Ireland became an increasingly violent place in which to live, more than a thousand more murders would occur, and many of these too would remain unsolved.

07 | THE MURDER OF CATHERINE BRENNAN AND EDDIE McCABE

The murders of 29-year-old Catherine Brennan and 35-year-old Eddie McCabe were cold and clinical. The gunman shot Eddie first, pointing the gun at his chest and firing at point-blank range; as Eddie fell backwards onto the side of the road the killer pointed the gun at his head and fired again. The second bullet entered Eddie's left temple.

Catherine Brennan struggled to open the passenger door of the car. In the previous few seconds she may have looked behind her and seen Eddie being shot as he stood at the back of the car; or she may have been looking straight ahead of her and suddenly heard the two gunshots coming from the back of the car. The fear that engulfed her must have been incredible. She had met Eddie a little more than an hour earlier after accepting a lift home from a night club, and now she was trapped in a nightmare from which there would be no way out.

The killer shot Catherine once in the head, the bullet entering through her right temple. Over the previous few seconds she had managed to get the car door open, but before she could step out of the car and try to run to safety the gunman fired. Catherine died instantly; she lay half in and half out of the car, her legs still inside and the rest of her body on the tarmac. It was shortly before

4:30 a.m. on Friday 24 November 1995 at Cookstown Road in Tallaght, Co. Dublin, and two lives had just been taken, including that of an innocent mother who was simply in the wrong place at the wrong time.

When I met two of Catherine's sisters in Killinarden, the continuing grief caused by her meaningless death was clear. Marie and Helen are the two eldest in a family of eight girls and three boys born to Bridget and Jimmy Brennan. Catherine was the second-youngest and is still fondly remembered as a bubbly character, always in good form, someone who made people smile and laugh. She adored her two young children, and as a single mother she worked hard to provide for them. At the time of her murder she worked as a cleaner in Killinarden Community School, and with Christmas only a month away she was saving to help Santa surprise her children with new bikes. Anthony was seven; he had been born in England when Catherine and Anthony's father had moved from Dublin to Rochdale, Lancashire, for a few years. Eventually the relationship broke down. Catherine and Anthony had come home, and Stacey was born in Dublin. Stacey had contracted meningitis when she was a baby but had pulled through. By November 1995 she was two years old.

Catherine's sister Marie says the entire family has been devastated by her savage and unexplained loss.

> Our mother and father were broken-hearted by what happened. Our mother later passed away, and I think that is what killed her: to lose a child like that, and for it never to be solved. There was no justice for Catherine. When people die naturally you can try and come to terms with it, but when someone is murdered like that it is just unbearable. We were all so close as well, and all our children were close, all the cousins. When Catherine was killed it affected her nieces and nephews terribly as well. Everyone was and is devastated by what happened. We all miss her so much.

On the night of Thursday 23 November 1995 Catherine Brennan and a friend went out for the night, and the two women enjoyed a dance and a few drinks at JJ's night club at the Embankment on the Blessington Road near Tallaght. Catherine hadn't been out for a night since she and her sisters and mother had gone to Tramore the previous month. Catherine loved to have a 'bop'; even if she didn't have much money for a drink she'd go out to have a dance. She was in great form that Thursday night. Like most people, she was looking forward to the weekend.

Catherine kissed Anthony and Stacey goodnight and headed out. One of Catherine's nephews was sleeping in the house to babysit his two young cousins. Though the Brennan family was originally from Walkinstown, Dublin, a number of the siblings had moved to Killinarden, and the family were a close-knit group. After saying goodnight to her son and daughter Catherine closed the door of her house at Knockmore Crescent and headed out to JJ's.

———

Eddie McCabe spent much of that Thursday night socialising with his wife, Linda, and some friends. Two of Eddie's friends called to the McCabe house at Glenshane Crescent in Jobstown in the early evening. Eddie gave someone out on the road some money and asked them to bring him back twenty cans of lager from an off-licence. He and his friends were enjoying their evening and planning to have a long one. Linda went off to bingo for a while and came home about 10 p.m. A babysitter arrived to look after Eddie and Linda's young children. One of their friends invited Eddie and Linda to come round to his house, which was also in Jobstown, and at about 11 p.m. the couple and their friends drove to the house, travelling in the car that Linda owned. They stayed there until about 1 a.m., when Linda decided to head home to let the babysitter go. Eddie said he'd drive her home and then go back to his friends.

For many years Linda and Eddie had a volatile relationship, breaking up and getting back together only to break up again. They had met in a pub in Ballyfermot in the early 1980s, when

Linda won a disco-dancing competition and Eddie approached her to congratulate her. He was from Ballyfermot and she was from Drimnagh, and they started going out straight away. By November 1995 they had been married ten years and had four children. Eddie junior was ten, the twins George and Wayne were seven, and Ciarán was two.

Linda had stuck by Eddie when he was given a prison sentence for assault in the mid-1980s. He had turned himself in to the Gardaí after attacking someone on a footpath; he had expressed remorse, kept his head down in prison and learnt carpentry. Linda visited him twice a week when he was in Mountjoy Prison and looked forward to his release. When he came out he put his carpentry skill to use, building beds and presses for his young family, and he did not come to the attention of the Gardaí for anything serious during the rest of the 1980s or into the 90s. At the time of his murder he was officially unemployed.

Hours before Eddie was shot dead he told Linda he loved her. The couple were not fighting as much any more, and the relationship was getting stronger. They both understood the importance of having four young boys to care for together.

That Thursday night the couple had enjoyed a good night socialising with their friends. Shortly after 1 a.m. Eddie and Linda drove back to Glenshane Crescent from their friend's house in Linda's car. It was a 1985 light-green Nissan Micra, and Linda kept it spotless. As Eddie dropped her at their gate Linda asked him not to drink too much and to look after the car. He replied, 'Don't worry, Linda. I love you, and I'll look after the car.' He blew her a kiss as he headed back to his friends to continue their night out.

After picking up his two friends, Eddie drove the car to another place to visit another friend, but he wasn't in. The three men then decided to take a spin up to JJ's night club, and they arrived there at about 2 a.m. As they pulled in to the car park they met a man and woman who had just started walking down the Blessington Road towards Tallaght. Eddie recognised the man, and he turned the car around and picked up the man and woman, and the five then travelled back into Tallaght, stopping at the Primo garage near the Square Shopping Centre. At 2:37 a.m. the five people—Eddie, his two friends, and the man and woman to whom they had given a lift—were sighted on CCTV at the garage. The man and woman got out of the car and the man had a brief conversation with Eddie at the back of the car. This man and woman then walked off over a bridge across the Tallaght Bypass. Eddie put £5 worth of petrol into Linda's car, and he and his friends headed off again, going back up towards JJ's.

When they arrived back at JJ's at about 3 a.m. they met Catherine Brennan and her friend, and they offered them a lift back to Killinarden. The two women had missed the last bus home and were happy to accept the offer of a lift. The five headed first to Catherine's home at Knockmore Crescent, where they had a smoke and a chat.

At 3:50 a.m. one of Eddie's friends said he was going to call it a night and head home to Jobstown. Catherine had run out of cigarettes, and Eddie offered to drive her down to the Primo garage. They dropped Eddie's friend close to his home and continued on to the garage, a mile away at the Square.

Were the killer or killers watching Eddie McCabe as all this was going on? Had they been following him for long as he drove around Tallaght in the early hours of that Friday morning? Did the gunman or gunmen wait until Eddie was separated from his two friends before deciding to attack him? If the killers saw that Eddie's friends were no longer with him as he drove from Killinarden down the Blessington Road to the Square they would also have seen clearly that there was a woman in the front passenger seat. This would mean that the killers made a plan over minutes rather than seconds to kill the front-seat passenger as well as Eddie.

It's also possible that Eddie's killers just stumbled on him at some point. Perhaps they were driving along the Blessington Road and Tallaght Bypass looking for him and came upon him by chance. Perhaps they heard he had been driving around and had a description of his vehicle. Did Eddie's killers simply spot him as he drove from Killinarden to the service station near the Square, then follow him and wait?

CCTV film shows that at 4:08 a.m. Catherine bought cigarettes at the Primo service station. The interior of the shop was closed for the night, so the shop assistant served Catherine at the service hatch outside. The black-and-white CCTV film of Catherine standing at the shop window is the last sighting of her alive. Within fifteen minutes Catherine Brennan and Eddie McCabe would be shot dead.

The most likely route that Eddie and Catherine took after leaving the garage was through the Springfield estate, along the Alderwood and Maplewood Roads, passing the Raheen and Whitebrook estates on the left-hand side before turning left along Cookstown Road. What has intrigued detectives investigating the double murder is that this was a winding and circuitous route back to Catherine's house in Killinarden: the more direct route would have been simply up the Tallaght Bypass. Did Eddie drive this alternative route because he spotted someone he feared near the Primo garage? Did he think a car was acting suspiciously in the area and fear that somebody was after him? Or had he arranged to meet somebody in the early hours of that morning and, not realising the imminent danger, brought Catherine with him?

Two doormen heading home after a night's work at a pub found Catherine's and Eddie's bodies. It was 4:30 a.m., and John and Noel had driven up the Cookstown Road from the Belgard Road. At the junction near Fortunestown Shopping Centre they had turned right, keeping on the Cookstown Road, and then turned left near the Whitebrook estate. As they turned the corner near Whitebrook they saw a car pulled in on the left-hand side of the road. It was facing the same direction that they were travelling, and as they looked closer they saw that a man was lying on the ground at the back of the car. John stopped his own car and he and Noel got out and moved closer. Within seconds they were dialling 999.

At exactly the same time Garda Frank Lee and Garda John Hickey were in a patrol car in the Rossfield estate, half a mile away. Across a large expanse of open ground they saw the lights of two cars stopped in the distance. Thinking it might be a traffic accident, they drove swiftly down the Cheeverstown Road towards the junction with Cookstown Road. As they approached, John and Noel waved a torch to signal to the gardaí the seriousness of what they had stumbled on.

Eddie McCabe lay on his back, with his head towards the kerb and his feet towards the middle of the road. The post-mortem examination would later confirm that he had been shot twice, but it was already clear to the gardaí at the scene that he had bullet wounds to his head and chest. The 35-year-old had been shot at point-blank range; he had not had time to run or even to turn away from his attacker, and he had fallen straight back onto the ground.

Catherine Brennan lay on the ground at the passenger side of the car, with her legs still inside it and with her head against the kerb. Her seat belt was also hanging out of the car, caught up with her body. It appeared that she had managed to get the belt off but had not had time to get out of the car before the gunman came towards her, firing once and killing her instantly.

The double murder had taken only seconds, and the killer or killers were gone in an instant. Given that Catherine was seen on CCTV at the Primo garage at 4:08 a.m., and that John and Noel came upon the immediate aftermath of the murders at 4:30 a.m., the killings most probably occurred at about 4:20 a.m. This would allow for the five-minute journey Catherine and Eddie would have taken to travel from the garage to Cookstown Road, and would also allow for the fact that the killer or killers had success-fully fled the scene by the time John and Noel made the shocking discovery.

One woman living in the nearby Whitebrook estate would later confirm that at about 4:20 or 4:21 a.m. she heard two loud bangs and the screech of tyres. This woman had been awake at the time and had looked at the clock because her daughter had just arrived in. A man who was in a truck in Whitebrook also told of hearing two bangs at about 4:20 a.m. But nobody ever came forward to say they had witnessed the killings. The fact that two loud bangs were heard may have been two of the bullets being fired; or perhaps the two sounds were in fact the three bullets, if Eddie McCabe was shot twice in quick succession before the killer walked towards Catherine Brennan, still trapped in the passenger seat of the car.

Linda McCabe was asleep when gardaí called to her door at Glenshane Crescent shortly before 5 a.m. She knew immediately that something was wrong: she knew her husband was somehow in trouble. Everything ran through her mind. Perhaps Eddie had crashed the car; perhaps he was hurt.

The gardaí asked Linda if she owned a green Micra, and she said she did. They read out a registration number to her, SZS 76, and she confirmed that it was her car. She told them her husband had borrowed her car, and asked why they were at her house. The gardaí said there had been an incident and asked if she had any photographs of Eddie.

Linda was now feeling uneasy and said she had no photographs right there and then. She began to get upset and asked what was wrong. They asked whether Eddie had a goatee beard. Linda again demanded to know what was going on, and she was then told that a man and woman had been found shot in her car, and the man had a goatee. Linda collapsed, telling the gardaí that her husband did in fact have a goatee. She was distraught, and a female garda sat with her and tried to comfort her as she began to scream.

Eddie junior was ten when he woke up in the early hours of that November morning as gardaí called to the front door. He heard the commotion downstairs and managed to pick up bits of the conversation. As neighbours began arriving at the house to comfort Linda and look after her children, young Eddie managed to get out of the house and to run across fields from Glenshane Crescent to Cookstown Road. When he got there the crime scene was now cordoned off, but his father's body still lay on the ground.

In October 2006 I interviewed Linda McCabe about the unsolved murder of her husband. She spoke about her family's continuing grief at the loss of her husband in such brutal and unexplained circumstances. Her motivation in speaking to me was partly to put on record the truth about her husband, so that his positive qualities would be remembered as well as the negative. He wasn't an angel, she told me, but he had been a good father and good husband. She was deeply upset by newspaper reports at the time of the murder that had tried to link his name with drugs. She stressed that Eddie had no convictions for drug offences. She was also upset that in the days after the double murder a photograph of her husband's body lying on the road had been published by a number of newspapers.

Linda spoke openly and frankly to me about the effects Eddie's murder had on herself and her children. In particular, she spoke of how Eddie junior had spent his teenage years running away from home and abusing drink and tablets, and how he had spent much of his young life in prison. He never intentionally harmed people, but he did commit offences, including travelling in stolen cars. Linda didn't seek to excuse what her son had done, but there was clearly an explanation for why his life had gone off the rails. She said that Eddie junior was glad I was writing about his father's unsolved murder and about the effect it had on all of them.

When I met Linda her eldest son was in Mountjoy Prison, but she had a real hope that he might finally be about to turn his life around. Two weeks earlier his girl-friend, Donna, had given birth to a baby boy, who they also called Eddie, in memory of his murdered grandfather. Linda said that her son had asked her on the phone if she could help him get into rehab; it was the first time he had ever admitted an addiction to tablets.

In November 2006 I travelled to Naas Circuit Court to make contact with Eddie McCabe Junior. The 21-year-old was on bail and was due to appear on remand on charges connected with the unauthorised taking of a car and causing criminal damage to the vehicle the previous March. Eddie had agreed to speak to me about his father. He was due to appear in Naas on 14 November, but because of a mix-up in court dates he didn't appear in court that day and I planned to make contact with him on another occasion, but we would never get a chance to talk.

On the night of Friday 1 December 2006 Eddie McCabe Junior was found critically injured in a laneway at Tyrconnell Road in Inchicore. He had been severely beaten, suffering horrific injuries to his face, in particular to his eyes. The Gardaí believe he was viciously assaulted at another spot and then thrown out of a vehicle into the lane.

He was rushed to hospital and survived for a week before he died on 8 December. Hours after his death a family friend, speaking on behalf of Linda and her three remaining sons, tearfully told RTE news that they wished 'all this violence would just stop.' Eddie's family and friends are still shocked by the loss of a young man who was beginning to try to get his life back on track and make amends to society. The Gardaí at Kevin Street continue to investigate this second violent death to hit the McCabe family.

On 25 November 1995, the day after his father was shot dead, ten-year-old Eddie junior sat beside his mother as an RTE reporter and cameraman conducted an interview with her at her home in Jobstown. Tears streamed down her face as Linda told the reporter that her husband had been a good father and was well liked in the area. She said there was no reason why anyone could have had a grudge against him, and she appealed for those with information to speak to the Gardaí. As she held one of her other sons on her lap and spoke to the reporter, Eddie junior looked shyly at the camera and squinted against the light. Over the following years few other reporters came knocking on Linda's door to see how Eddie junior and the rest of the family were coping.

———

As gardaí were telling Linda McCabe that her husband had been murdered that Friday morning in November 1995, detectives were also making contact with the family of Catherine Brennan to tell them that their loved one had also been shot dead. The Gardaí didn't know at first what set of circumstances had brought Catherine and Eddie into contact, but over the first few hours of the murder investigation it became apparent that Catherine Brennan had been a totally innocent victim. While the motive for the murder of Eddie McCabe has not yet been established, it was immediately clear that he had been the target of a gunman who had acted in the most brutal fashion. After killing Eddie the gunman had not hesitated before killing Catherine Brennan. It's almost certain that the killer would not have known her name or anything about her: she was simply a witness to the murder of Eddie McCabe. And so, having taken one life, the cowardly killer took a second life to protect his own skin.

As dawn broke on the morning of 25 November gardaí were calling to the houses of Catherine Brennan and her sisters in Killinarden. It was a difficult but essential task to break the awful news to Catherine's family as quickly as possible, before they heard through word of mouth or the media. Catherine's sister Helen clearly remembers the morning that all their lives changed for ever.

> Gardaí called to my door and they said that Catherine had been in an accident. I was in bits. They asked if there was someone I could go into and I went into a neighbour's house, and when I was there the gardaí told me what had really happened, that Catherine had been shot.

Catherine Brennan was a decent person who had never been in trouble. Her family were well-respected and law-abiding citizens. All of a sudden gardaí were trying to tell the family that Catherine had been shot in the head and that it had been a deliberate killing. Her sister Marie remembers the shock at being told the news.

> I had gone out to work early that morning, and we'd heard the news that two people had been shot dead. I'd actually spoken to a man at work and I was saying how awful it was about that woman being shot, never dreaming it was my own sister. I got a call to say I had to go home, but I still didn't know what was wrong. It was only when I got back that my husband told me. I couldn't believe it; I wouldn't believe him; and then I saw my two lads roaring crying, and that's when I knew it was true.

Marie had to tell Catherine's two children that something terrible had happened to their mother.

I remember how Stacey was crying for her ma, and I couldn't control Anthony. He was very upset and wanted to know where she was. I had to tell him that his mother had been shot and it was a bad man who had done it. We told both of them immediately. The kids in the area would have been talking about it, so we had to tell them. Myself and my husband, Jimmy, took Anthony and Stacey in to live with us immediately, and they've been with us ever since. Anthony was very close to my youngest boy before that, and I think over the years growing up with other children did help them.

Anthony was seven when his mother was taken from him and his sister. He was close to his mother and has his own special memories of her. His aunts told me that Catherine used to buy long cream cakes for herself and Anthony, and that she had got him a computer for his bedroom. By 2006 Anthony was seventeen and had started a college course and gone to his debs' ball. His grandfather Jimmy said that Catherine would be proud of her son and daughter. Down through the years all the family gathered around to wish them well, and there had been many tears.

Stacey is also now a teenager and reminds Catherine's sisters very much of her mother. She loves music and dancing and is very chatty and friendly. Stacey was only two-and-a-half when Catherine was murdered; now she's in secondary school. In recent years she has begun to ask more and more about her mother.

Marie's husband, Jimmy, and her brother Patrick had to identify Catherine's body. To this day they refuse to talk to the rest of the family about what they had to do that day. If somebody asks them they refuse to discuss it; they say they will take it to their graves.

In the days and weeks after Catherine's death her family tried to come to terms with the fact that she had been brutally murdered simply because she was in the wrong place at the wrong time. Helen acknowledges that they did at first partly blame Eddie McCabe for the loss of Catherine.

You do say that if she hadn't met him that night she'd still be alive. There's no point saying that we don't. We do say that. In the beginning we put some of the blame on him, but then we moved on. He lost his life as well, and he had a family and parents who were going through what we were going through. The real people responsible are the killers. Our mother used to talk about the fact that his family were going through the same grief as us. We met his parents at the inquest and they were very nice people, a lady and gentleman.

Helen smiled as she remembered some of the happy times they all had with Catherine.

About twelve of the girls went down to Tramore the October bank holiday weekend before she was murdered. We went down for a long weekend, and our mother was with us and some of our aunties. We stayed from a Friday to a Monday and it was just a brilliant weekend, a mad women's weekend. We played darts and we went to a disco. We had a great laugh. We hired a bus to bring us down and back. Catherine was always in good form. When I think of Catherine I think of all the great craic we had. She was a very caring woman. If she had a row with you she'd feel terrible; if you were low she'd bring you up.

Marie remembers another great holiday they all went on to Butlin's.

We all went to Butlin's, and the kids were with us too. Catherine was in a bikini, and some fellow came over to her and took her photograph and told her she'd be in the *Sunday World*. She was buying the paper for the next two months to see if she was in it! Catherine was just a naturally nice person. The type of girl she was, if she saw myself and my husband heading out she'd shout across the green, asking us where we were going, and she'd come out with us if she could. She wasn't a heavy drinker but just loved to meet up and have a bit

of craic. She had an open house for children. She used to let
Anthony and my lads get changed in her house when they
were playing football out on the green. She'd been in her house
about three or four years. I still find it hard going past her
house.

When post-mortem examinations were carried out on the bodies
of Catherine Brennan and Eddie McCabe it was established that
they had been shot with bullets of the same calibre. In the absence
of any direct witnesses to the murders it seems possible that there
were two gunmen and that Catherine and Eddie were shot with
separate guns. However, it is much more likely that the same
person, using the same gun, shot both victims. It is still possible
that the gunman did not act alone: perhaps there was a getaway
driver and perhaps other people in the car that was heard screeching away from the scene at about 4:20 a.m.

To this day the Gardaí are trying to make out what made Eddie
McCabe stop his car and go to the back of the vehicle, where he
was then shot dead. Did somebody flash their lights at him from
the rear to signal for him to pull in? Was there some obstacle on
the road preventing his car moving any further? The car had not
broken down, and it had not been disabled in any way. It had not
been shunted, and its tyres had not been shot or burst. The car was
parked parallel to the kerb, and all the indications are that Eddie
McCabe made a conscious and willing decision to stop the car and
get out of it. If he had been threatened at gunpoint as he sat in the
car it seems likely that he would have tried to speed away; but the
keys were still in the ignition when the car was later scientifically
examined.

It seemed that Eddie got out and walked to the back of the car,
unaware that the person or persons who had somehow convinced
him to stop had a loaded firearm. Perhaps the gun was hidden
behind the killer's back or in his jacket.

The possibility that Eddie willingly got out of the car doesn't
seem to tally with suggestions that he might have driven through
the Springfield estate as a detour because he was in fear of some-

one he spotted driving around Tallaght. If he was in fear, surely he would not then have got out of the car to talk to whoever it was, unless he felt he couldn't shake them off as he was driving and decided that whatever disagreement there was could be sorted out through a conversation, or, at worst, with their fists.

One of first possibilities ruled out by the Gardaí was that the double murder might have been a case of mistaken identity. Detectives were conscious that there have been a number of cases of people being shot because they looked like the intended victim or walked the same route or worked in the same place as a murderer's target. But there seemed no mistake about the murders of Catherine Brennan and Eddie McCabe. Somebody had somehow managed to convince Eddie McCabe to get out of his car, and the killer would have had a clear look at him before pulling out his gun. There seems no doubt that the target of the gunman was Eddie McCabe, while the killer's decision to end Catherine Brennan's life without a second thought suggests somebody who most probably had killed before and indeed may well have committed further killings since the double murder.

The fact that Catherine Brennan was shot dead because she was a witness to Eddie McCabe's murder opens up the strong possibility that the killer or killers were not wearing masks. This could have been for two reasons: that the killer knew Eddie and wasn't masked so as to put his intended victim at his ease before pulling out the gun, or that the killer was acting on the spur of the moment and hadn't time to cover his face before he began shooting. Perhaps elements of both these explanations could be put together to explain what happened. If the killer was known to Eddie, perhaps he was travelling in his own car and feared that even if Catherine couldn't identify him she might identify his car. Perhaps the killer didn't realise that Eddie wasn't alone in the car until after he began shooting. There are many different possibilities; but one certainty is that the killer or killers had no mercy.

In the early days of the murder investigation the Gardaí began examining various explanations for why someone might have attacked Eddie McCabe. One possibility was that he had been involved in a verbal dispute with the brother of a prominent criminal. Detectives confirmed through CCTV film from a shop that Eddie had met the man in the hours before his death and that they had words. This man left the country with his girl-friend for Britain in the days after Eddie and Catherine were shot. In February 1996 he returned to Ireland and presented himself at Tallaght Garda station, where he was promptly arrested under section 30 of the Offences Against the State Act. He was sub-sequently released without charge.

In late 1995 and early 1996 at least eight people were arrested by the gardaí investigating the double murder. Two women were among those detained. The arrests covered a number of different groups of suspects. However, no charges were brought against any person.

When the Gardaí examined the scene of the murder they found a .22 bullet and a large piece of wood. Subsequent inquiries would show that this bullet had nothing to do with the murders: Catherine and Eddie were shot with a firearm of a different cali-bre. It was never established whether the wood was of significance to the attack. The gun used to murder Catherine and Eddie has never been found.

———

Killinarden is a ten-minute walk from the scene of the double shooting. It's hard for Catherine Brennan's family to pass by the spot. Any time her sisters travel that direction they say a prayer. One sister, Noeleen, put up a cross at the spot on the Cookstown Road, but someone took it away. Marie told me that her mother, Bridget, was tormented by thoughts of Catherine's last few seconds.

Any time the rest of us got together for family occasions after the murder we could see that our mother was in a world of her own. She was missing Catherine from the gang. The big fear Mam had was of picturing Catherine screaming in the car, screaming and trying to get out of the car and being caught with the seat belt. Our mam passed away in 2005. If our mam was alive now and someone was caught for the murder she would love to ask them one thing: Why? Why not just leave Catherine alone?

Linda McCabe often thinks of the murders too. She told me that many times down the years she has wished that it was her in the car with her husband that night and nobody else. She has the greatest sympathy for the Brennan family. To this day she doesn't know why her husband was shot dead. As part of the grieving process she has often been angry with her husband, hating him and loving him at the same time. She'd like to know why he was killed, even if someone could contact her anonymously.

Linda spent a number of years in darkness, lashing out at people, while trying to come to terms with losing her husband. Eventually she found the strength to deal with her anger and grief. When we met in October 2006 she was working with the Dublin Christian Mission, doing voluntary work. She found a joy working in an environment that helped children like Eddie junior. She spoke with obvious love for her four children. Her three youngest had never been in trouble and were all now teenagers. The twins, George and Wayne, were looking forward to their eighteenth birthday that December, and her youngest son, Ciarán, was fourteen and in his second year of secondary school. George was studying to be a carpenter, and Wayne had plans to be an electrician. Her hopes for her eldest son, Eddie junior, turning his life around were clear and heartfelt.

The next time I spoke to Linda her eldest child had been beaten to death. She was broken-hearted, the loss of her son bringing back memories of the loss of her husband. Linda was also deeply upset about inaccurate and insensitive newspaper reports about her son and his father. And, just as they had done eleven years before, some newspapers reporting on the violent death of Eddie junior chose to publish graphic photographs of his father's body as he lay at Cookstown Road on 25 November 1995. Such insensitivity compounded the family's grief. It's clear that the McCabe family, like the Brennan family, have suffered more than any family should ever have to suffer in a lifetime.

In the days after Eddie McCabe was shot dead his ten-year-old son, Eddie junior, couldn't sleep. He told his mother that he could hear the sounds of gunshots going off in his mind and he could picture his father being shot. He would say to Linda, 'Mam, I always wonder what was he thinking when it happened.'

————

The killer or killers of Catherine Brennan and Eddie McCabe had a number of possible escape routes. The section of the Cookstown Road where the murders occurred is close to a number of housing estates and also close to the Tallaght Bypass. One of the few escape routes ruled out is the Cookstown Road heading for the Belgard Road. This is the road that the two doormen, John and Noel, had driven along before they discovered the two bodies, and they had not encountered any car travelling in the opposite direction. This left three possible escape routes for the killer. He could have turned back down the Cookstown Road and, rather than heading for the Belgard Road, driven into the Springfield estate, perhaps coming back out of the estate towards the Square. Alternatively, he could have driven in the opposite direction along the Cookstown Road and turned either right, towards Rossfield, Fettercairn or Fortunestown Lane, or left, towards Jobstown, Killinarden or indeed the Tallaght Bypass, which could have brought him back towards the city centre. Unfortunately there were no CCTV systems at any of these roads, so the escape route of the double killer remains a mystery.

This assumes that the killer drove away from the scene. It seems likely that he was travelling in a vehicle: this would explain the sound of screeching tyres at about the time of the loud bangs at 4:20 a.m. But in the absence of any eyewitnesses it seems possible that one or more of the attackers left the scene on foot while the murder weapon was driven from the scene.

Is it possible that the killer or killers were cruising, looking for Eddie's car? Perhaps they knew the model and knew he would be out that night. If they didn't spot him that night, perhaps they'd try again the following night or another time. Had the killers cruised around Tallaght on previous nights looking for Eddie?

The Gardaí have considered the possibility that more people could have been killed that night. If the killer or killers had spotted Eddie McCabe an hour earlier and attacked him when not only Catherine Brennan but her friend and Eddie's two friends were also in the car, five people might have lost their lives. The motive for the cowardly shooting of Catherine Brennan was simply that she was a witness to a murder. If other people had also been in the car when Eddie was shot without warning they could also have become targets simply because they were witnesses. The killers of Catherine and Eddie had shown a particular disregard for human life that demonstrated a capacity to murder without a second thought.

——

The murders of Catherine Brennan and Eddie McCabe were among a number of gun murders in the Dublin area in 1995 that have never been solved. In the summer of that year Francis Preston was shot dead as he got into his car in Baldoyle, and David Weafer was shot dead in Finglas. The next murder victim was Gerry Connolly in Ballyfermot. In November another gun murder occurred in Ballyfermot when Eric Shortall was killed while walking with his girl-friend. On the same night that Catherine Brennan and Edward McCabe where shot dead another murder inquiry was established after Christy Delaney was gunned down on his doorstep in Finglas. Similar murders continued in Dublin in 1996 with the shooting dead of Gerry Lee in March and the separate murders of John Reddin and John Kelly in April.

Catherine Brennan was shot seven months before another hard-working mother was gunned down on an Irish street. The journalist Veronica Guerin was sitting in her car at traffic lights on the Naas Road outside Dublin in June 1996 when a pillion passenger on a motorbike shot her dead in broad daylight. It was only after this brutal killing that greater investigative powers were given to the Gardaí to tackle the country's major criminal gangs. The establishment of the Criminal Assets Bureau and the Witness Protection Programme would in time have a considerable effect in tackling a number of gangland crimes that would occur after 1996. The dedication of almost unlimited resources to the Gardaí meant that the gang that murdered Veronica Guerin was slowly but surely brought to its knees. Sadly, there had not been a similar political outcry and response when a hard-working mother of two was gunned down, along with a father of four young boys, at Cookstown Road, Tallaght, on 24 November 1995.

———

Of the murders that have occurred in Tallaght in recent decades the Gardaí have successfully solved a number. These include the shooting of Joseph Cummins in the centre of the old village on St Stephen's Day 2001 and the murder of a fifteen-year-old girl in Killinarden in 1988—the first case in which DNA evidence was used. Detectives in Tallaght have often shown a determination to pursue criminal cases many years after a murder. It was in 1997, fifteen years after the murder of Garda Patrick Reynolds at Avonbeg Gardens in Tallaght, that a murder charge was brought against a suspected INLA man from Belfast who had been on the run since 1982. The suspect was subsequently found not guilty by the Special Criminal Court, but at least the prosecution evidence had finally been tested.

In the case of the double murder of Catherine Brennan and Eddie McCabe the Gardaí have unfortunately not yet come close to securing enough evidence to bring a prosecution. Despite the passing of time, most of the original main suspects are still alive, but without more evidence it seems that a murder charge will never be brought. The case is one that could perhaps greatly benefit from a complete re-investigation, using the latest legislative powers that were not available when the killings occurred.

Linda McCabe moved out of Jobstown many years ago and now lives in Drimnagh, where she originally came from. She now grieves the loss of her eldest child as well as her murdered husband. She still has three other sons who will soon be young men, and they will all continue to support each other. Linda is also now a grandmother, but the third-generation Edward will grow up without his father or grandfather. Linda doesn't know how people who commit murder can live with something like this on their conscience. When we first met she told me that while her husband suffered a brutal death, those left behind also suffer greatly. They have to pick up the pieces and go on.

A terrible twist of fate brought Eddie McCabe and Catherine Brennan together in the early hours of Thursday 24 November 1995. In the following years the McCabe and Brennan families would meet only once, when the inquests into the murders were formally adjourned in April 1996 while Garda inquiries continued.

In Killinarden, Helen told me that she, Marie and their mother once went to a seminar where families of murder victims were telling their stories. None of the three could stand up and talk: it was too upsetting. Some of the family have had counselling and, as time goes on, talking about what happened becomes easier, though the pain never dulls.

Christmas Day 1995 was a particularly sad time for the Brennan family. By that time Anthony and Stacey were now living with Marie, Jimmy and their children. Normally Catherine, Anthony and Stacey would have walked the short distance to Marie's house in Killinarden for Christmas dinner and then gone down to the original family home in Walkinstown for St Stephen's Day. That Christmas was a horrible time, and it's been a difficult time ever since.

Catherine Brennan was looking forward to celebrating her thirtieth birthday in April 1996. When she was in Tramore with her sisters weeks before she was murdered she told them of plans for a big party to celebrate her birthday.

In the years since Catherine's brutal killing the Brennan family have been hit by a number of tragedies, including the loss of Catherine's brother John, who was only forty-seven when he died from leukaemia. Catherine's mother, Bridget, died in 2005 without seeing her daughter's killers brought to justice.

As I sat with Marie and Helen they both spoke of all the opportunities that were taken from Catherine when her life was taken so violently. She missed out on her children growing up, and they missed out on her. Helen said it is disgraceful that the people responsible for Catherine's murder have not been caught.

I don't know how people can live with themselves and keep information about what happened. I don't know how they sleep at night. Catherine didn't stand a chance when she was shot. She was executed. They were probably afraid she might identify them, and out of that they wasted a life. They are really heartless people. They are still walking the streets now, and no-one seems to give a damn.

08 | THE MURDER OF BRIAN STACK

Brian Stack never saw his killer. He approached Brian from behind without warning. It was 10:49 on the night of Friday 25 March 1983. The gunman pointed the gun at the back of Brian's head and fired once, hitting his victim in the neck. As Brian fell to the footpath, his killer walked quickly to a waiting motorbike.

In a matter of seconds, on a busy Dublin street, one of the country's most senior prison officers had just been gunned down. The wound was fatal, but Brian did not die immediately: he would suffer for another eighteen months, paralysed and brain-damaged, before his body could no longer cope with the internal injuries caused by the bullet.

Minutes before the attack Brian and five friends were at the National Stadium on the South Circular Road attending the Irish senior boxing championships. A passionate sportsman, he had been instrumental in resurrecting the boxing club in Port Laoise. Well known on the amateur boxing circuit, he had only recently received his international boxing referee licence. Brian was forty-seven and the proud father of three boys. By this stage in his life his sporting abilities centred on organising and motivating the younger generation.

Sport also gave him an outlet for escaping from the pressure cooker that was Port Laoise Prison. As chief prison officer he was the highest-ranking uniformed officer at the prison. He loved his job and had clear ambitions to get to the top. With youth on his side, he knew he could yet become governor.

As Brian left the stadium there were many people on the street heading back to their cars having attended the night's boxing. Brian crossed over the South Circular Road from the stadium to meet his friends where they had parked in nearby Washington Street. They had already gone to the car and were waiting for him. Brian had been delayed talking to people. It wasn't uncommon for him to get caught up in a chat or sometimes a heated debate about boxing. He'd walked around the stadium for much of the night, meeting trainers and young boxers from all over the country. Now he was heading back to meet his fellow-members of Port Laoise Boxing Club.

The plan was to drive to a restaurant, Joe Wong's on the Naas Road, for something to eat. It would be well after midnight before they finally got home to Port Laoise, but it was a tradition that they always stopped at Wong's, near Newlands Cross, whenever they were travelling back from Dublin.

As Brian turned into Washington Street the killer struck. He had followed Brian around the corner from the South Circular Road. The gunman was wearing a balaclava with distinctive white colouring around the eye sockets. He moved quickly to catch up with Brian, who was still unaware of the imminent danger. The killer stopped a short distance behind Brian, who was now a few yards down Washington Street. He used both hands to hold the gun, and a second later he fired at point-blank range at the lower half of Brian's head.

Brian's friends witnessed the shooting, but everything happened so fast that they saw the gun only after it had been fired. They had seen Brian walking towards them and had seen the man running behind him. Suddenly they heard a loud bang and saw Brian fall forward on his face. Then another man appeared on a motorbike at the nearby corner. The gunman ran to the motorbike and jumped on the back. In a matter of seconds it was driving off at speed, mounting a footpath as it went and nearly colliding with a car on the South Circular Road. It sped away towards the nearby junction with Clanbrassil Street, popularly known as Leonard's Corner.

Thirteen-year-old Christopher Ging witnessed his father's friend being shot. He ran towards Brian and shook him, but there was no response. Christopher's father, Joe, and Brian's other friends—Tom Timmons, Jimmy Sullivan and Garda Séamus Fitzgerald—also jumped out of the car and ran to Brian. Seconds earlier they had started the car and were already moving towards Brian when they saw the masked man approach him from behind and saw Brian fall to the ground. For a moment after the sounds of the gunshot and the motorbike roaring away there was total silence. Then people began to scream.

Corporal Joseph O'Brien raised the alarm. He was standing inside the main gate of the nearby Griffith Barracks when he saw a flash in the darkness. He ran to the gate and looked across the road and saw a man in dark clothes running from Washington Street back out onto the South Circular Road. The man jumped on the back of the getaway motorbike, which headed in the direction of Leonard's Corner. The motorbike had a prominent red light on the back, below the seat. Corporal O'Brien could smell cordite and knew immediately that a weapon had been fired. He saw a man lying on the footpath across the road and people running towards him. He rushed back into the guardroom and made an emergency call to the switchboard operator.

Brian Stack might have died immediately were it not for the work of three doctors from Belfast. Eugene Maguire and the brothers John and Martin Donnelly were medical advisers to the Ulster Boxing Council. They were still in the National Stadium when they heard the commotion across the road. John and Martin grabbed medical bags, and the three ran across the road to Washington Street. More than a dozen people were now gathered around Brian Stack and they cleared a way for the doctors to get in. Eugene Maguire turned Brian onto his right side and saw that he was bleeding from a wound above his right eye. This had

happened when he had fallen to the ground. Brian lay beside a
street light, so despite the dark night the doctors were able to
study his injuries quite quickly. Martin Donnelly found the entry
wound at the back of Brian's neck on his left side at shoulder level.
Eugene Maguire meanwhile was listening for a heartbeat but
could not hear one. He began thumping Brian's chest and mas-
saging his heart. John Donnelly took a long piece of tubing from
the medical kit and inserted it into Brian's mouth and down his
throat. Martin began mouth-to-mouth resuscitation through this
airway, and John took over after a few moments. Eugene Maguire
checked again and could now hear a low heartbeat and felt a very
faint pulse. Through their prompt actions Brian Stack was still
alive, but only barely. An ambulance arrived at about 11:10 p.m.

———

Sheila Stack had said goodbye to her husband about four hours
earlier when she dropped him off at Joe Ging's house in Port
Laoise. They normally rotated the cars for the drive to Dublin, and
it was Joe's turn tonight. There were six of them heading to Dublin
in the one car, five men and Joe's son Christopher. Though they
would be home quite late, Brian knew he had an early start the
next day. A local bus-driver used to organise shopping trips to
Newry, and Brian, Sheila and the boys were due to go on the
Saturday morning. They'd have to be up at the crack of dawn to
get ready and meet the bus.

Brian dressed in his best for the boxing tournament. It didn't
matter whether he was in work or attending a sports event or
another social occasion, Brian was known for dressing well. When
he headed for Dublin that night he was wearing a dark-brown
suit, white shirt and brown-and-beige tie. He was also wearing a
long fawn-coloured overcoat.

By 11:17 p.m. the now bloodstained coat was cut apart as doctors
battled to save Brian's life. Within seconds of the ambulance
arriving at the Meath Hospital in Heytesbury Street, surgeons

knew his life hung in the balance. His blood pressure was now almost non-existent and he was making no effort to breathe by himself, and so he was placed on a ventilator.

The lead bullet still rested in his neck, under the left side of his lower jaw. He was given a general anaesthetic before two surgeons explored his neck to assess the wound. They found the bullet resting beneath a muscle layer at the front of Brian's neck, and with delicate precision they successfully removed it. Their patient was now critical but stable. Brian was in a coma, and his head was twice its normal size.

The surgeons now knew that Brian had most probably suffered some paralysis as a result of the bullet injury to the neck. It had severely damaged his spine, and there was also a strong possibility of brain damage. As they saved his life that night the doctors knew that in the coming hours and days in the intensive care unit the full extent of his injuries would emerge. They could not yet tell that the shooting would ultimately prove fatal.

Sheila's brother Séamus broke the news to her in Port Laoise that something terrible had happened to Brian. Local gardaí, alerted by colleagues in Dublin, had called to Séamus, who in turn went to see Sheila. He told her that Brian had been in an accident and was in hospital. Sheila told me there was no other information until well after midnight.

> Séamus said he would go back out and try and find out more. I knew nothing at this stage about Brian being shot. It was later that night that I found out it was so much worse. It was some time after midnight that Séamus came back with my mother and another brother, Seán, and some detectives. That's when I found out.

Brian's sons—Austin, Kieran and Oliver—were fourteen, thirteen and twelve, respectively, when their father was shot. That Friday night the boys had gone to sleep excited about the following day's trip to Newry. Austin's room was at the front of the house. It was after midnight when he woke up as cars began to pull up outside their house. He could hear people calling to the house and he got out of bed to see what was going on. He remembers that in the early hours of that morning family and friends were trying to keep the news from the children.

> I went down to the kitchen, and Uncle Séamus was on the phone, and Granny was there and Uncle Seán too. I was told Daddy had been hit by a motorbike and to go back to bed. I went back to my room, but I knew there was something up. I put on the radio at six o'clock the next morning and I heard it on the radio. I went down to Kieran and Oliver's room and told them what I'd heard. They didn't believe me, so I put on the radio again, and we all heard it, and they were giving out Daddy's name, saying he had been shot.

By 2 a.m. that Saturday, while Sheila Stack was being comforted by family and friends in Port Laoise, the bullet had been removed from Brian's neck. Dr Dermot Hehir gave the distorted lead bullet to Detective-Superintendent John Reynolds; it would later be analysed at Garda Headquarters, and tests would prove that it had been fired from a revolver of .38-inch special calibre. An analysis of Brian Stack's overcoat revealed powder blackening around a bullet hole near the collar, proving that the gun had been discharged at very close range. This confirmed what detectives already knew from many eyewitnesses. Mindful that the killer might try to attack Brian again, armed gardaí were placed close to his bedside.

As detectives began their investigations in the early hours of that Saturday morning they studied the descriptions of the gunman and getaway driver. In particular the balaclava used by the gunman was quite distinctive. Witnesses described it as being white at the top, beige in the middle and white at the bottom, and it also seemed white around the eyes. The gunman was wearing a dark jacket zipped up to the chin. He was described as about 5 feet 8 inches tall, and one witness said he wore a green army-type jacket with a patch pocket at the front. The driver of the motorbike seemed taller to the witnesses. He was wearing a short black leather jacket with a zip on the sleeve and he wore a helmet, which seemed to be mostly white, perhaps with black colouring. One witness said he seemed to be in his mid-twenties but couldn't give a description of his face. He also wore leather gloves.

One witness described seeing a man on a motorbike in the vicinity about half an hour before the shooting. The man wasn't wearing his helmet at the time, and the witness described him as having an upturned nose, high cheekbones and what looked like a brown 'beauty mark' on his right cheek. He was in his twenties, and was wearing leather gloves.

Sheila Stack arrived at the Meath Hospital early that Saturday. By now she knew her husband had been shot and that he was seriously ill. When she saw him she was distraught. His eyes were open but he was in a coma. His whole body was swollen, and a ventilator was helping him breathe.

––––

Brian Stack joined the Prison Service twenty-four years before that fateful night. He first reported for duty in August 1959, serving first in Mountjoy Prison and later moving back to his home town of Port Laoise to work at the maximum-security prison. As he rose through the ranks he was moved to prisons in Cork and Limerick before returning once again to Port Laoise. By March 1983 he was the most senior uniformed officer in Port Laoise.

It was a high-pressure job in a tense environment. The prison held convicted members of the Provisional IRA and the INLA as well as members of some of the first organised criminal gangs from Dublin and Limerick. There were many life-sentence prisoners, including the IRA man Tommy McMahon, convicted of the murder of Lord Louis Mountbatten. His fellow IRA member Liam Townson was serving a life sentence for the killing of Captain Robert Nairac of the SAS, while Peter Rogers, also an IRA member, was serving forty years for the capital murder of Garda Séamus Quaid in Co. Wexford.

Among the INLA prisoners was Dessie O'Hare, who would later lead the gang that kidnapped the Dublin dentist John O'Grady. Another prisoner under Brian Stack's care in the early 1980s was Eddie Gallagher, serving a lengthy sentence for kidnapping the Dutch industrialist Tiede Herrema. Two other high-security prisoners were Colm O'Shea and Patrick McCann, who were not members of any organisation but were serving forty years each for the murder of Garda Henry Byrne, shot dead along with Garda Tony Morley in Co. Roscommon in 1980.

During the 1970s members of the IRA had attempted to break out of the prison many times. Nineteen of them had successfully escaped in 1974. A similar attempt was made in March 1975, using explosives smuggled into the prison. However, soldiers guarding the prison quickly responded and foiled the escape attempt, firing a number of shots above the prisoners' heads. One IRA member, Tom Smith, was killed during the escape attempt, apparently by a ricochet.

Tensions became even more heightened in the late 1970s when twenty IRA prisoners went on hunger strike in protest at conditions in the prison. Throughout the 1970s and into the 80s there were many occasions when people were found smuggling explosives into the prison. One woman visiting a prisoner was found to have explosives in a condom hidden inside her body. During other searches, explosives were found hidden in musical instruments given to prisoners by friends and family. Mindful of the embarrassment of nineteen prisoners escaping in 1974, the authorities implemented a policy of strip-searching prisoners in Port Laoise.

Prison officers at Port Laoise were doing a difficult and dangerous job on behalf of the state. Brian Stack was a good leader, a strong motivator for staff working in the powder keg that was Port Laoise Prison. He would never talk about work when he went home, but Sheila knows that in the weeks before he was shot Brian was troubled by something.

> You knew there was something going on. There was no question about that. He was thinking to himself a lot at home. He was dwelling on something. You might ask him and he'd say,

'There's a lot of hassle in work. If I'm silent it's nothing to do with you.' He could be irritable and silent sometimes and would always say it was to do with work.

Austin recounted a story about how a night's swimming was once rudely interrupted.

Dad and I were down in the Port Laoise swimming pool on a night that prison officers had it for their families. It was maybe nine or ten at night, and a guy came running in saying a riot had broken out at the prison. All the lads, including Dad, got out of the pool and got dressed without drying and went back up to the prison. I went up in the car with him, and I remember sitting in the car for maybe an hour and a half before a prison officer came out with Dad's keys and drove me home. Dad had to stay in the prison to deal with the riot.

The bullet that entered Brian Stack's neck severely damaged part of his spinal cord. It left him quadriplegic, severely brain-damaged, and with no control of his bowel or bladder. His kidneys stopped working for a time, and he had to undergo dialysis for thirty-four days. He was also now partially deaf. A week after the attack he developed bronchopneumonia; the hospital gave him an intensive cocktail of antibiotics and the illness passed. It would be another eighteen months before the pneumonia would resurface and Brian would not survive.

The day after Brian Stack was shot, a motorbike was taken from the Grand Canal near Portobello, Dublin. It was a Kawasaki Z400J, black, grey and red in colour. It had been stolen from the Pimlico area of Dublin on 21 January and was most probably the one used by the gunman and his accomplice. The bike had a large square-shaped back light, as described by witnesses to the shooting, while the original number plate had been altered to give it a false number, 76 GZI. It had travelled more than fifty miles since it had been stolen.

It is possible that in the weeks before he was gunned down Brian Stack was carrying out a private investigation within Port Laoise

Prison. Perhaps he knew something, or suspected something; if he did, he was on a solo run. He didn't fully confide in anyone. One former colleague told me Brian was trying to work something out relating to Port Laoise.

> Brian was forever trying to establish how contraband was get-
> ting into the prison. He was always thinking about security at
> Port Laoise and where any weak links might be. Some time
> before he was shot he told me he was working on something
> that 'if true will rock the foundations of the state.' He wouldn't
> tell me what it was; he said it was better not to say. He never
> got a chance to test whatever theory it was.

Three weeks after the shooting Brian was moved from the intensive care unit of the Meath Hospital to the National Rehabilitation Centre in Dún Laoghaire. It was now clear that he would need 24-hour care for the rest of his life. He would be confined to a wheelchair and, because of his brain damage, would never work again. A team of Brian's colleagues from Port Laoise Prison organised a rota to take Sheila to Dublin to visit her husband. Because of advice from the doctors it was at least three months after the shooting before his sons got to see him. Kieran remembers how badly he and his brothers wanted to see their father.

> We were being shielded by Mam and other adults. But we were
> looking for straight answers as well, but we weren't being given
> straight answers. We were arguing and arguing about when we
> could get up to see him.

Brain damage affects every victim in a different way. In Brian Stack's case it often seemed that he was like a four-year-old in his speech and his mannerisms; at other times there was more apparent brain activity and flashes of his old character. The first time he saw his sons in Dún Laoghaire he called Oliver by a special pet name he had. He began speech therapy, and was finally able to breathe unaided, but his short-term memory was poor. The

Gardaí tried to formally interview Brian but he couldn't remember the attack. He seemed to remember the earlier part of that Friday, but the next thing he remembered was being in the hospital. Because of his brain damage, if he had any clear suspicions about why he was shot he wasn't able to tell the Gardaí.

Eventually the doctors in Dún Laoghaire said Brian could go home. One of the rooms at the family home in Port Laoise was rebuilt as a self-contained unit with its own toilet and shower. A track system with a hoist was fitted to the ceiling so that Brian could be lifted from bed and brought along the hoist to the shower. A special wheelchair that he could control with his chin was bought. Sheila's sister Catherine, a nurse, would help Sheila with Brian's 24-hour care in Port Laoise, along with a team of male carers. The armed Garda protection that Brian had in hospital would also continue at home.

In spite of his brain damage, Brian was sometimes able to register the enormity of what had happened to him. On one occasion Austin was shaving his father with an electric razor when Brian suddenly began to cry. The realisation that he was now totally dependent on his teenage children and his wife would often leave Brian frustrated. Oliver remembers that despite his brain damage Brian still wanted to keep his sons away from the extent of his suffering.

> He didn't want us seeing him in certain situations. If you were trying to get him dressed and the male carers were there you were put out of the room. He'd be like, 'I'll see you in a few minutes.' I think it's just natural he instinctively wanted to shield his children from the reality of his condition.

Until the attack Brian had been a fit and active man. As well as a boxing referee he had previously been a GAA referee and officiated at inter-county level. He had played hurling and football as a younger man and organised athletic events, including inter-prison sports. When he wasn't playing or organising sport in his spare time he was heavily involved in politics, a committed Fianna Fáil

man. His life before the gun attack was in stark contrast to the 554
days that he lived after the shooting.

Brian and Sheila were married in September 1967. Both were
from Port Laoise and had met at a dance a few years before. Brian
was already working as a prison officer and was steadily climbing
the career ladder. In the early 1970s he was promoted and transferred
to Cork Prison, and the couple and their three young boys moved
to Cork for three years. In 1976 the family settled back in Port Laoise
when Brian was transferred first to Limerick Prison and a short
time later to Port Laoise, where he would again be promoted.

In the hours after Brian was shot in the back of the neck both the
IRA and the INLA issued statements denying responsibility for the
attack. Neither denial was taken at face value by the authorities.
There was also some speculation that a group of disaffected
members of one or both organisation had formed a new alliance
and might be responsible. So-called 'ordinary criminals' might
also have been responsible. Detectives were aware of the emer-
gence of a sinister organisation calling itself the Prisoners'
Revenge Group. This collection of criminals warned of attacks
against prison staff and their families. The group claimed responsibility for a number of assaults on prison officers and petrol-
bomb attacks on their homes in the early 1980s; but in a television
interview an anonymous spokesman for the group denied any
knowledge of the shooting of Brian Stack.

From the start of their investigations, detectives knew Brian
Stack was shot because of his job as chief prison officer in Port
Laoise. But what was the exact motive? Senior officers drew up
three possibilities, which still hold to this day. Was Brian shot
because of a personal grudge relating to a previous incident in
prison? Was he shot as a warning or threat to all prison officers? Or
was he shot because he had discovered or was about to discover
something relating to Port Laoise Prison?

Of the three possibilities, the least likely is that he was shot as a
warning to all prison officers. If this had been the motive, some
group would have claimed responsibility or issued threats of
further attacks. What is certain is that Brian was singled out for

assassination. But was this because of a previous personal encounter with a prisoner, or was he becoming a thorn in the side of a group of people?

A friend of Brian's who worked closely with him told me of three occasions on which Brian was involved in physical confrontations with prisoners. The colleague said that on each occasion Brian was struck first but managed to defend himself, on one occasion being forced to use his baton. Such confrontations were not uncommon in a highly charged prison environment, where many prisoners spent their time planning escape attempts and many violently resisted strip searches.

As investigations continued in 1983 information began to emerge suggesting that Brian may have been followed by his killers over a number of days. A friend of Brian's told the Gardaí of an incident that may have been a botched attempt to kill Brian as he sat in a chip shop.

> I was up in Dublin when he was refereeing the Leinster juvenile boxing championships. We went to a chipper in Crumlin, just a mile or two away from the National Stadium. I remember I was looking out the window and I saw this motorbike driving along. It seemed to swerve into traffic and a car clipped it. There were two people on the bike, but they weren't hurt, but the bike was on the ground. Suddenly a car pulled up and the two got into the car. Someone else must have taken the bike away. I asked Brian if he'd seen it, but he hadn't. He said something like, 'Funny things happen in Dublin.' I thought no more of it. It was only later that I wondered if it had been the killers coming for Brian back then. They could have been following us around the whole week, waiting for their chance.

One thing the Gardaí noted about the eventual attack was that the gunman did not appear to speak. All the witnesses who had been closest to the shooting described hearing the sound of the gunshot but did not hear anything being said by the attacker. If Brian was shot because of a personal grudge or vendetta, detectives thought the

gunman might have shouted something as he pulled the trigger. The
gunman had been cold and callous but also seemed professional and
organised. He was either a paid killer or part of a group of people
who thought nothing of shooting someone in the back of the neck.

Another possibility is that Brian was shot to simply get him out
of Port Laoise Prison for the immediate future. The gunman fired
only once at point-blank range. He was sure he had hit Brian, but
as he ran to the waiting motorbike he didn't know whether Brian
was dead or alive. Detectives wondered whether there was any significance in the fact that only one bullet had been fired. Did the gun
jam? Did the gunman not care whether or not he actually killed
Brian or simply paralysed him for life? Would firing a second shot
delay the gunman too much? Was he satisfied, having seen Brian fall
face forward, that he had simply followed his instructions to ensure
that Brian Stack would not be returning to Port Laoise Prison?

1983 was a year marked by considerable violence in Ireland. In the
weeks before Brian Stack was shot a large-scale investigation was
under way into the stealing by the IRA of the champion racehorse
Shergar. In August an IRA group was captured when the Gardaí
foiled an attempt to kidnap the businessman Galen Weston.
Elsewhere the career criminal Michael Boyle from Bray carried out
more than half a dozen kidnappings in the Dublin and Wicklow
area. In July 1983 a gang led by the Dublin criminal Martin Cahill
stole £2 million worth of gold and jewels during an armed raid on
a jewellery manufacturing plant. Meanwhile the INLA was at its
most violent, with its leader, Dominic McGlinchey, directing the
kidnap of a thirteen-year-old girl and her father in Co. Mayo in an
effort to force an informer to retract statements made to the RUC.

Then, in December 1983, a member of the Defence Forces and
a recruit garda were shot dead as they assisted in the rescue of a
kidnapped supermarket executive, Don Tidey. He was freed following a shoot-out with an IRA group at Ballinamore, Co. Leitrim.
Private Patrick Kelly and Recruit-Garda Gary Sheehan died at the
scene. Gary Sheehan is one of more than a dozen gardaí to have
lost their lives while serving the state, while Patrick Kelly is the
only Irish soldier murdered on Irish soil. Within a matter of

months the Gardaí would also be investigating what would officially become the only murder of a prison officer in the history of the Irish state.

——

On Sunday 9 September 1984 Brian Stack went to the Laois hurling final at O'Moore Park in Port Laoise. It was now a year and a half since he had been shot and paralysed. His family brought him to the ground in a specially adapted car that was allowed to park at the side of the pitch. After the match the winning Port Laoise minor team gathered round Brian to show him the cup. The replay of the senior match was scheduled for the end of the month, but Brian Stack would not live to see it.

Over the previous eighteen months Brian's body had suffered greatly. He was only able to move his head, and he had limited speech. His immune system had been depleted by failing kidneys. Doctors had warned that Brian's life expectancy would be curtailed, but they couldn't say by how long. The once fit and healthy man had been replaced by a shell. In a search for some sort of solace, Brian's family felt that perhaps it was a good thing that he was brain-damaged: the dynamic man he was before the attack couldn't have coped with this new reality.

On Tuesday 11 September 1984 Brian suddenly fell unconscious and stopped breathing. Sheila ran for a neighbour, Theresa, who was a nurse, and the two of them got Brian out of his wheelchair and put him on the floor. Theresa tried mouth-to-mouth resuscitation, and they rang for an ambulance. Brian was rushed to Port Laoise General Hospital; he was still alive but was in a coma. He was transferred to the Meath Hospital in Dublin, but he never regained consciousness. On Saturday 29 September 1984 he died.

Austin, Kieran and Oliver have many great memories of their father. Brian was a committed family man; his wife and sons were his focus. Kieran explained:

Dad would bring us all around the country. When we were eight, nine, ten years old he was bringing us to big sporting events. We'd go up to Croke Park. And there are lots of guys who wouldn't do that, who would prefer to go and have a few pints. Dad never thought bringing an eight-year-old anywhere was a hassle. We were literally his focus and attention. And that is missed.

Oliver told me that he and his brothers would always look forward to the weekends.

During the week sometimes you were getting ready for bed and might only have an hour with Dad. When he was working you didn't see a whole lot of him except for the weekends. At lunchtime he would have a snooze. He could have a snooze, watch the telly and read the paper all at the same time. It was at weekends that we did so much with him. He would bring all three of us to boxing training in the town on Saturday nights. And we would then be off to watch hurling or football matches on a Sunday. We travelled around the country with him, going to different boxing events and other sports. It was always a great thrill when the weekends would come.

Austin would later follow his father's footsteps and become a prison officer. He remembers a man with a keen sense of history.

Dad was very much into discussing the way the country had developed over the years, how it developed politically, and he would have passed that on to me. He brought us up knowing exactly how Ireland had developed. We all took that on board, and of course sport: boxing, GAA, athletics. We're all interested in sport—all kinds of sport.

Detective-Superintendent John Reynolds and Detective-Inspector Michael Connolly attended the post-mortem examination carried out on Brian's body. The state pathologist, Dr John Harbison, confirmed that Brian had died as a result of bronchopneumonia caused by partial respiratory paralysis, which in turn was due to a bullet injury to his cervical spinal cord. It was more than eighteen months since the gunman had fired at point-blank range into the back of Brian's neck, but Dr Harbison's examination proved beyond doubt that Brian's death was a result of the shooting.

Detectives at Kevin Street Garda station led the investigation into the murder of Brian Stack. A number of senior officers had got to know Brian during his time at the Rehabilitation Hospital in Dún Laoghaire and also when he returned home to Port Laoise. They hoped at first that Brian himself might be able to give them clues about why he had been attacked, but his brain damage left him unable to help. If he had learnt anything during his private investigations at Port Laoise Prison, it was lost when he was shot.

Brian Stack's death was reported on the lunchtime radio news. While people throughout the country felt sadness, a section of prisoners within Port Laoise Prison began jeering prison officers and banging their cell doors. It had been a similar scene eighteen months before when news reached the prison that Brian had been shot. Prison officers had been subjected to blatant threats of 'You're next' and more subtle but equally sinister taunts, such as 'You'd better get your bills paid.'

The Gardaí investigated the possibility that a Dublin criminal gang may have been responsible for Brian's murder. There was a possibility that such a gang might have enlisted the services of a hired killer. Such an arrangement had been made in January 1982 when the Dublin criminal Martin Cahill had planted a bomb under the car of Dr Jim Donovan, head of the Forensic Science Laboratory. Garda intelligence would eventually establish that Cahill had obtained the device from a member of the INLA who was originally from Belfast but was living in Dublin. Dr Donovan survived the blast but suffered severe long-term physical injuries. Cahill hoped the attack might be blamed on the IRA, but detectives later established that he was responsible.

The attack on Dr Donovan clearly illustrated the lengths to which criminal gangs were now prepared to go. But what did such a gang have to gain from killing Brian Stack? Dr Donovan's good work was helping to convict some of the country's most violent criminals, but Brian Stack was merely keeping them secure behind bars. Brian Stack was not a direct threat to the activities of criminals on the streets. A Dublin criminal gang would indeed be capable of shooting a person in cold blood, but what would be the motive? It would have to be personal; but would a grudge against a prison officer be worth the risk of serving forty years in prison? Austin Stack told me he doesn't think 'ordinary' criminals were behind his father's murder.

> You have the paramilitaries, the IRA and the INLA—two cohesive organisations that would have the capability to carry out the murder, would have the manpower, and would have the gumption to do it. It was a very organised murder. I would be very surprised if it was a Dublin criminal gang. It's possible they paid paramilitaries to do it if it was a personal issue. But I just don't think so-called 'ordinary' criminals would have the ability to keep quiet about it all this time. My own view is that it was one of the paramilitary groupings.

The IRA had repeatedly stated that its members were not permitted to kill gardaí, members of the Defence Forces or prison officers. However, by the time of Brian Stack's murder an IRA member had murdered Garda Séamus Quaid while resisting arrest in Co. Wexford. And nine months after Brian Stack was shot Recruit-Garda Gary Sheehan and Private Peter Kelly were shot dead by the IRA during the rescue of Don Tidey in Co. Leitrim. In August 1984, a month before Brian Stack died, an IRA group killed Detective-Garda Frank Hand in Co. Meath during the robbery of a post office van. Three men were later jailed for forty years for the capital murder of Garda Hand. These killings meant that the denial by the IRA of responsibility for the murder of Brian Stack was never accepted unconditionally.

Likewise, the INLA had proved itself capable of taking the life of a garda. In February 1982 Garda Patrick Reynolds was shot dead by a gang in Tallaght. The young garda was shot in the back as he responded to reports of suspicious activity at a flat. Like Brian

Stack, Garda Reynolds was shot with a .38 revolver. The leadership of the INLA issued a statement denying responsibility for Garda Reynolds's murder, saying the organisation was not responsible for 'the actions of rejects from our organisation.'

Brian Stack spent a number of weeks at Limerick Prison the year before he was shot. He had been asked to oversee the security plans at the prison as INLA prisoners were moved into the complex. This work, like the bulk of his work at Port Laoise, brought him into close contact with high-security prisoners.

A former IRA prisoner, in a recent interview, alleged that Brian Stack had shown violence towards Republican prisoners at Port Laoise. The man said that Brian directed other prison officers to hold down IRA prisoners while he struck them with a baton. Brian's colleagues say there was no truth in these allegations, which they described as 'despicable'. The person making the allegations acknowledged that prisoners felt strip searches were an infringement of their human rights, and they violently resisted such searches. Prison officers were merely following a directive from the authorities to ensure that explosives or firearms were not being smuggled into Port Laoise. What is clear from the comments on both sides is that throughout the 1970s and into the early 80s, IRA prisoners felt a large degree of hostility towards the prison officers guarding them.

A year after Brian Stack died, eleven members of the IRA tried to escape from Port Laoise. Tommy McMahon, serving a life sentence for the murder of Louis Mountbatten, led the escape attempt on 24 November 1985. Four other life-sentence prisoners were among the would-be escapers, along with six other IRA men. The prisoners had somehow managed to acquire two guns, more than twenty rounds of ammunition, three pounds of explosives and fake prison uniforms. More intriguingly, they also had copies of prison keys to open a number of gates leading to the outside world. How the prisoners managed to get duplicate keys, which worked in sequence, has never been fully established. But it seems highly likely that there was at least one IRA member or sympathiser working within the prison, or someone who was being threatened or coerced. The escape attempt was foiled when an explosive charge failed to blow out the final door.

Did Brian Stack know or suspect that there was an IRA supporter working in Port Laoise? Did he believe he knew who it might be? Was this what he was talking about when, weeks before his death, he spoke of something that if true 'would rock the foundations of the state'? Did he know about attempts to smuggle guns into the prison? Did he suspect there was a mole working to sabotage the work Brian Stack and the other prison officers were doing to protect society? Did the mole find out that Brian had discovered his identity, or was close to doing so? Has this person any information about Brian's murder?

There are so many questions and so few answers. In the absence of any contact by the state for more than twenty years, the family of Brian Stack can do nothing but speculate. Brian's sons were aged sixteen, fourteen and thirteen when their father died in September 1984. Sheila immersed herself in her family, raising her sons and doing her best to cope. All along they were waiting for answers, waiting for a call to say the killers had been caught. They coped with their grief privately. It is only in recent times that they've decided that the only way to get answers is to start asking questions publicly.

Brian Stack was an Irish volunteer in the true sense of the word. He gave countless hours of his time organising boxing tournaments. Like all sports enthusiasts, he would have enjoyed seeing Barry McGuigan take the world featherweight title in 1985, or indeed Michael Carruth and Wayne McCullough's successes at the Barcelona Olympics in 1992. Brian enjoyed nothing better than working with teenagers in Port Laoise, seeing young lads take Leinster titles or all-Ireland medals. The former international boxer and now boxing analyst Mick Dowling and his wife, Emily, were two of the first people on the scene the night Brian was shot. Mick knew Brian well.

> Brian was a nice man, a gentleman. He was doing a lot of good work as secretary of Port Laoise Boxing Club. He put a lot of time into it, working with young boxers. Sport is one thing

that keeps kids out of mischief, and without people like Brian amateur sports wouldn't work. What happened to Brian was awful. I don't know why anyone would want to harm him.

Brian Stack was given a state funeral. The governor of Port Laoise Prison, Bill Reilly, discussed it with Sheila. It was something Brian's colleagues wanted to do. The Prison Service singers attended the mass, while Oliver and Kieran did readings in the church. Sheila's brother Seán held her close and Austin stood by her side. The Taoiseach, Garret Fitzgerald, and the Minister for Justice, Michael Noonan, were among hundreds who attended the funeral mass at SS. Peter and Paul's Church in Port Laoise, a few hundred yards from the prison. Prison officers from the North, who had lost many colleagues in the Troubles, also attended. After the mass Brian's coffin, draped in the Tricolour, was carried from the church as fellow-officers formed a guard of honour.

The months after Brian's death were not easy for Sheila and her children. They never looked back or discussed in detail the trauma they had been through over the previous eighteen months. Soon Austin, Kieran and Oliver went back to school. The Salesian priests and brothers and the lay teachers in the school in Ballinakill were supportive, but no formal counselling was available. And with no leads emerging in the murder investigation, contact with the Gardaí became less frequent. As the years went by, the detectives originally involved in the case either retired or were transferred. Gardaí in the Kevin Street District had solved other murder cases, but they just seemed to hit a brick wall in Brian's case. Neither informers inside or outside jail were talking; nobody was offering information as part of a plea bargain. This led many detectives to move away from the idea that 'ordinary' criminals were involved. No-one was mouthing off about the killing; none of the egotistical criminal gangs were bragging about it. The so-called Prisoners' Revenge Group was claiming responsibility for almost every other attack on a prison officer but was actively distancing itself from Brian's murder.

As they pondered the case, more and more gardaí felt that the silence was because of involvement by the IRA or INLA, be it an officially sanctioned killing or not. With Garda resources being stretched, Brian's murder file began to gather dust.

Sheila Stack voted against the Belfast Agreement, as did Austin. Amid suspicions that many prisoners in Port Laoise had information about Brian's murder, neither Sheila nor Austin could bring themselves to vote for something that would see many paramilitary prisoners being released *en masse*. Kieran, however, voted in favour of the agreement, feeling it was the best option to try to ensure that other families would not be put in a similar situation to his. Kieran wants to see his father's killers brought to justice every bit as much as Sheila, Austin and Oliver. The Stacks are a strong family, where there are occasional and healthy differences of opinion but all are united in wanting the truth to emerge. Kieran explained his position.

> All I want is the answer to the question, why? As hard as it is to come to terms with, I've tried to reconcile in my mind that if the IRA or INLA were responsible, it was not personally against Dad but against his position. The shooter and the guy on the bike may be dead, due to the nature of their criminal activities. But the actual people who organised and directed it are possibly still alive and walking the streets. There has to be something additional in the motive. All I want to know is, why?

If Brian was shot by members of the IRA or the INLA, or some other group of people falling under the remit of the Belfast Agreement, Austin Stack says there would still be a form of justice in murder charges being brought at this stage.

> I would like to see a trial, and if a person was convicted of Daddy's murder and came under the Good Friday Agreement, they would have a life sentence hanging over them. Maybe they might only serve six months in jail before being released on licence, but at least they would have served some jail time. I would like to see our family getting a day in court and the killers having to stand in court and answer for their actions.

On the night Brian Stack was shot a senior IRA man attended a greyhound race at Shelbourne Park in Dublin. He was seen by a group of prison officers who had travelled from Port Laoise to the same event. In fact they thought it strange that they spotted him a number of times that night. He wasn't on the run at the time, having been released from Port Laoise some time before. He was entitled to be at the races; but the group felt it was as if he wanted them to see him. It was only when the prison officers heard about the attack on Brian that they wondered if there was any significance in their sighting of the man. Perhaps there wasn't, but in the absence of any hard facts about the killing, such information is analysed again and again.

Brian Stack was not under protection before he was shot. However, the governor of the prison did have armed protection after a bomb had been left under his car many years previously. The device had failed to explode. As the most senior uniformed prison officer, Brian enjoyed the same standing as an assistant governor, but he did not seek Garda protection, and the Gardaí had no information that he was specifically under threat. Indeed Brian's work with amateur boxing would have made his movements quite predictable. On the night of the shooting the killers knew exactly where he would be. Like all prison officers, Brian would be aware of his surroundings, especially at sports events and other large gatherings, but it seems that at the time of the shooting he did not feel any particular personal danger.

Hours before Brian was shot his son Kieran was pestering him to bring him to the boxing in Dublin. Like any boy wanting to do something with his father, he kept asking him. Brian said no, they had to get a good night's sleep before going to Newry and that they'd go to the boxing again. Oliver told me they are all thankful they didn't witness their father being shot.

> You wonder if it didn't happen that night, when might it have happened: could it have been three weeks before, or the following day, and you might have personally witnessed it. I'm glad I didn't see it.

The Stack family believe that if ever there was a case that could benefit from the recently established Cold Case Unit within the Garda
Síochána, it is the murder of Brian. This unit could interview every
prisoner still alive who ever came into contact with Brian Stack, and
could interview every prison officer he served with, as well as soldiers and gardaí who worked at Port Laoise. With the passage of
time certain people might give information in confidence that
could ease the suffering of Sheila and her sons. A complete review
of the case by detectives might be the solving of it, because without
doubt the answer lies in Brian's job as chief prison officer. Even if
the investigation did not yield criminal charges, a cold case review
might get some of the answers the Stacks desperately want. Austin
told me the family have been left totally in the dark about why Brian
was shot, and why nobody was ever caught for the crime.

> The people who did this are still walking the streets. Due to the
> callous nature of what they did, it wasn't their first time, and
> wasn't their last. There must be a number of people who know
> what happened. There must be a certain amount of intelligence
> with the Gardaí, pointing them in some direction. It does seem
> amazing that there was never any progress in the case. There
> would only have been a handful of people in the country at that
> time capable of such a cold-blooded murder. I think a greater
> effort must be made to solve crimes like this, and that means a
> cold case unit with a fresh mind, like in other jurisdictions.
> Cases should not be just left to gather dust.

Austin said that a number of older non-political prisoners have
often spoken highly of his father.

> Particularly in Mountjoy, where I did most of my service, any
> prisoner who linked my name with his and asked me if I was
> Chief Stack's son always spoke well of him. Ordinary prisoners
> would have been brought down to Port Laoise for a time to
> carry out the demeaning task of slopping out the IRA cells, as
> the IRA refused to empty their own chamber pots. Ordinary

prisoners volunteered for this work detail and got half remission
for carrying out this horrible task. I've spoken to two or three
such prisoners who only ever said good things about Daddy.
There was one who told me Daddy always managed to get him
temporary release for when there was a family occasion. These
were good prisoners, who were on good behaviour.

Sheila agreed, telling me that Brian always acknowledged that
prisoners were entitled to a second chance.

He respected people as people. He would always acknowledge
that every prisoner was a human being.

Sheila and her sons have watched the widow of Detective-Garda
Jerry McCabe bravely fight for justice on behalf of her husband,
who was shot dead by an IRA group in June 1996. The state later
accepted 'guilty of manslaughter' pleas from four men. Ann
McCabe has fought a vocal and public campaign to ensure that
each of the killers serves the longest possible time in prison. The
difference between the violent deaths of Jerry McCabe and Brian
Stack is that no-one has ever been charged in relation to Brian's
death, never mind being convicted.

Neither the Department of Justice nor the Gardaí have made
any contact with Brian's family in relation to the case in a long
time. The gardaí who led the investigation have long retired, and
it's clear that no-one was ever appointed to pursue the case with
the same vigour. No-one has ever come to Sheila with an update
on the progress, or lack of progress, in the case. Not one Minister
for Justice has ever called to her door.

Sheila and her sons accept that they never sought answers before
now. Sheila was a lone parent totally immersed in trying to raise
three teenage boys while privately trying to grieve. Now she's a
proud grandmother: Austin, Kieran and Oliver all have children of
their own. It goes without saying that Brian would love to have
brought his grandchildren to Croke Park, or the National Stadium.

Sheila is angry at the lack of contact from the state throughout these past years, but the bulk of her anger is still directed towards the killers. She would like to see them suffer the way Brian suffered.

> Brian was killed before he was fifty. I was deprived of a husband. The lads were deprived of a father. And there's somebody going around having a good laugh at the whole thing.

On any given day a prison officer faces the possibility of being attacked in the course of their work. Throughout recent years there have been many examples of prison officers being terrorised by prisoners. A number are still suffering the traumatic effects of having syringes held to their necks during the siege at Mountjoy Prison in the late 1990s. In January 2000 Alan Kavanagh had his throat slit during an attack by three prisoners at Limerick Jail; he survived the attack, receiving seventy-five stitches. Other prison officers have had petrol bombs thrown at their homes. The murder of Brian Stack remains the only killing of a prison officer in the recent history of the state, but it is one of countless attacks on men and women in that profession.

Every March a group of people gather in Dublin to remember the IRA prisoner Tom Smith, who was shot dead during an attempted break-out from Port Laoise in 1975. It is but one example of countless public events organised by those Republicans to remember members of their fold who died during the 'Troubles'.

There is no similar event for Brian Stack. There is no state event to honour his work, no plaque, no memorial. There is no official acknowledgement by the state of a man who gave his life for Ireland. Brian lives on in the hearts and minds of his family and his many friends. He is remembered in boxing and GAA circles. He is also fondly remembered in his home town of Port Laoise, and he is remembered and respected by his colleagues in the prison service throughout the country.

Kieran summed up the family view that the killers will eventually have to answer for what they have done.

> That includes the shooter, the guy who rode the bike, and whoever ordered the shooting. Because you can be damn sure

there was someone higher up who actually ordered it. My own view is those kinds of thugs, be they Provisionals or an organised criminal element, or someone who was working in the prison—they will get their come-uppance at the end of the day. My main question is more, Why? That's what I'd really like answered. Why take somebody's life like that—our dad, Mum's husband; a loving dad, a loving husband; a man who put so much back into the community, a dedicated senior prison officer.

In 2007 the Stack family wrote to the Garda Commissioner seeking answers about the status of the case. The family would like to see the case reopened, with a view to establishing answers about who was responsible for Brian's murder.

The killing of Brian Stack is one of a number of capital murder cases where little progress was ever made in bringing the killers to justice. Another such murder is that of Inspector Sam Donegan, who was killed by a bomb on the Cavan-Fermanagh border in 1972. There are other capital murders where arrests were made but no charges were ever brought. As well as the double murder of Private Kelly and Garda Sheehan in Co. Leitrim in 1983, another unsolved murder is that of Garda Michael Clerkin, killed by a bomb at Garryhinch, Co. Laois, in 1976. Garda Clerkin had previously been seconded to policing duties at Port Laoise Prison.

Sheila Stack and her family want action and answers from the state. In this more peaceful time she wants to ensure that those who gave their lives in the line of duty will be honoured and respected by the political leaders of today.

I want Brian's murder to be looked at properly again. I want to see every available resource being used to get to the truth of who killed him. I want to see every conceivable witness being spoken to again. My husband suffered greatly for eighteen months after being shot before he passed away. It was one of the most callous, cowardly, brutal attacks on a husband and father and a servant of this state.

| **THE MURDER OF
ARLENE ARKINSON**

Fifteen-year-old Arlene Arkinson didn't know that the man giving her a lift was a serial rapist. She didn't know he had committed violent attacks in Ireland and England against both girls and young women. She didn't know that Robert Howard was awaiting sentence for sexually abusing another teenage girl.

Arlene was tired and just wanted to get home. She had drunk some bottles of beer with her friend Donna and Donna's boyfriend, Seán. Bob Howard had given them a lift to the pubs in Bundoran and then brought them home to Co. Tyrone. Bob had drunk a pint of stout in one of the pubs but had drunk orange juice for the rest of the night.

Bob Howard was fifty years old but tried to act younger, buying alcohol for teenagers and chatting with them as if they were adults. Arlene didn't know much about him except that he was from the midlands and was now living in Castlederg, Co. Tyrone, and going out with Donna's mother.

Arlene, Donna and Seán had a good night dancing in Bundoran. On the drive home over the border Bob had to stop the car because Donna needed to get sick. He then drove to Seán's house at Scraghy, a few miles outside Castlederg. Donna was going to stay the night with Seán, and as the two of them got out of the car they invited Bob and Arlene in for a cup of tea. Bob said no, they better keep going. It was half past two on the morning of Sunday 14 August 1994.

Arlene got out from the back seat of Bob Howard's car, where she had been sitting with Donna, and waved goodbye to her two friends. Donna told Arlene she'd see her later in the week. Arlene got into the front passenger seat of the car for the journey back to Castlederg, and the car pulled away.

When Donna and Seán last saw Arlene she was wearing a grey Wrangler T-shirt with writing on it, blue jeans and lace-up boots with big clog heels. She was about 5 feet 4 inches tall and was wearing her blonde hair tied up.

Four hours earlier Arlene had been at home watching television. She had been babysitting at her sister Kathleen's house and had no other plans for that Saturday night until her friend Donna rang her at about 10 p.m. Donna told her that she and Seán were going to a disco in Bundoran, and she asked Arlene if she would like to join them. Donna's mother's boy-friend, Bob, had agreed to drive them to Bundoran and back. Donna was two years older than Arlene, but the two girls had travelled to discos over the border before, and Arlene readily accepted the latest invitation. When Donna called to the door an hour later Arlene's older sister, Kathleen, was back home and so Arlene was free to head out with her friend.

When I met Kathleen Arkinson in Castlederg, the depth of anger she feels at the circumstances of her sister's unsolved murder was immediately apparent. Over the last few years the Arkinson family have tried to come to terms with the fact that their young sister and daughter was abducted and murdered. But what is particularly upsetting for the family is that almost from the first day there was a prime suspect for the murder.

The name Bob Howard is one that makes their blood boil. This is the man who, by the time he found himself alone with Arlene that night, had committed sexual assaults on both children and women, sometimes using ropes or sheets to tie up his victims. The

Arkinsons knew nothing about Howard's crimes until after Arlene
had disappeared. They are particularly upset that the Irish and
British authorities did not keep such a violent sexual offender
under constant watch. Kathleen told me they firmly believe the
community of Castlederg should have been told by the RUC (as it
was at the time) that there was a rapist living among them.

> We should have been told about his background, about what
> he was capable of doing and what he did do. And all those
> years he had been in jail in the South, we were told nothing
> about that. Because if we had known there was no way Arlene
> would have gone out the door that night.

Twenty years before Arlene Arkinson vanished from Co. Tyrone,
Robert Howard raped a 58-year-old woman in her home in
Youghal, Co. Cork. He had been in the coastal town only a matter
of weeks when he struck on the night of 10 May 1973, breaking into
the woman's house under cover of darkness. He was then twenty-
nine and already had convictions in England for attempted
unlawful carnal knowledge and attempted rape. In March 1969 he
had been given a six-year sentence in Durham in north-east
England, but he was released early and deported to Ireland. He
had no connections with Youghal but had arrived in the town in
early 1973, getting a job in a local textile factory and living under a
false name, Leslie Cahill.

Nobody in Youghal suspected that Leslie Cahill was Robert
Howard from Wolfhill, Co. Laois. No-one had an inkling that the
quiet but friendly young man was a serial rapist. Nobody knew
that Howard had broken into a house in London in 1965 and got
into the bed of a six-year old girl, telling her he was a doctor and
that she should undress, and that he then tried to sexually assault
the child. Everyone was equally unaware of the fact that in 1969 he
had broken into a woman's house in Durham and attempted to
rape her.

By the time he arrived in Co. Cork, Robert Howard was showing a particular criminal cunning by using an alias and living a

seemingly quiet life. He was perfecting the ability to be considered a sociable and amiable man, masking his previous convictions and also masking plans for violent crimes he still intended carrying out.

His victim in Youghal was alone and asleep when Howard broke into her house. He had been lodging in a guesthouse next door and had simply jumped over the back wall and broken a downstairs window and within seconds was in the woman's home. The woman woke up after hearing a noise in her room; Howard jumped onto her bed and began his harrowing attack. Having raped the woman in her bedroom he then forced her down the stairs, breaking her ankle in the process. After finding the keys to her car, he forced the woman back upstairs. He tore up a sheet and tied the woman's hands and feet. He stuffed cotton wool in her mouth to gag her, then fled the house, leaving the woman still bound and gagged. He then stole the woman's car and drove to Cork.

It was a number of hours before the alarm was raised. Some of the woman's relatives couldn't contact her and became concerned. They had a key to her house and they found her in her bedroom.

An alert was immediately put out to all gardaí; the woman had been able to give a general description of her attacker. As gardaí began house-to-house inquiries in the neighbourhood Sergeant Willie Doyle soon discovered that a lodger in the house next door was missing: Leslie Cahill hadn't appeared for breakfast and hadn't turned up for work. The sergeant entered Leslie Cahill's room and among the sparse luggage he found a small travel clock. The clock was encased in a small leather case, and on the inside of the case he found the name *R. Howard.* Inquiries through the Crime Section revealed that a Robert Howard from Co. Laois had a conviction for attempted rape in England and had been released from prison some months previously.

The following morning the Gardaí in Cork found the woman's car abandoned near the quays. They had been keeping a close watch on the bus and train stations and the airport. They were in luck: a man answering Howard's description had boarded a flight for Dublin that had just left Cork. Willie Doyle remembers travelling to Dublin to bring Howard back to Youghal.

When we discovered Howard had got on a flight for Dublin we immediately contacted Dublin Airport, and they detained Howard when the flight landed. I went up to Dublin and arrested him. I remember he didn't speak a word on the journey back to Youghal. Later he held up his hands being interviewed and admitted committing the attack, but he would not go into detail. He claimed he broke into the house to commit a robbery and hadn't planned to rape the woman. He said if the woman hadn't woken up he wouldn't have attacked her. Howard was very quiet and came across to people as mild-mannered. After he was charged he was remanded in custody to Limerick Prison.

I was only in his company for a short time but I felt he was a strange and dangerous person, and I consider him to be the most dangerous person I ever encountered during my service with An Garda Síochána. Howard never showed any remorse for what he did. It was a horrific attack, and the unfortunate lady could easily have smothered. Her mouth was stuffed with cotton wool. Fortunately she survived and showed tremendous strength and courage after her ordeal. She continued to live in her home in Youghal, and she lived to be a great age. She died a few years ago.

In March 1974 Robert Howard pleaded guilty to raping the 58-year-old woman and was jailed for ten years. He was given concurrent sentences for robbery with violence and for wounding. The case had been delayed for a number of months after Howard was transferred for a time from Limerick Prison to the Central Mental Hospital. Judge Thomas Neylon noted the report of a psychiatrist, Dr David Dunne, who had interviewed Howard in Limerick Prison. The report showed that Howard was claiming that he did 'these terrible things when I lose my temper ... I blow up and can do anything.' Dr Dunne concluded that the now thirty-year-old Howard was 'a dangerous and explosive psychopath.'

For the rest of the 1970s society was safe from Robert Howard as he remained behind bars serving his sentence for rape. He kept his head down while in prison and associated only with murderers and with other rapists and thieves. In fact by the time he had been given the ten-year sentence by Cork Circuit Criminal Court, Howard was well used to being in prison.

Robert Howard was born at the family home at Slatt, Wolfhill, Co. Laois, on 19 April 1944 to Stasia and James Howard. He was one of a family of seven who grew up in the townlands of Swan and Wolfhill in the south-west corner of Co. Laois. The area is a maze of winding country roads and tracks. It is a scenic part of the country, with low, rolling hills, where sheep graze in small fields and where areas of thick forest are only a few minutes' walk away. Today in this peaceful place large new houses are beginning to appear, while the older stone houses are well maintained. Local people and strangers alike are greeted with a friendly wave.

All Robert Howard's brothers and sisters remained law-abiding people throughout their lives; but at an early age Robert left Wolfhill behind and embarked on a life of crime that would ultimately see him serving a life sentence for murder. He was thirteen when he received his first criminal conviction, in October 1957. He appeared at the District Court in Abbeyleix on a charge of breaking into a house and was sentenced to two years and seven months' detention in St Joseph's Reformatory School in Clonmel. He was only out of St Joseph's when, in early 1960, he was given a further two years at Athy District Court, also for housebreaking, this time being sent to Daingean Industrial School in Co. Offaly. It was a pattern that would continue for the next five years until Howard left for England.

While the criminal convictions he racked up during his teens were mostly for burglaries, Howard was already showing himself to be adept at travelling long distances to commit crimes. In March 1962, at the age of seventeen, he was given six months' imprisonment at Port Laoise District Court for breaking and entering. A further eight months were added the following December at the Circuit Court in Naas for similar offences, with Roscrea District Court giving him another nine months in June 1964. By now Howard was twenty and had spent almost the entirety of his teenage years in the custody of the state.

In early 1965, after completing his latest sentence at St Patrick's Institution for Young Offenders in Dublin, Robert Howard took his first trip abroad. He travelled to London, where he was soon arrested for attempted unlawful carnal knowledge of a six-year-old girl. He was now embarking on a path of travelling between different jurisdictions, committing ever more serious violent crimes. London Criminal Court gave him a lenient sentence of nine days' borstal training in April 1965 for attacking the six-year-old girl.

Howard next surfaced in Ireland in September 1967 when he appeared at the District Court in Sligo and was sentenced to nine months in Mountjoy Prison for larceny. After completing that sentence he travelled to England again, and in March 1969 he was given a six-year sentence for attempting to rape a woman in Durham. He was then deported from England, and it was only five years later that the now thirty-year-old was jailed for ten years for raping the woman in Youghal. For the rest of that decade Irish and British society could breathe a sigh of relief that this prolific violent criminal had finally been given a lengthy prison sentence. But as Robert Howard whiled away his hours in Mountjoy Prison during the 1970s, nobody knew that some of his worst crimes were yet to come.

———

On the evening of Sunday 19 September 1993 a sixteen-year-old girl jumped out of the bathroom window of a flat in Castlederg, Co. Tyrone, and ran as fast as she could. She had just escaped from a three-day ordeal of being sexually assaulted by a man she thought had been a friendly, harmless individual. She knew the man as Bob. He was from the midlands, like herself, and was the boy-friend of her friend's mother. Bob had seemed a nice man, but now she knew exactly what he was really like. She would later tell the police that Howard had tricked her into coming to his flat the previous Friday and had then kept her prisoner, putting a rope around her neck and tightening it as he raped her. She said he had first made her take tablets and drink poitín, and when she passed out he removed her clothes and began his attack. She reported that when she later woke up he continued the assault, producing a rope and placing it tightly around her neck as he raped her in a three-day ordeal that included oral and anal rape. It was late on the third day, after Howard fell asleep while watching a football match on television, that the girl bravely jumped from the bathroom window, and within an hour she had given a statement to the police.

Howard was arrested and charged with raping the sixteen-year-old girl, who would be referred to in court as Miss X. He was granted bail, and throughout 1994, as the case wound its way through the court system, he continued to live in Castlederg. It was while out on bail that he gave Donna Quinn, Seán Hegarty and Arlene Arkinson a lift to the disco in Bundoran.

Arlene Arkinson was the youngest of a family of seven. She had two older brothers, Adrian and Martin, and four sisters, Kathleen, Mary, Anita and Paula. Arlene was born on 20 April 1979 to Willie and Bridget Arkinson. Her mother died when Arlene was eleven. Arlene had been close to her mother and was deeply affected by her sudden loss.

Arlene was a bright, intelligent, articulate girl who was also considered giddy and had some difficulties with school attendance. As she grew into a young teenager she was close to the rest of her family but could sometimes prove a handful for her brothers, sisters and father. Like many teenagers, she was trying to act a lot older than she was. She loved clothes and music and especially loved make-up. Her sister Kathleen told me:

> She was just an ordinary fifteen-year-old. She loved life; she loved everything: going out with friends. When we think of Arlene now, she could have been married by now, she could have had children. She could have been anything. She had her whole life in front of her.

Arlene's father, Willie, told me he is often tormented by thoughts of what happened his youngest child.

I'm lying there in bed some nights, thinking about what happened to her. What way did she die, how long did it take her to
die?—thoughts like that. They go round and round in my
brain.

The early stages of the police investigation into Arlene's disappearance were hindered by a number of factors. It was some
days after Arlene vanished that she was officially reported as a
missing person. Some of her family thought she might be staying
with other family members or had slept at a friend's house, but it
was soon established that she was nowhere to be found. As the RUC
began their inquiries they soon came knocking on the door of
Robert Howard.

At the time of Arlene's disappearance Howard was living with
Patricia Quinn and her young adult children, Donna and Mark, at
Churchtown Park, Castlederg. Howard also had a flat in Main
Street in the town, where the previous September he had attacked
the sixteen-year-old girl who had jumped out the bathroom
window to escape him. In August 1994 Howard was still on bail
and was contesting the charge of rape.

Donna Quinn would later say that in the days after Arlene's disappearance Howard asked her to lie and say that Arlene had not
gone to Bundoran with them. She said that Howard referred to the
rape charges he was facing and said, 'They might try to blame me
for something to do with Arlene if she doesn't turn up.'

———

After being dropped off at Seán's house in the early hours of that
Sunday morning, Donna had stayed away from home until the
Wednesday. She later told the police that when she went home to
Castlederg she asked Howard where he had dropped Arlene off,
and he first said he'd left her at Spamount, an estate about a mile
east of Castlederg. Donna told detectives that when she asked
Howard again about Arlene he said he'd left her near Wall's bar in

the centre of Castlederg. She would say it was later that day that Howard asked her to lie and to say that Arlene had never been to Bundoran with them the previous Saturday.

Arlene might not have gone out that Saturday night if another girl had been able to go instead. Angie McDaid, another friend of Donna's, had at first said she would go to Bundoran, but she had to cancel at short notice, so Donna had then phoned Arlene. One moment Arlene was babysitting, with no real plans for the rest of the night, and the next she was en route to Bundoran with Donna and her boy-friend, Seán; and driving the three was Bob Howard.

They left Castlederg after 11 p.m. and headed for Co. Donegal, stopping at Belleek on the way and buying Bacardi and lemonade. They first went to a pub in Bundoran and then on to a night club. In the pub Donna and Seán drank six or seven Bacardis and lemonade. Arlene had some bottles of Budweiser, while Bob Howard drank one pint of stout and then had glasses of orange. When they went on to the nightclub Donna and Arlene got up to dance.

It was after 1 a.m. when the four of them left the night club and got back into Howard's blue two-door Mini Metro for the drive back to Castlederg. Having left Donna and Seán at Scraghy Road, Howard continued on in the direction of Castlederg. He would later maintain that he left Arlene in the centre of Castlederg and that he was home by 3:30 a.m. Prosecutors would allege that Howard did not arrive home until six hours later, at 9:30 a.m., and that during the early hours of that morning he had murdered Arlene and hidden her body.

In the weeks after Arlene's disappearance Robert Howard continued living in Castlederg. The police already knew of his violent background, and after speaking to Donna Quinn and Seán Hegarty they knew that Howard was the last known person to be in Arlene's company. Howard was arrested and questioned about where he had driven Arlene after dropping off Donna and Seán, but he stuck to his story that he had left her in Castlederg and had gone home himself. The police feared that Howard had murdered Arlene, but they had no body and no other real evidence, and he was released without charge.

On Saturday 27 August 1994, two weeks after Arlene's disappearance, a petrol bomb was thrown at the house Patricia Quinn shared with Robert Howard. They were not at home: they had gone out for a drink across the border to Castlefinn. When they returned in the early hours they could see smoke coming from a window, and the wooden window frame was burned. The wall above the front living-room window was also blackened, but the fire had already been put out. They went to bed, and Patricia reported the attack the next day.

Patricia would later tell a jury at Belfast Crown Court that she lied to the police when she gave Robert Howard an alibi for the night of Arlene's disappearance. She said that Howard told her to tell lies, and that doing so had been the biggest mistake of her life. She said that when she asked Howard about Arlene he told her, 'People have secrets and want to keep their secrets.'

On 31 August 1994 Robert Howard pleaded guilty to five charges of having unlawful carnal knowledge of sixteen-year-old Miss X and one charge of buggery. The charges of rape had been dropped after a decision by the prosecution counsel. The victim had told the police that Howard had put a rope around her neck and forced her to submit as he raped her. In a subsequent search of Howard's flat the police found two ropes—a length of blue rope and a tangled length of flex and twine—but the victim could not identify either as the rope that had been used against her.

After a review of the evidence the prosecution decided to drop the rape charges and accept a plea of guilty to the lesser charge of unlawful carnal knowledge. Years later this decision would be strongly criticised, because it was taken without consulting the victim of the attack, who had bravely come forward to expose Howard as a violent offender. Because Howard pleaded guilty, Miss X was not called to give evidence. It would be almost a decade before this young woman would be given the opportunity to tell a jury of her ordeal, as she gave 'similar fact' evidence when Howard would face trial for murdering a fourteen-year-old girl in London, found with a blue rope wrapped tightly around her neck.

By the end of September 1994 Howard was feeling the pressure.

The word was out about his previous convictions and the rape charge still pending. He moved over the border to live rough in Letterkenny. On 27 September he sold his car to a group of Travellers and bought a Hiace van. The Metro was seized by the Gardaí at the request of the RUC and underwent a full scientific examination. Detectives knew this was the car that Arlene had been in when she was alone with Howard; but no evidence of a violent attack was found in the car.

———

Arlene Arkinson was two-and-a-half years old when Robert Howard walked out of Mountjoy Prison, Dublin, on 7 December 1981. Though he had been given a ten-year sentence for raping the woman in Youghal in 1973, he was released after serving eight-and-a-half years. As he walked out through the prison gates a notice was circulated to each Garda division to alert them that the rapist was now out of prison. There was no sex offenders' register and no post-release supervision. Robert Howard, now thirty-seven, was free to go where he liked and associate with whomever he liked. The general public could not be alerted that such a dangerous individual was living in their midst.

A photograph of Howard taken during his detention in the 1970s shows him with long hair and a beard. During the 1980s and 90s and later Howard would perfect the art of changing his appearance. The only attributes that would remain constant were his height of 6 feet, his sallow complexion and his dark-brown eyes.

On his release from Mountjoy, Howard settled in Dublin, moving into a flat at Lower Beechwood Avenue in Ranelagh. He began an ANCO training course in carpentry in the city centre, which he completed in May 1982. He showed a particular ability at carpentry and got a job in a craft shop on the north side of the city. He left the job for a time in July that year and signed on the dole until the end of August, before returning to the craft shop until the end of December. Early in 1983 he got work as a labourer in Santry.

Robert Howard was a charmer. He had the gift of the gab, and his soft voice gave him a laid-back air that a number of women found attractive. They had no idea that he was a serial rapist.

On 4 April 1983 Howard married a thirty-year-old woman, Patricia, in a ceremony at a church in Ranelagh. She worked as a civil servant in the city and had no inkling of her husband's violent past. Whether it was genuine or part of his web of deceit, Howard was making an effort to gain employment and be a seemingly useful member of society. He got labouring, carpentry and cleaning jobs with three companies in Dublin and for the most part was in employment until November 1985. In the meantime he and Patricia moved into a house in Yellow Meadows Drive in Clondalkin. However, their marriage was not a happy one and would last only three years. They did not have any children.

One family who lived near Howard in Clondalkin remember that he used to visit them and regale them with tales of hunting and fishing while growing up in Co. Laois. The family knew him as Bob, and they still have photographs of some of the younger children sitting on his knee and smiling at the camera. No-one was aware of the vicious deeds this charmer had committed many years before.

From early 1986 until the end of 1988 Robert Howard did not work and often did not claim unemployment assistance. His marriage had ended, and he was living for a time in a caravan at Mayfield Park in Clondalkin. He then moved into a house in Primrose Grove in Darndale and later moved away from Dublin, settling for a time at Belgium Park in Monaghan, where he lived with a woman and her two young children. Then he returned to Dublin for a time and got a flat in James's Street in the south inner city.

His continuous movement around Ireland was the same style of life that he would continue years later when, after the disappearance of Arlene Arkinson, he began travelling extensively between Ireland, Scotland and England, stopping his travels only in 2002 when he was arrested and charged with murdering a fourteen-year-old girl in London.

———

In 1989 Garda Denis O'Sullivan and Garda Pauline Reid were in a patrol car travelling around Dublin. It was about 3 a.m. and the two gardaí, who were attached to the Bridewell station, were watching a Hiace van. Garda O'Sullivan knew there was something odd about the van: its registration number didn't seem to tally with the model of the van, and the number plate seemed too new. The two gardaí decided to pull the van over, but suddenly it sped away, and the Garda car gave chase. The van sped down the north quays past the Ha'penny Bridge and turned right over O'Connell Bridge, turning right again to go up the south quays. The Garda car followed at speed, the two gardaí feeling sure that their suspicions had been right.

They caught up with the van as it turned into a halting site at Bonham Street, near the Guinness brewery. One man jumped out of the van and got away, but the driver was still in the van. The gardaí arrested Robert Howard and took him to the Bridewell station. Inside the van they found crockery and other items that had been stolen some hours earlier from a house in Montpellier Hill, near Arbour Hill Prison. A subsequent search of Howard's flat in James's Street revealed a virtual Aladdin's cave of stolen goods. The Gardaí soon established that the van had been stolen in Edenderry, Co. Offaly. Howard admitted his part in stealing the property from Montpellier Hill, and he also admitted stealing drink and cigarettes from a pub in Ballylinan, Co. Laois.

He appeared in court, with the Gardaí strenuously objecting to bail, but bail was granted. Howard travelled over the border and enrolled in an alcohol treatment centre in Newry. He decided to stay in the North and soon left Co. Down and moved west to Castlederg, Co. Tyrone, where he rented a flat in Main Street and began a relationship with a local woman, Patricia Quinn.

On 21 October 1994 Robert Howard attended a psychiatrist in Co. Tyrone for an assessment. The clerk of Omagh Crown Court had asked for a full psychiatric report on Howard before sentence was imposed for the crime of having unlawful carnal knowledge of sixteen-year-old Miss X. This report was compiled almost twenty years after another psychiatrist had interviewed Howard at

Limerick Prison, following the rape of a 58-year-old woman in Youghal. That previous report, compiled when Howard was thirty, had described him as an 'explosive psychopath'. The new report described how the now fifty-year-old Howard was turning much of his attention to abusing teenage girls. He was found to have used a 'grooming' process to facilitate his latest sexual assault. Over time he had gained the girl's trust and manipulated situations where she would be alone with him, and he had meticulously planned the three-day attack. The report also stated that Howard claimed he himself had been sexually abused as a teenager in a reformatory school while serving a sentence for robbery. The new psychiatric report stated that Howard had

> a strong propensity for further offending … has admitted experiencing strong recurrent sexual urges directed towards teenage girls … He has a strong desire to dominate teenage girls both sexually and physically … He has the propensity not only to commit further offences but to escalate his offending behaviour … The risk of recidivism with respect to Mr Howard's present and previous sexual offending would be high.

On 13 January 1995 Robert Howard appeared at Omagh Crown Court to be sentenced for attacking the sixteen-year-old girl. It was now five months since Arlene Arkinson had disappeared, and Howard had been in effect run out of Castlederg as tensions boiled over following the discovery that a rapist had been living in the town. Howard had first fled to Co. Donegal and then back over the border to Cookstown.

Robert Howard had pleaded guilty to five charges of unlawful carnal knowledge and one charge of buggery. The judge in Omagh gave him a three-year sentence but suspended it on condition that Howard undertake to be of good behaviour for the next five years.

Within weeks of receiving the suspended sentence Howard took a ferry to Stranraer and travelled to Glasgow, where he obtained a council house at Bayfield Avenue in the suburb of Drumchapel after claiming he had fled the 'Troubles' in the North. His partner,

Patricia Quinn, joined him in Scotland, but soon the relationship broke down for good, and she travelled back to Ireland.

The Scottish police were alerted by the RUC to the fact that Howard was the prime suspect in the murder of Arlene Arkinson, and extensive surveillance was placed on his home. An official with the Glasgow Housing Resettlement Unit called to Howard, and they discussed the disappearance of Arlene Arkinson, but Howard denied all knowledge of her whereabouts. The council official noted that as he spoke to Howard on the street the Irishman stared at a young woman walking by and did not take his eyes off her until she was out of sight. The way Howard looked at the woman caused the official concern, and he reported it to Clydebank Police.

After Patricia Quinn returned to Ireland, Howard formed another relationship with a woman in Glasgow. He met the woman in a pub, and they soon began going out. She would stay in his flat on Friday nights. She had a ten-year-old daughter at the time, but she later told the police that Howard had never been alone with her child.

For most of 1995 Howard lived in Glasgow, occasionally travelling back to Ireland and moving north and south of the border. It was noticed that he could disappear for days at a time before resurfacing.

In November 1995 Howard fled Scotland when a newspaper published his photograph under the headline 'Face of evil' and revealed that he was a convicted rapist and also a murder suspect. The article gave his address and stated that he was living only yards from a primary school. Within hours a group of local people organised a vigilante-style eviction and smashed the windows of Howard's flat in Bayfield Avenue. Howard was at home when the group of angry residents arrived at his door, but he escaped from a back window, using a rope to lower himself to the ground.

On 27 November 1995 the Scottish authorities saw Howard onto a bus in Glasgow. He gave them back the keys to the flat in Bayfield Avenue and told them he was moving to London, and he gave them a forwarding address, that of a hostel at Lewisham in the south-east of the city where he would spend at least his first night. He probably knew that the London police would now be awaiting his arrival. In time he would disappear under the radar in London, and it would be another six years before he would murder a fourteen-year-old girl a short distance from Lewisham.

As Howard moved from Scotland to London the RUC and Garda Síochána were still conducting dozens of searches for Arlene Arkinson. It was now more than a year since Arlene had vanished, and excavations had been undertaken at bogland in Cos. Tyrone and Donegal. It was two miles outside Castlederg that Robert Howard and Arlene had driven off from Donna Quinn and Seán Hegarty that August night. The forests, bogland and rivers around this area of west Tyrone therefore formed the centre of most of the searches, which continue to this day.

Before Arlene disappeared Robert Howard was known to frequent Killeter forest, a few miles west of Castlederg, towards the Co. Donegal border. This was one of a number of woodland areas to be searched. Detectives also searched Scraghy Mountain, south of Castlederg. Remote areas along the Drumquin road to the south-east were also examined, as was the River Derg, which flows through the town towards Lough Derg in Co. Donegal. In the Republic, bogland at Pettigo was searched a number of times by the Gardaí. This area was of particular interest, because a short time after Arlene's disappearance Howard had visited the area, telling someone he had previously dropped his watch there while going to the toilet. Elsewhere, about fifteen acres of bogland were searched at Castlefinn on the Donegal side of the border. Despite all the searches by both police forces, no trace of Arlene or her clothing has yet been found.

Arlene's family have spent thousands of hours searching for her. They have maintained countless vigils, as firstly the RUC and later the PSNI excavated bogland and other open ground around Castlederg. While raising their own families, Arlene's sisters have continued to keep a public pressure on the authorities to do everything in their power to find the fifteen-year-old's remains. Arlene's sisters have spent hours analysing different ideas about what may have happened their sister. They have found themselves looking at different types of terrain to try to guess where the killer might have hidden her body. They have looked at rivers and lakes, bogs and forests. Kathleen says that every conceivable place must be considered.

> We're never going to give up until we find Arlene. We believe as a family that we need Arlene back, and we are not giving up. We have had great support from a number of police officers, especially one PSNI detective, Adrian McCombes. And we want to see the Gardaí and the police continue to search for Arlene until she is found.

Throughout the late 1990s Robert Howard travelled back and forth by ferry between Ireland and England. He lived mostly in the east end of London but never stayed in one place too long. When he had left Scotland for London in November 1995 the police in Glasgow had alerted their counterparts in Lewisham that the rapist and suspected killer was en route to a hostel at Hither Green. He didn't stay long at the hostel, and the police then kept tabs on him as he moved to a flat at nearby Brockley Rise. They asked the social services department to call Howard in for interview, the plan being to get up-to-date photographs of him and more information about his intentions. However, he failed to show up for his appointment. Another interview was arranged, with a stop being put on his unemployment assistance until he attended for interview, but again he failed to show.

By February 1996 the police had tracked Howard to a new address at Glensdale Road, a short distance from Lewisham. Detectives carried out video surveillance of him and secretly photographed him as he waited for a bus. They later kept tabs on him when he moved to another flat at Firs Close, also in south-east London. A report by the London police noted that Howard was

> a difficult subject to monitor. He is particularly surveillance conscious, would seem to have chosen his address due to the difficulties of observing it and disappears for days on end.

On 16 August 1996 Robert Howard applied for a replacement
passport. The Irish embassy in London approved a ten-year passport, which simply recorded Howard's date and place of birth and
incorporated a recent photograph. Howard was now fifty-two,
and for his photograph he wore a sports jacket and white shirt and
had his hair cut short.

In 1999 Howard was observed getting off the ferry at Rosslare,
Co. Wexford. He was driving a van similar to an old ambulance
and he was in the company of his new girl-friend, Mary, who was
also originally from Ireland. Also with them were Mary's daughter
and her boy-friend and their young child. The group rented a
house at Barntown, a townland a short distance outside Wexford.
The Gardaí immediately kept close surveillance on Howard, and
he obviously felt the heat, because he and Mary soon left the
house and travelled back to England. Before they had travelled to
Wexford, Mary and Robert Howard had lived in Mary's house at
Northfleet in Kent. By now another couple were renting the house
from Mary, and when she and Howard returned to England they
settled in Mottingham in south London. Howard would still visit
Northfleet to collect the rent and do repairs to the house.

———

On Friday 15 March 2002 workers were excavating land at a site
near Northfleet. As well as housing estates in this area, which lies
a few miles south of the River Thames and east of London, there
were also large sections of dense forest and woodland. The team of
workers who began clearing undergrowth with heavy machinery
at 8:30 a.m. that Friday were doing preparatory work for a new
railway line. They had only begun their work when one of them,
David Coleman, saw a black boot and then saw a skull.

The remains of fourteen-year-old Hannah Williams were
wrapped in a blue tarpaulin. She was still wearing her blue denim
jacket and black sleeveless top with gold leaf design. The thick
rope that had been used to murder her was still wrapped around

her neck. For eleven months Hannah's body had lain undiscovered in the thick woodland, and for those eleven months the London Metropolitan Police classified her as a missing person. She was last seen alive on Saturday 21 April 2001 when she left her home in Deptford in the east end of London, about twelve miles from where her body was found. A popular and outgoing girl, she was a familiar face at the stalls and markets in Deptford, where she loved to browse and chat with the stall-holders. Hannah lived at home with her mother, Bernadette, and brother Kevin, who had a stall at the market. Her father, Billy, had left the family home before Hannah was born, but he still kept in touch with her. When Hannah was a little girl her father had a girl-friend, Mary, and she and Hannah got on well. Hannah would go to visit her father and Mary in Northfleet, where they were living. Hannah loved to walk Mary's dogs and play near the big lake in the area, known as the Blue Lake.

When Hannah's father and Mary split up in the 1990s Hannah still kept in touch with Mary, who would often come to the Deptford market on a Saturday. Hannah got to know Mary's new boy-friend. He was from Ireland, and his name was Bob.

It was a fourteen-second phone call that brought Hannah Williams to her death. It was Bob calling her from Mary's mobile phone. Whatever he said to her, they must have made an arrangement to meet somewhere. It was the last known contact with Hannah before she vanished. She had given her mobile number to Mary and Bob two months beforehand, when she had bumped into them by chance. She had gone back to their home in Mottingham, and Bob had taken a video of Hannah cuddling their dogs. There was talk of Hannah possibly going to France with them on a short holiday, and she organised to get a passport application form.

Hannah Williams had some learning difficulties, and she had been to special-needs schools. At the time of her murder she was in part-time education at a local centre in Deptford. Her murder trial would hear that she had an emotional age much younger than her 14 years, but in contrast to that she looked older than her actual age. It was a combination that made her particularly vulnerable.

Mary was asleep when Robert Howard took her mobile phone and made contact with Hannah that Saturday morning. Mary worked as a care assistant in a residential home and had worked a shift through the Friday night into Saturday morning.

Hannah had left her home at about 11 a.m. and headed for the market, two minutes' walk from the house. She was spotted by a number of people while she was browsing at the stalls. But then she received a phone call from Bob Howard, and she was gone.

Bernadette expected her daughter home for tea that evening. Like many teenagers, Hannah would sometimes be late home, but by 10 p.m. Bernadette was worried. A friend of Hannah's had been expecting to see her that evening too, but she hadn't turned up, and he too wondered where she was. Hannah's friend came to Bernadette and they waited together; they tried ringing her phone but couldn't contact her. At 5 a.m. on Sunday 22 April, Bernadette went to the local police station to report her daughter missing.

In the weeks before Hannah Williams's body was discovered in Kent the police in Co. Tyrone were reviewing the case relating to Arlene Arkinson's disappearance. Though Robert Howard had been the prime suspect almost from the first day, the police had also followed up other leads. The back garden of a house in Castlederg had been excavated as part of the investigation. This search had caused much upset for the family involved, but at least the police could now say they believed they had exhausted all other lines of inquiry. In the eight years since Arlene's disappearance she had not shown up in Ireland, Britain or beyond. Both her family and the police believed she was dead, and that she had been killed in August 1994. As searches continued for her remains, detectives were now considering the feasibility of bringing a murder charge, whether or not Arlene's body was found.

Within weeks of Hannah Williams's body being found, Robert Howard was arrested in London and charged with her murder.

The Kent Police had established that they could bring a murder case against the convicted rapist purely on circumstantial evidence. Meanwhile the PSNI were making progress in their investigation into the murder of Arlene Arkinson. In May 2002 Howard was flown from England to Belfast and taken to Enniskillen police station, where he was questioned about Arlene's disappearance. At the end of his period of questioning the Public Prosecution Service directed that Howard be charged with Arlene's murder.

It was decided that the Hannah Williams murder trial would proceed first, and Howard was flown back to England and remanded in custody to Belmarsh Prison. When his trial eventually began in September 2003 a reporting ban was imposed, because Howard was still due to face trial for the murder of Arlene Arkinson. Journalists were allowed to take notes at the Hannah Williams trial but could not report the evidence or the outcome until after the Arlene Arkinson trial.

At the opening of the Hannah Williams trial at Maidstone Crown Court in Kent the jury were told that Hannah's body had been found with a blue rope wound tightly around her neck, with her hair still entangled in it. The prosecution was permitted by the trial judge to introduce 'similar fact' evidence of how Robert Howard had placed a rope around the neck of a sixteen-year-old girl, Miss X, whom he had abused for three days in his flat in Castlederg in September 1993. In 1995 this woman had been denied the opportunity to give evidence in her own case because, without consulting her, the prosecution had dropped the rape charges and accepted a plea of guilty of unlawful carnal knowledge. Finally the woman, now twenty-six, entered the witness box in Kent to tell how Robert Howard had put a rope around her neck and tightened it to force her to submit to his assaults. In detail she described the rope as 'blue, not as thick as ordinary rope and about two-and-a-half rulers long.' She said she last saw the rope on the bottom of Robert Howard's bed.

Arlene Arkinson's family also attended the murder trial in Kent. The 'similar fact' evidence allowable in the Hannah Williams trial extended to the jury being told that Robert Howard was the last known person to have been in the company of fifteen-year-old Arlene Arkinson, who had disappeared nine years before. The prosecution barrister, Wendy Joseph, put forward a case that Howard had 'an unwholesome interest in young, vulnerable teenage girls.' She told the jury about the fourteen-second phone call made from Howard's girl-friend's mobile phone to Hannah's phone on the day she disappeared. Only two people had access to that phone, the jury were told: one was Mary, who was asleep at the time after a night's work at a care centre; the other was Robert Howard.

> After that phone call nothing is really known about Hannah. There is no-one who's seen her or spoken to her. From that point that morning, she simply disappeared.

Accepting that the entirety of the case against Howard was circumstantial, prosecuting counsel argued that

> when you have enough circumstantial evidence, it can be the most compelling of all.

After the jury had retired to consider their verdict it took them 3 hours and 20 minutes to return to the court, where they announced their unanimous verdict, finding Robert Howard guilty of the murder of Hannah Williams. Many members of the jury began to cry when the full list of Howard's previous convictions was now read out in the court. They heard of his convictions for robbery in Ireland from the age of thirteen onwards; they heard how he had attacked a six-year-old girl in London in 1965, how he had attempted to rape a woman in Durham in 1969, and how he had raped a 58-year-old woman in Co. Cork in 1973.

Howard showed little emotion as Mr Justice McKinnon imposed a life sentence, saying, 'It is plain to me you have no mitigating circumstances whatsoever, and it is clear you are a danger to teenage girls and women and have been for a long time.' The media could not report the judge's comments: indeed not even the outcome of the trial could be reported, as Howard still awaited trial in Belfast for the murder of Arlene Arkinson. He was soon flown to Maghaberry Prison in Lisburn to await his second murder trial.

On 24 May 2005 a now 61-year-old Robert Howard was brought into Court 11 at Belfast Crown Court. He sat in the dock in the centre of the room as a jury of nine men and three women entered the court. Prosecuting counsel, Gordon Kerr, outlined the case against Howard. The defendant was facing five charges: one charge was that he had murdered Arlene Arkinson on Sunday 14 August 1994 at an unknown place, and the other four charges were that he had perverted the course of justice. The prosecution had decided that although it could bring an application to introduce 'similar fact' evidence in the trial, it did not believe such an application would be successful and so did not do so. The jury in the Arlene Arkinson trial, therefore, never heard Miss X's evidence about how she had been abused by Howard in Castlederg a year before Arlene Arkinson disappeared. They were also unaware that the defendant had been convicted of murdering a fourteen-year-old girl in Kent nine years after Arlene's disappearance.

A retired judge, Sir John MacDermott, would later be asked to review the decision taken by the prosecution in Arlene's case not to seek to introduce 'similar fact' evidence. He concluded that it had been correct not to try to introduce evidence of Howard's bad character from the Miss X case and the murder of Hannah Williams. The main problem faced by the prosecution was that 'assuming that the death of Arlene Arkinson could be established, there was simply no evidence as to the circumstances in which she had died.' He found that while there was a common link between the Miss X and Hannah Williams cases, in that there was evidence of sexual assault and of a rope being involved, there was no such evidence in Arlene's case. He concluded that if ever Arlene's body was discovered 'such evidence might emerge and the material for a fresh prosecution might exist.' The cases of Miss X and Hannah Williams had also been similar in that Robert Howard had 'groomed' both victims, seeking to put them at their ease for a time before beginning his attacks. There was no evidence of such 'grooming' in Arlene Arkinson's disappearance: in fact she went to Bundoran with Howard and her two friends that night only because another teenage girl cancelled at the last minute.

The trial of Robert Howard for the murder of Arlene Arkinson, therefore, was based largely on circumstantial matters and witness evidence. Howard was the last person known to have been in Arlene's company, he had allegedly asked his former partner and her daughter to lie to protect him, and he had allegedly lied to a policeman about the case. The four charges of perverting the course of justice all related to events alleged to have occurred in the week after Arlene disappeared. The prosecution claimed that Howard had asked Patricia Quinn to lie and say he had been at home all night on 14 August 1994 and had also urged her to say she had seen Arlene in a car some days after her disappearance. The prosecution also alleged that Howard had asked Patricia's daughter, Donna, to lie and say Arlene had not gone with them to Bundoran that night.

The nine men and three women listened carefully as Gordon Kerr outlined the prosecution case. He told the jury that there would be compelling circumstantial evidence that the missing fifteen-year-old was dead and that she had died in the early hours of 14 August 1994. He said there had been extensive searches in Co. Tyrone and Co. Donegal for her body but that she had not yet been found. The last that was known of Arlene was her heading off in the car with Robert Howard after leaving her friends, Donna Quinn and Seán Hegarty. The jury would hear from Patricia and Donna Quinn how Robert Howard asked both of them to lie for him when the police came asking questions. He had tried to persuade people to hide the fact that he had been the last person to see Arlene alive, and an inference could be drawn that he had killed Arlene and was attempting to avoid responsibility for the killing.

Arlene's father, William, and her brothers and sisters all attended the murder trial in Belfast. After maintaining countless vigils at the scene of so many searches for Arlene, the family were now beginning a vigil at Belfast Crown Court. They had watched as

Howard stood trial in Kent for the murder of Hannah Williams and were now hoping for some breakthrough relating to Arlene.

The Arkinson family sat at the back of the courtroom. Howard had his back to them as he sat in the dock facing the presiding judge, Mr Justice Hart. The jury sat to one side of the room, and the first piece of evidence they were shown was a video tour of Castlederg to familiarise them with the geography of Arlene's home town.

A number of Arlene's sisters left the courtroom in tears when Donna Quinn was giving her evidence. Donna began to cry as she spoke about the last time she saw Arlene. She told of asking Robert Howard about where he had left Arlene and that he had first said Spamount estate and had later said Wall's bar in the town centre. She said Howard had asked her to lie and to tell the police that Arlene had not gone to Bundoran with them.

Patricia Quinn entered the witness box and said that Howard had asked her to lie and to provide a false alibi for him for the night of Arlene's disappearance. She said Howard had asked her to say she had seen Arlene in a car some days after she had disappeared. She told the jury she had followed Howard over to Scotland in 1995 and lived with him for a number of weeks, before they finally broke up. She said she went to Scotland to 'see if he would tell me anything about Arlene.'

Detective-Sergeant Alan Bailey travelled from Dublin to give evidence on behalf of the Garda Síochána. He described the extent of searches that had been undertaken in the Republic for Arlene. There had been many physical searches of open land but there had also been extensive computer searches of databases of banks, shops, credit unions and businesses. Arlene had never come into contact with the Gardaí, the Department of Social Welfare or any other authority. The jury heard similar evidence relating to Britain: the prosecution said that in the more than ten years since Arlene's disappearance all 'proof of life' inquiries had been exhausted. The prosecution argued that the jury could draw a reasonable inference that Arlene had died soon after getting into the car alone with Robert Howard.

During the trial Howard took notes and occasionally conferred with his solicitor, who passed on messages to the defence barrister. When the prosecution case concluded he exercised his right not to give direct evidence. The jury heard taped interviews from when Howard was originally questioned about Arlene's disappearance in 1994. In a soft midlands voice he had told the police, 'I deny all of it—absolutely.'

In closing speeches, Howard's defence counsel argued that there was no evidence to connect Howard with the crime of murder. Arlene might have run away from Castlederg, or some other person might have attacked her. He pointed out that there was no scientific evidence relating to the case, and no crime scene. If Arlene had been killed there was no way of knowing if she had been strangled or shot, for example, or drowned. Even if the jury believed Arlene had been killed, could they decide whether it had been an accident or had been murder?

Before he sent the jury out to consider their verdict, Mr Justice Hart told them that the trial had been a source of great distress but that a jury must approach deliberations without any feelings of sympathy or prejudice. 'A calmly, thoroughly and conscientiously considered verdict is needed,' he said. After a four-week trial the jury retired to consider their verdict. They had much to debate. The judge had asked for a verdict on all five charges against Robert Howard.

The jury's deliberations went into a second day, and then into a third, and a fourth. Unlike practice in the Republic, the members of the jury were allowed to go home to their families each night, under strict instructions not to discuss the case with anyone. They would then return to court each morning and continue their deliberations.

On the fifth day the jury stated that they had reached a verdict on one of the charges. Arlene's family went back into court, and Howard was brought from the holding cell to sit in the dock once again. The jury came back into the courtroom; they had now been deliberating for a total of seventeen hours over a period of five days. By a majority verdict the jury found Howard not guilty of one of the charges of perverting the course of justice—the charge that he had asked Donna Quinn to tell the police that Arlene had not gone to Bundoran with them. They then retired to continue considering the other verdicts.

On the afternoon of Monday 27 June 2005 the jury came into the courtroom once again. They had now been deliberating for twenty-three hours over a period of six days. They had reached a verdict on another of the charges on the indictment. Nobody in court knew which of the charges the verdict related to until it was formally read out seconds later. By a majority of ten to two the jury found Robert Howard not guilty of the murder of Arlene Arkinson.

Howard showed no emotion as the verdict was read out. Members of Arlene's family stormed out of the courtroom, and in the corridor outside they cried and hugged each other. The court staff gave the family a room in which to be alone for a while. Later, Arlene's family met the media outside the court building, and in an emotional statement Arlene's sister Kathleen gave the family's reaction.

> We have always said our top priority has been to recover Arlene's body. This is still the case, and we are calling on the police to continue the searches and we will not rest until our sister is found.

Meanwhile the jury had retired to continue considering their verdict on the three other charges Howard still faced of perverting the course of justice. But after such lengthy deliberations they were exhausted, and they would eventually be unable to reach a verdict on the remaining charges.

While the media were able to report that Robert Howard had been found not guilty of the murder of the missing teenager Arlene Arkinson, a 'gagging order' still existed, banning journalists from revealing any detail of Howard's previous convictions, including the fact that he was serving a life sentence for murdering fourteen-year-old Hannah Williams in England. The publication ban existed because Howard was also facing separate charges of rape and buggery against another schoolgirl. These offences were alleged to have occurred in Northern Ireland in the late 1980s and had been brought following the fresh police investigation into Howard in 2002. However, on Tuesday 20 September 2005, three months after Howard was acquitted of murdering Arlene Arkinson, the prosecution counsel, Ciarán Murphy, told Belfast Crown Court that the prosecution was not proceeding with those charges and asked for them 'to remain on the books.' Judge Tom Burgess then formally lifted the publication ban relating to Robert Howard, and within minutes journalists were reporting that the man found not guilty of murdering Arlene Arkinson was a convicted murderer and rapist. Finally, two years after he was convicted of murdering Hannah Williams, the verdict in that case could be made public.

One month later Robert Howard was taken from Maghaberry Prison and flown to England. The prison authorities had decided that he should be transferred to the high-security Frankland Prison in Durham to continue serving his life sentence. Howard's life had come full circle: it was from Durham that he had been deported back to Ireland after attempting to rape a woman in 1969. Frankland Prison houses a number of convicted killers and other high-risk prisoners among its population of more than seven hundred. On arrival in October 2003 Howard was given a cell of his own, and he remains there to this day. By December 2006 he had exhausted all avenues of appeal against his conviction for murdering Hannah Williams.

The Gardaí, the PSNI and the British police have spent countless hours examining Robert Howard's movements during the parts of his life when he was not in custody. In particular they would like to learn a lot more about where he travelled during the twenty years and four months from when he walked out of Mountjoy Prison in Dublin on 7 December 1981 until he was arrested and charged with the murder of Hannah Williams in Kent in March 2002. Much is known about his life during certain parts of those two decades, but other periods are unaccounted for. Naturally, because of his murder conviction and the randomness of his crimes, detectives have tried to analyse his movements at times when particular unsolved violent incidents occurred. He is one of a number of random killers to have been looked at by detectives working on Operation Trace, which investigated the disappearance of a number of women from the Leinster area in the 1990s. Those investigations continue, and the Gardaí have requested permission to visit Howard in Frankland Prison.

The man who led the investigation by the Kent Police into the murder of Hannah Williams, retired Detective-Superintendent Colin Murray, has met gardaí on a number of occasions to discuss Howard's movements. He says Howard tried to convince detectives that he wouldn't hurt a fly.

Howard tried to come across as a pitiful figure. He would shuffle into a room, he was softly spoken and he almost seemed to think that he could charm his way out of things. This man was a prolific sex offender, and he travelled around without using credit cards or the like. I do believe he must be looked at to see if he's been involved in any other murders. Poor little Hannah Williams suffered a terrible death.

One garda says it is imperative that the force be given the proper resources to conduct a meticulous investigation into Howard's life.

I think the people of this country and the North, and Scotland and England, deserve nothing less. Here we have a proven paedophile and child-killer who also has a conviction for raping a 58-year-old woman. And he has travelled so extensively: he first travelled from Ireland to England in the mid-1960s and was still travelling back and forth until his arrest in Kent in 2002. I think we need to look closely at Howard for everyone's sake, even including his. For example, Howard was once the prime suspect for the horrific sexual assault of a young woman in the south-east of Ireland in 1988. A man driving a green Hiace van abducted this woman. The attacker put a jumper around the woman's neck and tightened it as he raped her. He then tied her hands with rope and threw her out of the van. Robert Howard drove a Hiace van at the time of this attack, and the crime would match the scale of his proven crimes. But we eventually got a DNA sample and checked it and it actually eliminated Howard. He went from being a prime suspect to being eliminated. We need to do the same research in other cases, either rule him in or rule him out. His name has been suggested in relation to unsolved crimes in Mayo, Sligo, Dublin and Bray, for example.

And even if he wasn't responsible for any other crimes we could learn a lot from getting inside the mind of someone like Robert Howard, someone who has more than one *modus operandi*. Yes, he 'groomed' Hannah Williams before murdering her, and he 'groomed' Miss X before attacking her in Castlederg; but what about the random rape of the woman in Youghal in 1973, or the attempted rape of the woman in Durham in 1969? There is a lot in the mind of Robert Howard, and it is not right that he can just while away his hours and years in a high-security prison and not give something back to society.

The woman formerly known as Miss X now lives in the midlands, where she is originally from, and has now built a happy and fulfilled life. In late 2006 this woman received a visit from a representative of the North's Public Prosecution Service. She was told that a review of the handling of Robert Howard's prosecution for attacking her in his flat in Castlederg in 1993 had found that it was wrong that she was not consulted before the prosecution dropped the rape charges in favour of the lesser charges of unlawful carnal knowledge.

In the months after she had made her complaint to the RUC in Castlederg she had not been kept properly informed about the case and was ultimately denied the opportunity to give evidence before Howard was sentenced. She was only sixteen when she was attacked, but in later years she would show great bravery and maturity in giving evidence at the Hannah Williams murder trial.

The police in Kent were thankful that Miss X had kept faith with the justice system, and in turn she was grateful that a jury could finally hear of the appalling abuse she had suffered over the course of three days in September 1993.

After Howard was found not guilty of murdering Arlene Arkinson, her family returned to Castlederg, still broken-hearted. It had taken three years from the time Howard was first charged with the murder of Arlene until the trial had been held and a verdict reached. In the meantime the Arkinsons had travelled to Kent and seen Howard given a life sentence for murdering Hannah Williams. They had met Hannah's mother, Bernadette, and they had cried together. Bernadette understood what the Arkinsons were going through: she knew how it felt to grieve for a missing child. She knew that if it hadn't been for excavation work undertaken for a railway line Hannah's body might not have been found. At least the Williams family were able to lay Hannah to rest, when she was buried in a white coffin carried by a white horse-drawn carriage.

In the years since Robert Howard was found not guilty of murdering Arlene her family have continued to keep watch as the police carry out searches throughout Co. Tyrone for her body. The family have also looked at possible places in Co. Donegal where Arlene's killer may have left her body. They have urged the Gardaí and the PSNI to continue to work together to find the fifteen-year-old's remains.

The Arkinsons have seen how the police using sniffer dogs have had success in finding the bodies of other murder victims. A police dog called Eddie found the shallow grave of 65-year-old Attracta Harron near Sion Mills, Co. Tyrone, in April 2004. Mrs Harron had been abducted and murdered the previous December while walking back to Strabane from mass in Lifford. Her killer was a 21-year-old known sex offender, Trevor Hamilton; he was charged with Mrs Harron's murder a number of days before her body was found by Eddie, a 'victim recovery' dog with South Yorkshire Police. Eddie and his comrade Frankie and their police handlers have also spent considerable periods in Co. Tyrone searching for Arlene Arkinson.

At the PSNI headquarters I met two of the senior officers involved in the continuing search for Arlene. Detective-Superintendent Raymond Murray and Detective-Inspector John Gilmore stress that future investigations into the murder of Arlene will be professionally and properly focused. As well as using the dogs from Yorkshire the PSNI have also had assistance from sniffer dogs attached to Strathclyde Police in Scotland; but that is only one aspect of a detailed search strategy. The PSNI have also used aerial photography, behavioural analysis and geographical profiling as well as physical digs to try to find Arlene. They have also used ground-penetrating radar to try to find her durable personal effects: she was wearing some rings when she disappeared and had an Irish £1 coin with her. Conscious that more than fifty detailed searches have previously been conducted, Detective-Superintendent Murray says future searches have to be 'reason-led' and cannot be speculative.

I could put twenty people in a bog cutting away at turf and it might look good for the TV cameras, but it is not always the best way to conduct searches. The ongoing search for Arlene is a professional investigation, involving new scientific methods. We are searching for human isotopes, we are checking if there is water beneath the surface of search areas, if there has been soil disturbance. We have sunk pipes into the ground to draw water and test if there is any chemical material suggesting the presence of human remains. We are working extensively with scientists from Queen's University. We are faced with searching rural, rugged countryside in Co. Tyrone, and we are using new scientific methods, using geography and hydrology to assess whether human remains might be present in soil or water.

We are committed to this case for a number of reasons. Naturally we want to find Arlene's remains and return her to her family, and we want to catch the person responsible for her murder. And we also want to make up the ground in restoring confidence in policing. If there is one case that I and my colleagues want to bring to a resolution it is this one.

One scientist involved in the search for Arlene told the police that apart from the searches for mass graves at war crime sites such as in Bosnia, the search for the fifteen-year-old is one of the most detailed continuing searches for the remains of one person. Similar searches have been undertaken in England at Saddleworth Moor near Manchester for the body of Keith Bennett, the twelve-year-old boy killed by the serial killers Ian Brady and Myra Hindley in 1964. The English police have long wished to bring closure to Keith's family by finding his remains. They were able to bring this comfort to another family in 1987 when they recovered the body of another victim of Brady and Hindley. Sixteen-year-old Pauline Reade had vanished in the early 1960s, and her body was found on Saddleworth Moor only after Myra Hindley began to co-operate with a fresh investigation.

_____

The disappearance of Arlene Arkinson is one of two cases of long-term missing children in the north-west of Ireland. In March 1977 six-year-old Mary Boyle disappeared from Cashelard, near Ballyshannon on the southern tip of Co. Donegal. Mary was visiting her grandparents' home when she vanished from the quiet countryside on a Friday afternoon. When she disappeared she was wearing a lilac-coloured hand-knitted cardigan, and her brown jeans were tucked into her wellington boots. Her disappearance left her parents, Ann and Charlie, and her twin sister and her brother all broken-hearted. In the decades since Mary's disappearance there have been numerous searches of rivers, lakes and bogland along the border area. As more recent searches have been conducted, detectives have also hoped that such investigations might also bring some news about Arlene Arkinson if, as some suspect, she is buried in the Republic, close to the border.

From the late 1960s to the late 1990s Northern Ireland was the scene of countless acts of violence as part of the 'Troubles'. As part of the reconciliation process now under way a Historical Inquiries

Team has been established to investigate more than 3,200 deaths related to the conflict. However, the desire by members of the PSNI to get answers about 'cold cases' is not confined to the Historical Inquiries Team. In recent years detectives with the PSNI have carried out fresh reviews of a number of mystifying cases not connected with the political conflict. The disappearance of thirteen-year-old John Rodgers and of eleven-year-old Thomas Spence from Belfast on 27 November 1974 has been the focus of much police work in recent years. The two boys vanished from a Belfast street one morning while waiting for a school bus. As part of the renewed police investigation, detectives have excavated gardens close to where the boys disappeared and have also issued age-progression photographs of how the boys might now look as adult men.

Another case still actively under investigation is the murder of nine-year-old Jennifer Cardy from Ballinderry, Co. Antrim. Jennifer was cycling to a friend's house when she disappeared in August 1981. Six days later her body was found near Hillsborough. As part of a fresh investigation a Scottish man was arrested in May 2005 and brought to Northern Ireland to be questioned about the murder.

In Co. Tyrone, Arlene Arkinson's father looks through a collection of photographs of his youngest child. One shows Arlene hugging her mother and looking up into her eyes. There's also a picture of Arlene making her first Holy Communion, and another of her in her school uniform.

In recent years the PSNI have carried out searches for Arlene's body at a number of places in Co. Tyrone. They have been to Lurganboy Wood, outside Castlederg. They have travelled southeast along the Drumquin Road and also looked at open ground closer to the town centre. They have searched lanes off the main roads in the area, cutting back weeds and grass, assessing where the next dig should be.

Arlene's sister Kathleen remains angry that her little sister lost her life in circumstances that have not yet been fully explained. The family's grief has been compounded by the failure to find Arlene's remains.

I hope no other family ever goes through what we have gone through. It should never happen again. We need Arlene back; we need to give her a Christian burial.

Arlene's mother, Bridget, is buried in a church cemetery in the centre of Castlederg, across the road from the police station. William and his sons and remaining daughters would dearly love to see Arlene laid to rest in the same plot. There's a small plaque at the spot with a photograph of Arlene and a candle. The plaque reads:

In Memory of Arlene Arkinson who disappeared on the 13th of August 1994. Will those who think of Arlene today, a little prayer to Jesus say.